BT
6/9/10
P9-CQT-541

fP

PRIOR BOOKS BY TONY SCHWARTZ

The Power of Full Engagement:
Managing Energy, Not Time, Is the Key to High Performance and Personal Renewal (with Jim Loehr)

What Really Matters: Searching for Wisdom in America

Risking Failure, Surviving Success (with Michael Eisner)

The Art of the Deal (with Donald Trump)

The Way We're Working Isn't Working

THE FOUR FORGOTTEN
NEEDS THAT ENERGIZE
GREAT PERFORMANCE

Tony Schwartz
with Jean Gomes and Catherine McCarthy, Ph.D.

Free Press
New York London Toronto Sydney

fP

Free Press
A Division of Simon & Schuster, Inc.
1230 Avenue of the Americas
New York, NY 10020

First Free Press hardcover edition May 2010

Designed by Mspace/Maura Fadden Rosenthal

Manufactured in the United States of America

10 9 8 7 6 5 4 3 2 1

Library of Congress Cataloging-in-Publication Data

Schwartz, Tony, 1952–
The way we're working isn't working : the four forgotten needs that energize great performance / Tony Schwartz, with Jean Gomes and Catherine McCarthy.— 1st Free Press hardcover ed.
p. cm.
1. Performance. 2. Work—Psychological aspects. 3. Organizational effectiveness. 4. Personnel management. I. Gomes, Jean. II. McCarthy, Catherine, 1968– III. Title.
HF5549.5.P37S39 2010
658.3'128—dc22 2009045655
ISBN 978-1-4391-2766-7
ISBN 978-1-4391-4121-2 (ebook)

To The Energy Project Team
with love and admiration

Contents

PART III: SECURITY/EMOTIONAL

PART IV: SELF-EXPRESSION/MENTAL

PART V: SIGNIFICANCE/SPIRITUAL

PART I

A NEW WAY OF WORKING

CHAPTER ONE

More and More, Less and Less

The way we're working isn't working.

The defining ethic in the modern workplace is more, bigger, faster. More information than ever is available to us, and the speed of every transaction has increased exponentially, prompting a sense of permanent urgency and endless distraction. We have more customers and clients to please, more e-mails to answer, more phone calls to return, more tasks to juggle, more meetings to attend, more places to go, and more hours we feel we must work to avoid falling further behind.

The technologies that make instant communication possible anywhere, at any time, speed up decision making, create efficiencies, and fuel a truly global marketplace. But too much of a good thing eventually becomes a bad thing. Left unmanaged and unregulated, these same technologies have the potential to overwhelm us. The relentless urgency that characterizes most corporate cultures undermines creativity, quality, engagement, thoughtful deliberation, and, ultimately, performance.

No matter how much value we produce today—whether it's measured in dollars or sales or goods or widgets—it's never enough. We run faster, stretch out our arms further, and stay at work longer and later. We're so busy trying to keep up that we stop noticing we're in a Sisyphean race we can never win.

All this furious activity exacts a series of silent costs: less capacity for focused attention, less time for any given task, and less opportunity to think reflectively and long term. When we finally do get home at night, we have less energy for our families, less time to wind down and relax, and fewer hours to sleep. We return to work each morning feeling less rested, less than fully engaged, and less able to focus. It's a vicious cycle that feeds on itself. Even for those who still manage to perform at high levels, there is a cost in overall satisfaction and fulfillment. The ethic of more, bigger, faster generates value that is narrow, shallow, and short term. More and more, paradoxically, leads to less and less.

The consulting firm Towers Perrin's most recent global workforce study bears this out. Conducted in 2007–2008, before the worldwide recession, it looked at some 90,000 employees in eighteen countries. Only 20 percent of them felt fully engaged, meaning that they go above and beyond what's required of them because they have a sense of purpose and passion about what they're doing. Forty percent were "enrolled," meaning capable but not fully committed, and 38 percent were disenchanted or disengaged.

All of that translated directly to the bottom line. The companies with the most engaged employees reported a 19 percent increase in operating income and a 28 percent growth in earnings per share. Those with the lowest levels of engagement had a 32 percent decline in operating income, and their earnings dropped more than 11 percent. In the companies with the most engaged employees, 90 percent of the employees had no plans to leave. In those with the least engaged, 50 percent were considering leaving. More than a hundred studies have demonstrated some correlation between employee engagement and business performance.

Think for a moment about your own experience at work.

How truly engaged are you? What's the cost to you of the way you're working? What's the impact on those you supervise and those you love?

What will the accumulated toll be in ten years if you're still making the same choices?

The way we're working isn't working in our own lives, for the people we lead and manage, and for the organizations in which we work. We're guided by a fatal assumption that the best way to get more done is to work longer and more continuously. But the more hours we work and the longer we go without real renewal, the more we begin to default, reflexively, into behaviors that reduce our own effectiveness—impatience, frustration, distraction, and disengagement—and take a pernicious toll on others.

The real issue is not the number of hours we sit behind a desk but the energy we bring to the work we do and the value we generate as a result. A growing body of research suggests that we're most productive when we move between periods of high focus and intermittent rest. Instead, we live in a gray zone, constantly juggling activities but rarely fully engaging in any of them—or fully disengaging from any of them. The consequence is that we settle for a pale version of the possible.

How can such a counterproductive way of working persist?

The answer is grounded in a simple assumption, deeply embedded in organizational life and in our own belief systems. It's that human beings operate most productively in the same one-dimensional way computers do: continuously, at high speeds, for long periods of time, running multiple programs at the same time. Far too many of us have unwittingly bought into this myth, a kind of Stockholm syndrome, dutifully trying to mimic the machines we're meant to run, so they end up running us.

The limitation of even the highest-end computer is that it inexorably depreciates in value over time. Unlike computers, human beings have the potential to grow and develop, to increase our depth, complexity and capacity over time. To make that possible, we must manage ourselves far more skillfully than we do now.

Our most basic survival need is to spend and renew our energy. We're hardwired to make waves—to be alert during the day and to sleep at night, and to work at high intensity for limited periods of time—but we lead increasingly linear lives. By putting in long, continuous hours, we expend too much mental and emotional energy without sufficient intermittent renewal. It's not just rejuvenation we sacrifice along the way but also the unique benefits we can accrue during periods of rest and renewal, including creative breakthroughs, a broader perspective, the opportunity to think more reflectively and long term, and sufficient time to metabolize experiences. Conversely, by living mostly desk-bound sedentary lives, we expend too little physical energy and grow progressively weaker. Inactivity takes a toll not just on our bodies, but also on how we feel and how we think.

THE PERFORMANCE PULSE

In 1993, Anders Ericsson, long a leading researcher in expert performance and a professor at Florida State University, conducted an extraordinary study designed to explore the power of deliberate practice among violinists. Over the years, numerous writers, including Malcolm Gladwell in his best-selling *Outliers,* have cited Ericsson's study for its evidence that intrinsic talent may be overvalued. As Gladwell puts it, "People at the very top don't just work harder, or even much harder than everyone else. They work much, *much* harder."

But that conclusion doesn't begin to capture the complexity of what Ericsson discovered. Along with two colleagues, he divided thirty young violinists at the Music Academy of Berlin into three separate groups, based on ratings from their professors. The "best" group consisted of those destined to eventually become professional soloists. The "good" violinists were those expected to have careers playing as part of orchestras. The third group, recruited from the music education division of the academy, was headed for careers as music teachers. All of them had begun playing violin around the age of eight.

Vast amounts of data were collected on each of the subjects, most notably by having them keep a diary of all their activities, hour by hour, over the course of an entire week. They were also asked to rate each activity on three measures, using a scale of 1 to 10. The first one was how important the activity was to improving their performance on the violin. The second was how difficult they found it to do. The third was how intrinsically enjoyable they found the activity.

The top two groups, both destined for professional careers, turned out to practice an average of twenty-four hours a week. The future music teachers, by contrast, put in just over nine hours, or about a third the amount of time as the top two groups. This difference was undeniably dramatic and does suggest how much practice matters. But equally fascinating was the relationship Ericsson found between intense practice and intermittent rest.

All of the thirty violinists agreed that "practice alone" had the biggest impact on improving their performance. Nearly all of them also agreed that practice was the most difficult activity in their lives and the least enjoyable. The top two groups, who practiced an average of 3.5 hours a day, typically did so in three separate sessions of no more than 90 minutes each, mostly in the mornings, when they were presumably most rested and least distracted. They took renewal breaks between each session. The lowest-rated group practiced an average of just 1.4 hours a day, with no fixed schedule, but often in the afternoons, suggesting that they were often procrastinating.

All three groups rated sleep as the second most important activity when it came to improving as violinists. On average, those in the top two groups slept 8.6 hours a day—nearly an hour longer than those in the music teacher group, who slept an average of 7.8 hours. By contrast, the average American gets just 6.5 hours of sleep a night. The top two groups also took considerably more daytime naps than did the lower-rated group—a total of nearly three hours a week compared to less than one hour a week for the music teachers.

Great performers, Ericsson's study suggests, work more intensely than most of us do but also recover more deeply. Solo practice undertaken with high concentration is especially exhausting. The best violinists figured out, intuitively, that they generated the highest value by working intensely, without interruption, for no more than ninety minutes at a time and no more than 4 hours a day. They also recognized that it was essential to take time, intermittently, to rest and refuel. In fields ranging from sports to chess, researchers have found that four hours a day is the maximum that the best performers practice. Ericsson himself concluded that this number might represent "a more general limit on the maximal amount of deliberate practice that can be sustained over extended time without exhaustion."

Because the number of hours we work is easy to measure, organizations often default to evaluating employees by the hours they put in at their desks, rather than by the focus they bring to their work or the value they produce. Many of us complain about long hours, but the reality is that it's less demanding to work at moderate intensity for extended periods of time than it is to work at the highest level of intensity for even shorter periods. If more of us were able to focus in the intense but time-limited ways that the best violinists do, the evidence suggests that great performance would be much more common than it is.

It's also true that if you're not actively working to get better at what you do, there's a good chance you're getting worse, no matter what the quality of your initial training may have been. As Geoffrey Colvin points out in his provocative book *Talent Is Overrated,* simply doing an activity for a long time is no guarantee that you'll do it well, much less get better at it. "In field after field," Colvin writes, "when it came to centrally important skills—stockbrokers recommending stocks, parole officers predicting recidivism, college admissions officials judging applicants—people with lots of experience were no better at their jobs than those with very little experience."

In a significant number of cases, people actually get worse at their jobs over time. "More experienced doctors," Colvin reported, "reliably score lower on tests of medical knowledge than do less experienced doctors; general physicians also become less skilled over time at diagnosing heart sounds and X-rays. Auditors become less skilled at certain types of evaluations." In some cases, diminished performance is simply the result of a failure to keep up with advances in a given field. But it's also because most of us tend to become fixed in our habits and practices, even when they're suboptimal.

OUR FOUR PRIMARY NEEDS

If sustainable great performance requires a rhythmic movement between activity and rest, it also depends on tapping multiple sources of energy. Plug a computer into a wall socket, and it's good to go. Human beings, on the other hand, need to meet four energy needs to operate at their best: physical, emotional, mental, and spiritual.

By moving rhythmically between activity and renewal in each of these four dimensions, we fulfill our corresponding needs: sustainability, security, self-expression, and significance. In the process, we build our capacity to generate more and more value over time.

The problem is that few of us intentionally address each of our four key needs on a regular basis and organizations often ignore them altogether. When we fuel ourselves on a diet that lacks essential nutrients, it shouldn't be a surprise that we end up undernourished and unable to operate consistently at our best.

"Value" is a word that carries multiple levels of meaning. The ultimate measure of our effectiveness is the value we create. The ultimate

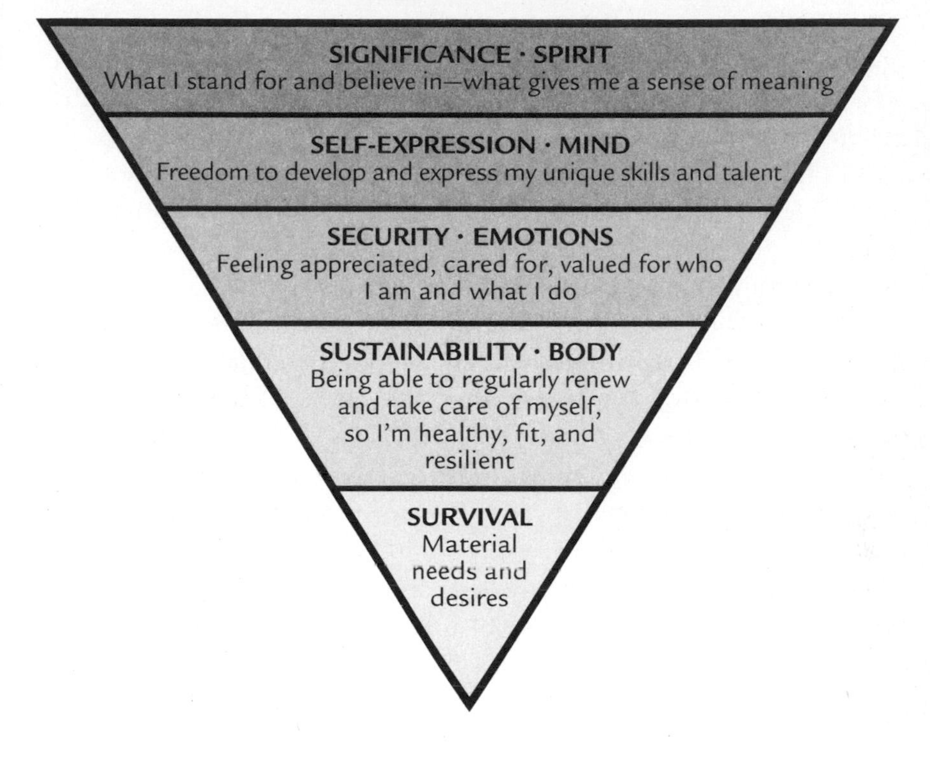

measure of our satisfaction is the value we feel. The ultimate measure of our character is the values we embody.

The primary value exchange between most employers and employees today is time for money. It's a thin, one-dimensional transaction. Each side tries to get as much of the other's resources as possible, but neither gets what it really wants. No amount of money employers pay for our time will ever be sufficient to meet all of our multidimensional needs. It's only when employers encourage and support us in meeting these needs that we can cultivate the energy, engagement, focus, creativity, and passion that fuel great performance.

For better and for worse, we've cocreated the world in which we work. Our complicity begins, ironically, with how we treat ourselves.

We tolerate extraordinary disconnects in our own lives, even in areas we plainly have the power to influence. We take too little responsibility for addressing our core needs, and we dissipate too much energy in blame, complaint, and finger-pointing.

We fail to take care of ourselves even though the consequence is that we end up undermining our health, happiness, and productivity.

We don't spend enough time—truly engaged time—with those we say we love most and who love us most, even though we feel guilty when we don't and we return to work more energized when we do.

We find ourselves getting frustrated, irritable, and anxious as the pressures rise, even though we instinctively recognize that negative emotions interfere with clear thinking and good decision making and demoralize those we lead and manage.

We allow ourselves to be distracted by e-mail and trivial tasks rather than focusing single-mindedly on our most high leverage priorities and devoting sacrosanct time to thinking creatively, strategically, and long term.

We are so busy getting things done that we don't stop very often to consider what it is we really want or where to invest our time and energy to achieve those goals.

Of course, we can't meet our needs and build our capacity in a vacuum. Most organizations enable our dysfunctional behaviors and even encourage them through policies, practices, reward systems and cultural messages that serve to drain our energy and run down our value over time.

When the primary value exchange is time for money, people are fungible—units that can be replaced by other units. An increasing number of organizations pay lip service to the notion that "people are our greatest asset." Call up the phrase on Google, and you'll find more than a million listings. But even among companies that make the claim, the vast majority off-load the care and feeding of employees to divisions known as "human resources," which are rarely accorded an equal place at the executive table. As a consequence, the needs of employees are marginalized and treated as perquisites provided through programs that focus on topics such as "leadership development," "work-life balance," "wellness," "flexibility," and "engagement."

In reality, these are largely code words for nonessential functions. They're funded when times are flush, but they're the first programs that are slashed when cost cutting begins. The vast majority of organizations fail to make the connection between the degree to which they meet their employees' needs and how effectively those employees perform.

The principles at the heart of this book grow out of a rich body of research across disciplines ranging from nutrition to cognition; strength training to training strengths; emotional self-regulation to the role of the right hemisphere of the brain; extrinsic to intrinsic motivation. These findings, generated by subject-matter experts, remain mostly isolated from one another. Our mission has been to bring the evidence together underneath one umbrella to better understand how our varied choices influence one another.

We've also learned a great deal by studying great performers in various professions. In the corporate world, we've worked with senior executives at companies including Sony, Toyota, Novartis, Google, Ford, Ernst & Young, Grey Advertising, and Royal Dutch Shell. We've also worked with cardiovascular surgeons and ICU nurses at the Cleveland Clinic, police officers at the Los Angeles Police Department and high school students in the Bronx. When we published an article about our work in *Harvard Business Review* in the fall of 2007, we received inquiries from companies and individuals in more than two dozen countries around the world including Singapore, Colombia, Russia, China, Korea, Germany, Austria, Italy, Thailand, Denmark, India, and Australia. Across disparate cultures and at all levels, people share both a visceral sense that the way they're working isn't working and an intense desire for more satisfying, productive, and sustainable ways to work and live.

Beyond survival, our needs begin at the physical level with *sustainability*. Four factors are key: nutrition, fitness, sleep, and rest. They're all forms of renewal, either active or passive. Our physical capacity is foundational, because every other source of energy depends on it.

At the individual level, our key challenge is to create a healthy rhythmic movement between activity and rest. The left-hand quadrants in the figure on the next page represent dysfunctional ways of generating and renewing energy. The optimal movement is between the upper-right and lower-right quadrants. Even then, too much of one at the expense of the other is suboptimal. Physically, most of us

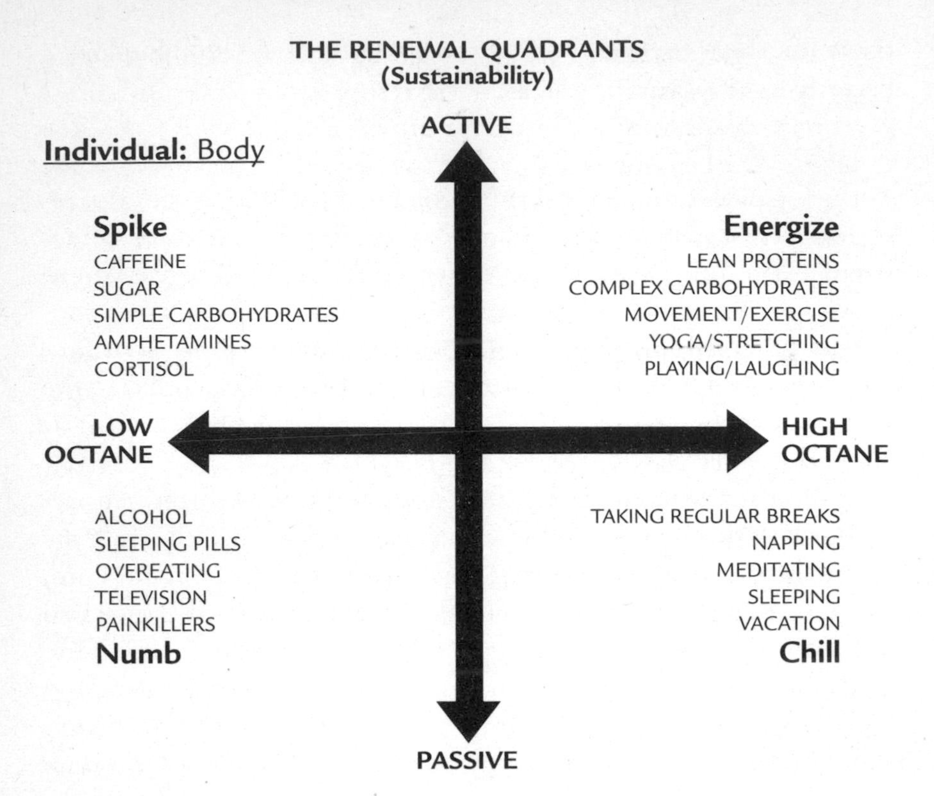

tend to fall on the side of not moving enough (lower left). By contrast exercise (upper right) raises our heart rate and in so doing builds our physical capacity. It also provides a form of mental and emotional renewal, quieting the mind and calming the emotions. That's why exercise in the middle of a workday—especially after an intense period of work—can be such a powerful form of rejuvenation. On the other hand, too much exercise, too continuously, is called "overtraining" and can lead to breakdown and burnout.

The best violinists in the Ericsson study renewed themselves physically not just by sleeping more hours than their less accomplished fellow students, but also by taking more afternoon naps. Eating more energy-rich foods, more frequently—at least every three hours—is a means of stabilizing blood sugar. Many of us attempt to run on too little food for too long and then overeat to compensate. Eating too little deprives us of a critical source of energy we need to operate at our best, and eating too much pushes us into a state of lethargy.

At the organizational level, we work with leaders to build policies, practices, and cultural expectations that support employees in a more rhythmic way of working. When we introduced our work to the top officers at the Los Angeles Police Department it rapidly became clear that sleep deprivation and exhaustion were defining issues for many members of Chief William Bratton's leadership team. Until we addressed this basic problem, nothing else we suggested was getting much traction.

At the conclusion of our work, Bratton and his team agreed on a series of nine policy changes that included limiting off-hours nighttime calls to commanding officers, in order to increase the quality and quantity of their sleep; changing the schedules for key meetings to ensure that they were held at times when the energy levels of participants were likely to be highest; and creating a series of new policies aimed at giving the commanding officers more opportunities to renew themselves during the workday. "What's happened is that our people come to work feeling more rested," Bratton told us a year after our intervention. "They were more able to focus, think clearly, and remain calm in the face of the crises that are part of our everyday work."

Our core need at the emotional level is for *security*, the sense of well-being that depends, in significant part, on the experience of being accepted and valued. How we feel profoundly influences how we perform. Feeling devalued pushes us into the Survival Zone—the upper left quadrant shown on the next page—which increases our fear, distracts our attention, drains our energy, and diminishes the value we're capable of creating. The optimal rhythmic movement in this dimension is between the positive energy we feel when we're operating at our best—the Performance Zone—and the Renewal Zone, where emotional recovery occurs. The more we renew ourselves emotionally, the better we feel about ourselves and the more resilient we are in the face of life's challenges and stresses.

Before we began working with heart surgeons and ICU nurses at the Cleveland Clinic, several of our Energy Project team members spent twenty-four hours shadowing three shifts of nurses on a cardiac intensive care unit. During that time, we asked each of the nurses we encountered to describe their primary dissatisfaction with their jobs. They were unanimous in their response: lack of appreciation from the surgeons.

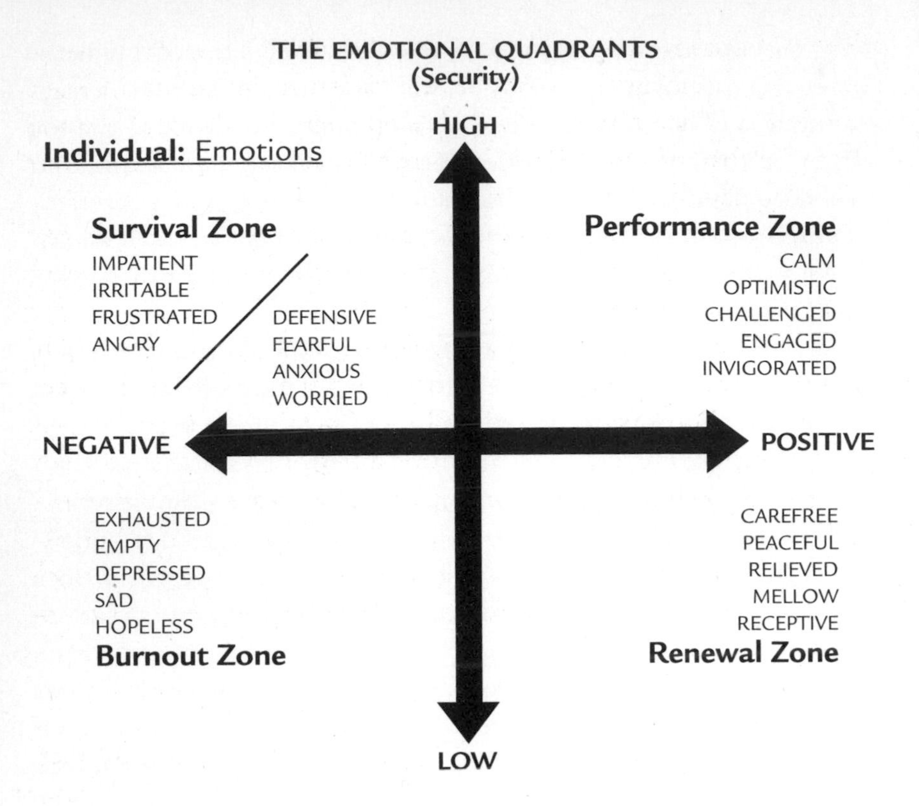

"We're the ones who keep their patients alive day in and day out, but the docs don't talk to us or seek out our opinion," one nurse told us, echoing many others. "They treat us like handmaidens. It's demeaning and frustrating." Later, we had the opportunity to ask the same question to more than a half-dozen surgeons on the same unit. They, too, were nearly unanimous in their response: lack of appreciation from hospital administrators.

Perhaps no human need is more neglected in the workplace than to feel valued. Noticing what's wrong and what's not working in our lives is a hardwired survival instinct. Expressing appreciation requires more conscious intention, but *feeling* appreciated is as important to us as food. The need to be valued begins at birth and never goes away. Failure to thrive is a syndrome in which newborns don't gain sufficient weight to develop normally. One key cause, research suggests, is the absence of touch, stimulation, and care from the primary caregiver. Without love and attention, babies become depressed and withdrawn. Very quickly, they lose the motivation to eat and to interact with others. They also begin to develop cognitive deficits, become more prone to infections, and, in extreme cases, even die. They literally become flatliners.

Most of us obviously have better coping mechanisms, but the deep need for connection and warm regard persists through our lives and influences our performance to a remarkable degree. The single most important factor in whether or not employees choose to stay in a job, Gallup has found, is the quality of their relationship with their direct superiors. Gallup has uncovered twelve key factors that produce high engagement, productivity, and retention among employees. Fully half of them are connected to the issue of feeling valued—including receiving regular recognition or praise for doing good work, having a supervisor or someone at work who "cares about me as a person," "having a best friend at work," and having someone "who encourages my development."

Happily, it turns out that we have far more influence over how we feel, regardless of what is going on around us, than we ordinarily exercise. Our first challenge is to become more aware of how we're feeling at any given moment. The more we can observe our feelings, the more we can choose how to respond to them. The second challenge is learning to intentionally and regularly renew the positive emotions that best serve high performance.

Our hardwired response to perceived threat drains us of positive energy. The bigger our reservoir of value and well-being, the less emotionally vulnerable we are to the challenges we encounter every day. Resilience, the ability to recover quickly from an emotional setback, depends less on what occurs in any given circumstance than on the story we tell ourselves about what's happened to us. Although we're hardwired to be alert to danger and threat, we can also systematically train ourselves to be more aware of what's worth appreciating in our lives and to actively seek out people and activities that make us feel better about ourselves. Consciously cultivating a more realistically optimistic perspective refuels our emotional reservoir.

Our core need at the mental level is *self-expression,* the freedom to put our unique skills and talents to effective use in the world. Self-

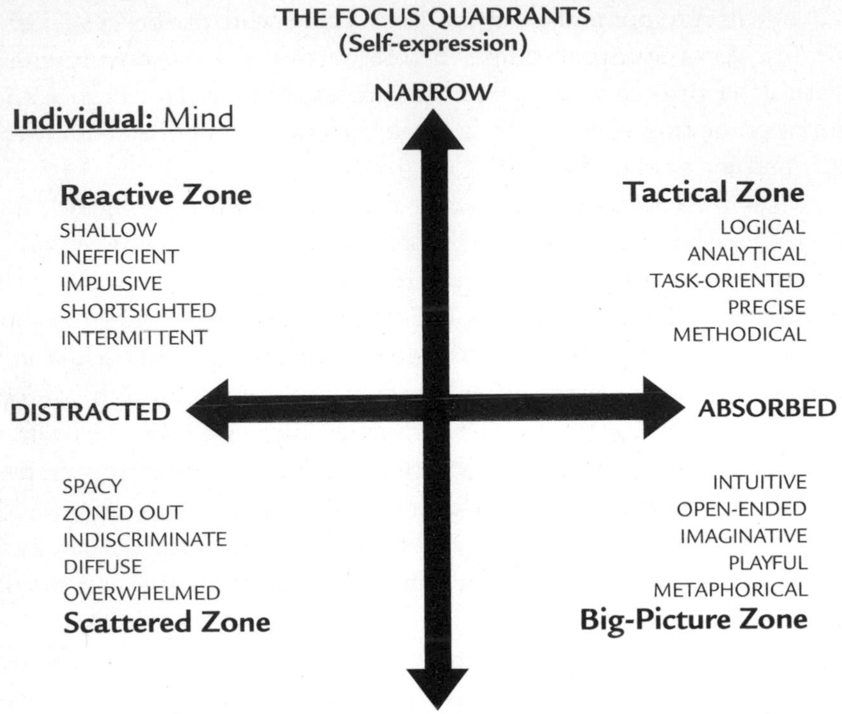

expression is fueled by our capacity to control the placement of our attention and to focus on one thing at a time. The optimal movement in this dimension is between deductive, analytic thinking, aimed at accomplishing a specific task—the Tactical Zone—and wider, more open focus which prompts creative and strategic thinking—the Big-Picture Zone.

We live in a world of infinite distractions and endless demands. Many of us juggle several tasks at a time and struggle to focus on any one of them for very long. Lack of absorbed focus takes a toll on the depth and quality of whatever we do, and it's also an inefficient way to work, extending the time it takes to finish any given task.

At the individual level, the work of self-expression begins with recognizing that our minds have minds of their own. To tame them, we must systematically build our capacity for focus. The more control we have of our attention, the freer we are to make purposeful choices about where to put it and for how long. That's what the best violinists in Ericsson's study accomplished by setting aside uninterrupted periods of time in which to do their most challenging work. In the process, they not only developed their musical skills but also their capacity for absorbed focus. Eventually, they discovered that 90 minutes was the longest period of time for which they could sustain the highest level of attention.

From an early age, we're taught a form of tactical attention that we use to solve problems logically and deductively and to work step-by-step toward a desired outcome. To do so, we depend largely on the left hemisphere of our brain, where language resides. In order to think more creatively, imaginatively and strategically, we need to cultivate a more intuitive, metaphorical attention that calls preeminently on the right hemisphere of the brain. It's only by learning to move freely and flexibly between right and left hemisphere mode—the upper-right and lower-right quadrants—that we can access the whole brain and achieve the highest and richest level of thinking.

The parallel challenge for leaders and organizations is to create work environments that free and encourage people to focus in absorbed ways without constant interruptions. One obvious way is to encourage more frequent renewal. At Ernst & Young, we conducted two pilot programs in which groups of employees were given the opportunity to regularly renew themselves in the middle of their busiest tax season. In large firms like E&Y, young accountants are typically expected to work twelve- to fourteen-hour days in the highest-demand months between January and April, six and seven days a week. It's often debilitating and demoralizing.

We taught teams of E&Y accountants to work instead in more focused, efficient ways for ninety minutes at a time and then take breaks. We also encouraged them to renew intermittently throughout the day. Many of them began taking off an hour in the afternoons to work out at a nearby gym, an unthinkable option before we launched the pilot. When they returned to work at 4 or 5 P.M.—a time at which their productivity typically began to diminish dramatically—they consistently reported feeling reenergized and better able to focus. Because they were able to get more work accomplished in the later afternoon, they were often able to leave work earlier in the evening. The result was more time to relax at home and more time to sleep, which allowed them to return to work the next day more energized and better able to fully engage.

Encouraging employees to set aside sacrosanct time to think creatively, strategically, and long term is even more countercultural in most organizations, which are characteristically focused on immediate results and urgent deadlines. Google is a company that specifically encourages more creative thinking. Its engineers have long been permitted to invest up to 20 percent of their time in projects of their own choosing, based on whatever interests them. Even so, many feel such urgent pressure from their everyday responsibilities that they struggle to get around to their own projects.

The need for *significance* at work is a manifestation of our inborn hunger for meaning in our lives. We call this spiritual energy, and it is fueled by deeply held values and a clear sense of purpose that transcend our self-interest and which we embody in our everyday behaviors. The optimal movement in this dimension is between nurturing our awareness of what we stand for, in the lower-right quadrant on the next page, and expressing those values through our actions, in the upper-right quadrant. Values are aspirations, and they come to life only through our behaviors.

Meaning and significance may seem like luxuries, but they're a unique source of energy that ignites passion, focus, and perseverance. Tapping spiritual energy begins with defining what we stand for amid all the forces that press on us. At his sentencing for the crimes he committed, the Watergate coconspirator Jeb Stuart Magruder told the judge, "Somewhere between my ambition and my ideals, I lost my moral compass."

Deeply held values help us to avoid being whipsawed by whatever winds happen to be blowing around us. Values provide an internal source of direction for our behaviors. Unlike Magruder, most of us don't cross the line into breaking the law, but we're all confronted with opportunities to make expedient choices and to rationalize them after the fact. The antidote is taking the time to reflect not so much on what we want right now but what will make us feel best about ourselves over time—not just on our self-interest but also on how to add value to the greater good.

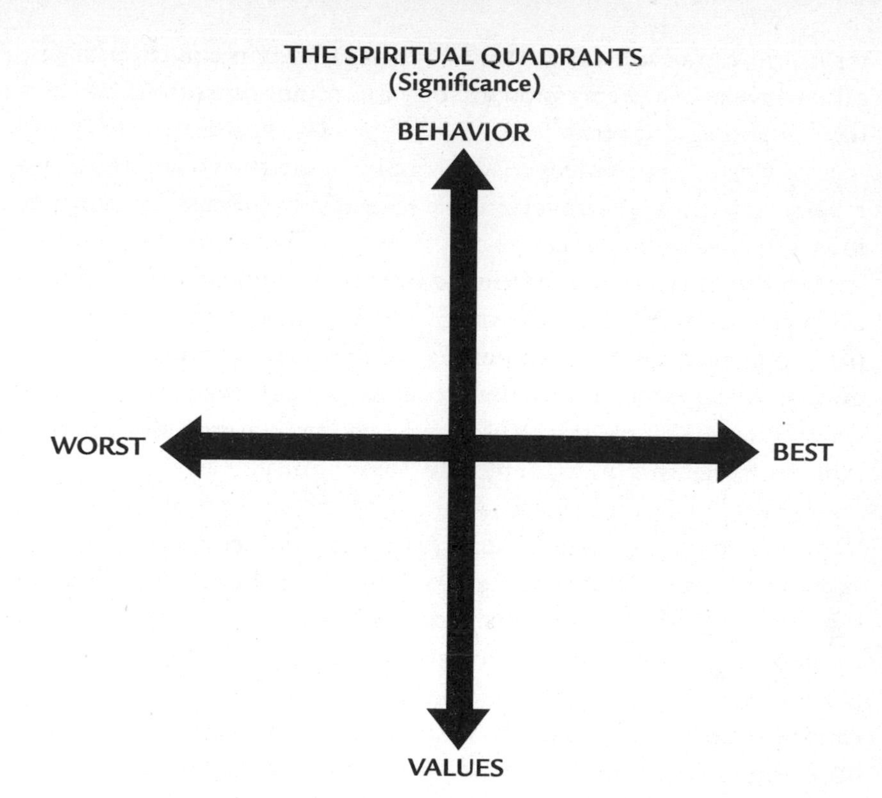

Unlike the other three quadrants, the spiritual quadrants contain no descriptive adjectives. That's because the qualities that fuel spiritual energy are more subjective than those in the other three quadrants. You'll choose these adjectives for yourself in chapter 18.

Purpose is the external expression of what we stand for. The majority of people we meet lack a strong sense of purpose in their jobs, beyond taking home a paycheck and building their careers. Many of us are so busy trying to serve clients and customers—to simply do our jobs—that we don't spend much time or energy thinking about what we really want or how our choices affect others.

While selfishness makes us smaller and takes a toll on others, the costs of *selflessness* can be equally depleting. That's especially true for nurses, teachers, social workers and others who work in the helping professions. Serving others can become so preoccupying that it occurs at expense to our own well-being and eventually to those we're committed to serving. "Compassion fatigue" is characterized by symptoms such as depression, inability to focus, decreased effectiveness, burnout, and breakdown. For people who spend their lives giving to others, the challenge is to equally value their own needs—to renew themselves both for their own sake and so they can serve others more effectively.

The intrinsic mission of service organizations such as hospitals, nonprofits, and schools can powerfully fuel people's need for meaning and purpose. But what about the vast majority of companies that don't so obviously manufacture products or offer services that clearly contribute to the greater good? Leaders of such companies can still build cultures that give people the opportunity to live their values and to feel purposeful at work.

Take Zappos.com, which sells shoes and other clothing. Not long ago, I spent a day visiting the Zappos headquarters, which are located in a bland industrial park in a suburb of Las Vegas. The vast majority of its employees are customer service representatives paid between $12 and $18 an hour, but many find their jobs very satisfying. Zappos inspires employees not only by treating them exceptionally well and by giving them an opportunity to express themselves as individuals, but also by generating a shared mission around providing an extraordinary level of service to customers.

In most call centers, employees are evaluated partly by how quickly they can get onto and off of calls with customers. These employees typically work from a tight script. At Zappos, agents are encouraged to stay on the phone in order to genuinely connect with customers and to build a relationship that is more likely to endure. This approach not only serves customers well but also makes employees proud to work at Zappos. Employees find significance less from the products they sell than from the relationships they nurture.

MEETING PEOPLE'S CORE NEEDS

"How can we get more out of our people?" leaders regularly ask us. We suggest they pose a different question: "How can I more intentionally invest in meeting the multidimensional needs of my employees so they're freed, fueled, and inspired to bring the best of themselves to work every day?" As this book gets published, the perilous state of the economy has exacerbated people's fears everywhere. We live in a vastly more complex world that is changing at warp speed. The systems that worked in the past won't in the future.

To build competitive advantage, organizations must help employees to cultivate qualities that have never before been critical—among them authenticity, empathy, self-awareness, constant creativity, an internal sense of purpose, and, perhaps above all, resilience in the face of relentless change. And whatever our employers do, we serve ourselves well to cultivate these same qualities in order to be more effective and more satisfied, both on the job and off.

CHAPTER ONE ACTION STEPS

- Reflect on the four key energy needs: sustainability (physical); security (emotional); self-expression (mental); and significance (spiritual). How well are you meeting these needs? Where do you feel you're falling short? What are the costs to you and to others in your life?
- Think of a typical day at work. How much of your day do you spend working without breaks for long periods of time? Schedule a midmorning and midafternoon break to experiment with refueling.
- Identify one of your employees whose work isn't as good as you think it could be. Which of the four core needs could you do a better job of helping that person to meet? If you're not certain, sit down and have a conversation with this person about what he or she needs more of from you. If you don't supervise anyone, think about these questions in regard to your best friend at work.

CHAPTER TWO

We Can't Change What We Don't Notice

Human beings have continued to evolve by leaps and bounds in terms of what can be externally measured and observed. Athletes keep breaking records. Scientists understand ever more deeply the causes of diseases and discover new ways of treating them. Technology is more powerful, more multifunctional, and less expensive to produce than ever. But for all these extraordinary external advances, we've devoted remarkably little attention to better understanding our inner world. We've accumulated vast knowledge but woefully little self-knowledge.

"We are already the most overinformed, underreflective people in the history of civilization," argue Robert Kegan and Lisa Lahey, Harvard-based psychologists and leading adult developmental thinkers. "True development is about transforming the operating system itself, not just increasing your fund of knowledge or your behavioral repertoire." The same principle applies at the organizational level. Our current capacities, say Kegan and Lahey, "no longer suffice in a world that calls for leaders who can not only run but also reconstitute their organizations—its norms, missions and culture."

"Flatland" is the name that the writer and philosopher Ken Wilber has given the arid, two-dimensional worldview that prevails in so many organizations and in our culture more broadly. This view grew, Wilber argues, out of a much earlier inflection point: the Enlightenment and the resulting rise of scientific materialism. "If something couldn't be studied and described in an objective empirical fashion, then it wasn't 'really real,' " Wilber explains. "All knowledge had to be objective *it*-knowledge, and so all of reality began to look like a bunch of 'its' with no subject, no consciousness, no selves, no morals, no values, no interiors, no depths." Even Albert Einstein recognized the limitations of the extraordinary discoveries he made. "It would be possible to describe everything scientifically," he wrote, "but it would make no sense; it would be without meaning, as if you described a Beethoven symphony as variation of wave pressure."

Our expanding knowledge of the external world got us to where we are. Without a richer understanding of *who* we are and the full range of needs we must address, we'll remain insufficiently equipped to address the huge challenges we face. Fortunately, there is a way out. It's begins with self-awareness. As Daniel Goleman has written, inspired by the psychiatrist R. D. Laing,

The range of what we think and do
Is limited by what we fail to notice
And because we fail to notice
That we fail to notice
There is little we can do
To change
Until we notice
How failing to notice
Shapes our thoughts and deeds.

The failure to connect behavior to its inevitable consequences shows up in our lives every day. We begin our work with clients by asking them to undertake an "energy audit" and answer questions like these:

- To what extent do you eat right, work out regularly, and get enough sleep?
- Are you eager and excited to get to work in the morning?
- Do you focus your attention on your most important priorities, and are you as productive as you could be?
- Are you motivated by a clear sense of purpose at work—something beyond your self-interest?
- Do you positively energize and inspire those you lead and manage?

In most cases, our clients find they're uneasy and dissatisfied with their answers. It isn't that they discover anything they didn't already know. The discomfort comes from recognizing how they've resisted connecting the dots in their lives and seeing all the examples of how they're selling themselves short aggregated in one place.

It's no different for leaders. During the past decade, we've asked hundreds of them this question:

"Do you think your people perform better when they're healthier and happier?" Almost invariably, the answer is "Yes." Then we ask one more question:

"Does your organization regularly invest in people's health and happiness?" The answer is nearly always "No."

In both sets of questions, to individuals and leaders, our goal is to create discomfort. As people begin to connect the dots, the picture that emerges is rarely pretty. Most of us work long hours and feel a relentless sense of urgency. We juggle multiple demands without feeling we're devoting sufficient time to the most important tasks. We arrive home in the evenings with little energy left for our families. We spend too little time thinking strategically and long term, too little time taking care of ourselves, and too little time simply enjoying our lives. In many cases, the thirty minutes or so our clients invest in answering our list of questions is the first time they've ever stopped long enough to examine the benefits and costs of the choices they're making.

We conclude the exercise by asking them to wrestle with this question:

Is the life you're leading worth the price you're paying to live it?

RICHER, DEEPER, MORE REFLECTIVE

Several years ago, I met with a fifty-something senior executive at a large company to discuss the increasing demands on his organization's consultants, particularly due to their fierce travel demands and long hours.

This executive—we'll call him Carl—began by speaking enthusiastically about the strategies he had devised for making his own travel easier: the right time to get to the airport, the best hotels to stay in and the best restaurants to eat at, and the trick to fitting in meetings in two cities in the course of a single day. It was clear that he was deeply invested in his work.

But Carl was also significantly overweight. In the course of our conversation, he acknowledged that he rarely took time to exercise on the road, skipped meals, and then often ate too much, almost never got a full night's sleep, and seldom spent more than a day at home during any given workweek. On this particular afternoon, it so happened, he was about to fly home a day earlier than usual in order to drive his only child to college, which she was due to start that week.

"What does your family think about your travel schedule?" I asked.

Carl thought for a moment; began to answer and then his voice got caught in his throat. Tears formed in his eyes. In that brief and fleeting moment, just as his daughter prepared to leave home Carl recognized a cost he hadn't allowed himself to feel before.

Two weeks later, Tony found himself standing in the back of a large conference room as the chief executive of Carl's company gave a welcoming talk to several hundred of his employees who'd gathered for a meeting. A charismatic man, proud of the several hundred thousand miles he flew every year, this CEO—let's call him Bill—opened his remarks with a story about how he'd returned a few nights earlier from an extended overseas business trip and landed back home at 4 A.M. "It was dark outside, and I could have gone home to get some sleep, take a shower, and change clothes," Bill explained exuberantly. "But I realized that this was an incredible opportunity to go straight to the office and get a couple of hours of work done, with no interruptions, before anyone else arrived. And that's exactly what I did."

Carl was a product of that culture, and he had mostly gone numb to the consequences, just the way his CEO had. What Bill failed to recognize is that he might have been reenergized by a few more hours of sleep, by relaxing over breakfast at home, or by reconnecting with his wife and children after having been on the road for a week. Nor did it dawn on him that by taking some time to renew he might have been more alert, productive, creative, and even inspiring to others once he did get to work. Finally, whether he intended it or not, Bill's story sent a message to his employees that the path to success at this company was to follow his lead, even if that meant inexorably draining their energy and engagement.

As the CEO of the accounting firm KPMG, Eugene O'Kelly lived his life much the way Bill still lives his. "My calendar was perpetually extended out over the next eighteen months," O'Kelly has written. "I was always moving at a hundred miles per hour. I worked all the time. I worked weekends. I worked late into many nights. I missed virtually every school function for my younger daughter. My annual travel schedule averaged, conservatively, 150,000 miles. Over the course of my last decade with the firm, I did manage to squeeze in workday lunches with my wife. Twice."

In 2004, at the age of fifty-four, O'Kelly was diagnosed with a terminal brain tumor. During the final months of his life, he wrote a book entitled *Chasing Daylight,* about the life he'd lived. "What if I hadn't worked so hard?" he wondered. "What if, aside from doing my job and doing it well, I had actually used the bully pulpit of my position to be a role model for balance? Had I done so intentionally, who's to say that, besides having more time with my family, I wouldn't also have been even more focused at work? More creative? More productive? . . . But I didn't. Not in the many years I was pushing. It took inoperable late stage brain cancer to get me to examine things from this angle." O'Kelly died shortly after writing those words.

The limitation of many people we meet begins with a lack of awareness, a failure to see the consequences of the choices they're making in their own lives and in the lives of those they care about most. It's nearly axiomatic that the more continuously we work, the less likely we are to notice how we're feeling.

Awareness has multiple dimensions. We typically ask our clients to consider it from three angles: How long is your perspective? How wide is your vision? And, perhaps most important, how deeply are you willing to look? Taking a longer view requires moving beyond our instinctive focus on immediate gratification. A wider view means regularly moving beyond our narrow self-interest to take into account the impact of our everyday behaviors on others. Seeing more deeply requires *seeing in*—the willingness to observe ourselves with unflinching honesty.

Awareness increases our knowledge, and knowledge enriches us. The more we're willing to see, the bigger our world becomes. Learning to observe our feelings as they arise, rather than simply acting them out, allows us to make more reflective, intentional choices about how we want to show up in the world.

Each of us has an infinite capacity for self-deception. We become skilled at denial because it helps us avoid discomfort. "Our efforts at self-justification are designed to serve our need to feel good about what we have done, what we believe, and who we are," explain Carol Tavris and Elliot Aronson in their wonderfully titled book *Mistakes Were Made (but Not by Me)*. "To err is human," they go on, "but humans then have a choice between covering up or fessing up. We are forever being told that we should learn from our mistakes, but how can we learn unless we first admit that we have made any?" Or as the psychologist Sandra Schneider puts it, "Self-deception is marked by a lack of attempt to gain reality checks. It relies on an exclusively confirmatory approach to information processing."

The fear of what we'll see keeps us from looking at ourselves more honestly. Denial prompts a cycle that feeds on itself. "Each violation of one's standard brings negative affect that makes it unpleasant to be self-aware," writes the psychologist Roy Baumeister. "The person avoids monitoring his or her own behavior, which makes further violations possible. The longer this goes on, the more unpleasant it is to resume monitoring oneself, because one must recognize that one has severely violated desired patterns of behavior."

Instead, we squander energy in rationalizing, minimizing, and justifying our expedient behaviors. It's notable, for example, that almost no major players in the recent financial meltdown have stepped forward to take personal responsibility for the catastrophic decisions so many of them made. "The greatest of faults," said the philosopher Thomas Carlyle, "is to be conscious of none." By contrast, the willingness to take responsibility for our missteps and shortcomings frees up energy to learn, grow, and add value.

EMBRACING OPPOSITES

Above all, seeing more depends on excluding less. We each have a tendency to choose sides: right or wrong, good or bad, black or white, win or lose. Certainty makes us feel safer, especially in times of anxiety and change. But the consequence is that we create a narrow, more two-dimensional world for ourselves even as the world around us grows ever more complex.

By embracing our own opposites and getting comfortable with our contradictions, we build richer, deeper lives. This is especially crucial for leaders, who must weigh multiple points of view, balance conflicting priorities, serve numerous constituencies, and make decisions about issues with no easy answers. "I don't do nuance," George W. Bush was often quoted as bragging. But nuance is precisely what we need now more than ever: the willingness to recognize shades of gray, grapple with paradox, acknowledge ambiguity, make subtle distinctions, and resist premature certainty. "Do I contradict myself?" Walt Whitman asked in "Song of Myself." "Very well, then I contradict myself. I am large, I contain multitudes."

Consider, for a moment, the following qualities:

Extroverted	Introspective
Decisive	Open-minded
Confident	Humble
Logical	Intuitive
Tactical	Reflective
Pragmatic	Visionary
Discerning	Accepting
Honest	Compassionate
Courageous	Prudent
Tenacious	Flexible
Tough-minded	Empathic

Which quality do you most value in each pair? Circle your choices before you read any further.

Is there any doubt that most of us tend to choose sides between qualities, valuing one in preference to its opposite? Many companies value the whole constellation of qualities on the left side far more than those on the right. But by celebrating one set of qualities and undervaluing another, we lose access to essential dimensions of ourselves—and others.

Many organizations build leadership programs around "competency models," a list of core skills they expect all leaders to cultivate.

Far more of the qualities in the left-hand column appear in these competency models than do those in the right-hand column. No leadership model we've come across acknowledges the value of being able to move freely and flexibly between the opposite qualities we need to perform at our nuanced best.

In direct reaction to the competency models, the Gallup Organization began focusing a decade ago on something it calls "strength-based" leadership. Gallup's premise is that we're better served by cultivating our intrinsic strengths rather than by trying to fix our weaknesses. It's a seductive notion, but also a limited one.

The research of Anders Ericsson and others makes it clear that excellence depends above all on practice and less so on intrinsic talent. With the right kind of practice, we can develop nearly any skill. But the deeper limitation of the Gallup focus on strengths is that it's a classic choosing up of sides. Doing so creates a false choice, much the way competency advocates do by focusing solely on fixing weaknesses. Neither approach is sufficient by itself. On the one hand, it's undeniably more demanding and frustrating to improve in our areas of weakness than to build on our existing strengths. It's also true that we're likely to be most effective doing whatever it is we already enjoy most and do best. On the other hand, a sole focus on strengths creates its own problems. "There is always an optimal value," explained the philosopher Gregory Bateson, "beyond which anything is toxic, no matter what: oxygen, sleep, psychotherapy, philosophy." The Stoic philosophers referred to this paradox as *anacoluthia,* the mutual entailment of the virtues. No virtue, they argued, is a virtue by itself. Even the noblest virtues have their limits.

Honesty in the absence of compassion becomes cruelty. Tenacity unmediated by flexibility congeals into rigidity. Confidence untempered by humility is arrogance. Courage without prudence is recklessness. Because all virtues are connected to others, any strength overused ultimately becomes a liability. Inhaling deeply is useful, but only if we're equally capable of exhaling just as deeply. Even pleasure and pain are connected. Pushing beyond our comfort zone is uncomfortable, but it's the only means by which we can learn and grow, and ultimately perform better and experience deeper satisfaction. This understanding has ancient roots. In Chinese philosophy, *yin* and *yang* refer to opposing forces that are actually interdependent and part of a greater whole. Seng-ts'an, a Chinese Zen master, put it this way: "If you want the truth to stand clear before you, never be for or against. The struggle between 'for' and 'against' is the mind's worst disease."

We create the highest value not by focusing solely on our strengths or by ignoring our weaknesses, but by being attentive to both. Nowhere is this more critical than in the way we see ourselves. "Loving oneself is no easy matter . . ." writes the psychologist James Hillman, "because it means loving all of oneself, including the shadow where one is inferior and socially so unacceptable. The care one gives this humiliating part is also the cure, but the moral dimension can never be abandoned. Thus is the cure a paradox requiring two incommensurables: the moral recognition that these parts of me are burdensome and intolerable and must change, and the loving, laughing acceptance which takes them just as they are, joyfully, forever. One both tries hard and lets go, both judges harshly and joins gladly." It is through this embracing self-acceptance that we're freed to both acknowledge the obstacles we face and build the capacities we need to perform at our best.

CHAPTER TWO ACTION STEPS

- Go to www.theenergyproject.com and take the Energy Audit to gauge how effectively you are currently managing your own energy across the four key energy dimensions. Identify the specific behavior that you feel is most getting in the way of your greater effectiveness and satisfaction. Why haven't you addressed it before now?
- Start a journal to build your awareness about how you are feeling at different points during the day. Choose one or two specific times during the day to check in with yourself. Observing our emotions allows us to be more intentional about our behaviors and more effective with others. How are you feeling right now? Can you identify why?
- Strengths overused eventually become liabilities. List three of your greatest strengths on a sheet of paper, giving yourself room to write underneath each one. Now identify the way you tend to behave when you overrely on these strengths. Ask a colleague at work for feedback about how you overuse one of the strengths you've identified.

CHAPTER THREE

We're Creatures of Habit

Will and discipline are wildly overrated. That's why we struggle so hard to make changes that last. Even when the need for change is obvious and our intentions are strong we often fall short. Consider:

- Ninety-five percent of those who lose weight on a diet regain it, and a significant percentage gain back more than they originally lost.
- Even after a heart attack, only one of every seven patients makes any enduring changes around eating or exercise.
- Twenty-five percent of people abandon their New Year's resolutions after one week. Sixty percent do so within six months. The average person makes the same New Year's resolution ten separate times without success.
- Seventy percent of organizational change initiatives ultimately fail.

Despite the vast evidence that our efforts rarely yield good results, we keep right on trying to fix what's wrong in our lives, in other people's lives, and in organizations. It is possible to make change that lasts but it depends less on using our conscious minds and more on coopting the more primitive part of our brain in which habits are formed.

No one has demonstrated the limits of willpower more cleverly and convincingly than Roy Baumeister, who has spent much of his career studying self-control. In 1998, Baumeister and his colleagues did a study in which they invited subjects into a room on the pretext that they were going to participate in a taste perception test. The subjects had been deprived of food for several hours, so they were hungry. As they sat down, the researchers brought in a large plate of fragrant chocolate chip cookies, fresh out of the oven, along with a plate of radishes. Half of the subjects were invited to eat at least two or three cookies but no radishes. The other half was asked to eat two or three radishes but no cookies. The researchers then left the room. None of the subjects, it turned out, violated the rules, although several radish eaters did stare longingly at the cookies.

After five minutes, the researchers returned. This time, they asked each of the subjects to complete a puzzle, which had been rigged so it was impossible to complete. What the researchers really wanted to know was how long the subjects would persist at the challenge before giving up. As it turned out, the chocolate chip cookie eaters hung in for an average of nineteen minutes, compared to just over eight minutes for the radish eaters. The explanation, Baumeister theorized, was that the radish eaters had burned down their reservoir of willpower resisting the chocolate chip cookies and therefore had less energy available to persist on the puzzle.

"Acts of choice," Baumeister and his colleagues concluded, "draw on the same limited resource used for self-control." In short, we each have one reservoir of will and discipline, and it is depleted by *any* act of conscious self-regulation—whether that's resisting a cookie, solving a puzzle, or doing anything else that requires effort. "The implication," Baumeister writes, "is that many widely different forms of self-control draw on a common resource, or self-control strength, which is quite limited and hence can be depleted readily."

This finding helps explain why diets so consistently fail. In another series of experiments, dieters who were offered appealing foods proved much more likely to break their diets than those who were not exposed to similar temptation. Dieting effectively creates a continuous demand for self-control. Not surprisingly, people on diets perform worse than nondieters on tasks that require focus and vigilance.

A series of studies has demonstrated that uncontrollable stress of any kind—for example, frustration when trying to deal with a government bureaucracy—leads to breakdowns in other areas in which individuals have been trying to exercise control, such as dieting or smoking. In a similar way, not eating for extended periods, getting too little sleep, or feeling distracted by noise that we can't control each diminishes people's self-regulatory reserves. In turn, we become less effective at any given task we undertake.

Self-control, Baumeister hypothesized, operates the same way a muscle does during resistance training. Exposed to continuous stress, the muscle becomes progressively depleted of strength, until ultimately it can't exert any more energy and fails. If we have to rely on willpower to sustain a new behavior the overwhelming likelihood is that we'll eventually fail.

Contained in this insight is a hint at its solution. If self-control does indeed operate like a muscle, then repeated exposure to stress, followed by sufficient recovery, may subsequently lead to greater strength. That's precisely what happened with the best violinists in Ericsson's study. During their practice sessions, they subjected themselves to intense demand, but never for more than ninety minutes at a time, at which point they rested. They didn't become capable of practicing for longer, but they did get better at practicing for finite periods of time at the highest levels of focus. As a consequence, they became progressively better musicians, just as if you regularly lift weights, offset by periods of recovery, you systematically gain strength.

But if conscious will and discipline are rarely sufficient to make enduring change, why were the top violinists able to persist in their practice with an intensity and regularity that their less skilled counterparts did not? The answer is that they didn't rely solely on willpower. Rather, they were carried along by the largely invisible pull of the routines they built over time.

THE UNBEARABLE AUTOMATICITY OF BEING

For better and for worse, we are deeply creatures of habit. Fully 95 percent of our behavior occurs out of habit, either unconsciously or in reaction to external demands. We're run by the automatic processes of the primitive parts of our brain far more than we rely on the complex conscious capacities of our prefrontal cortex. In short, we think we're in charge of our lives, but often we're not.

It is our evolutionary heritage, for example, to move toward pleasure and away from pain. "Human beings," explains historian John Gray, "are an animal species much like any other, more inventive and destructive, no doubt, but like other animals in using their resources to survive and reproduce." For thousands of years avoiding pain *was* critical to staying alive in a world full of dangerous predators. Rather than reflecting on our future, we reacted to our needs in the present. When we came across food, we ate as much of it as possible, not least because it wasn't clear when we'd find food again. Storing it in our bodies for potential later use was a survival behavior, and it still is for animals. For most human beings today, it's just a prescription for gaining weight. Even so, the instinct to keep eating after we're full remains powerfully encoded. "We have to be mistrustful of our brains," argues former FDA commissioner David Kessler. "We have to recognize they are the vehicle to invite us to do things that at some point in our evolutionary past may have been very useful, but have gotten completely out of control."

In a similar way, tolerating discomfort in the short term to reap a richer reward in the future requires overriding our powerful and primitive instinct to seek immediate gratification. This challenge shows up in our lives every day, in nearly every way: the temptation for indulgence when it comes to food, alcohol, and sex; the avoidance of regular exercise; our Pavlovian response to the beep of an incoming e-mail rather than maintaining our focus on a challenging task; and the tendency to default to impatience, irritation, and even anger as a way to mobilize others to action.

The irony is that our efforts at self-control fail in large part because we overrely on our prefrontal cortex, where our highest cognitive capacities reside. We're often better served by replacing our negative habits, formed in the more primitive parts of our brain, with positive rituals—highly specific behaviors that become automatic over time. The more these behaviors are repeated and routinized, the more they recur without conscious effort and the less energy they require. The less conscious willpower we have to expend to make things happen, the more effective we become.

In 1911, the mathematician Alfred North Whitehead brilliantly intuited what scientific research would begin to confirm nearly a century later:

> It is a profoundly erroneous truism . . . that we should cultivate the habit of thinking of what we are doing. The precise opposite is the case. Civili-

zation advances by extending the number of important operations, which we can perform without thinking about them.

Every great performer we've encountered—musicians, heart surgeons, dancers, FBI agents, athletes, and leaders—instinctively understands the power of making key behaviors automatic. This is especially valuable under pressure, when fear tends to undermine performance if our skills aren't deeply ritualized. Self-consciousness interferes with the ability to perform any complex task. "To pay attention to their own internal processes—to how they are executing their performance—is often disruptive to highly skilled people," explains Baumeister. "The increased conscious attention merely interferes with the automatic quality of the well-learned response." If you play golf or tennis, for example, you're well aware that thinking about your swing during play only makes you more awkward in your execution.

Much of what we think of as spontaneous behaviors actually contain a significant degree of what's called automaticity. "Even when engaged in creative processes, such as writing papers, speaking spontaneously or driving to novel destinations, the component acts and movements are routinized responses," explain psychologists Irving Kirsch and Steven Jay Lynn. "Their automaticity is evidenced by the speed and fluidity with which they are produced. There simply is not enough time for a conscious decision prior to the initiation of each component response." Or, as psychologist and philosopher William James put it, "Consciousness deserts all processes where it can no longer be of use."

John Bargh, one of the leading researchers into the phenomenon of automaticity, takes this insight a step further. "Most of moment-to-moment psychological life must occur through nonconscious means if it is to occur at all," he writes in his cheekily titled paper "The Unbearable Automaticity of Being." In Bargh's view, we are best served by using our limited capacity for conscious self-regulation highly selectively on tasks that require complex thinking and creativity. Similarly, Ericsson argues that one of the values of building expertise in basic skills is to release "cognitive resources for other, higher, functions." Think about a great jazz musician. The capacity for improvisation emerges only from a deep, rich foundation in basic musical skills that have long since become automatic and unconscious.

BITE OFF ONLY WHAT YOU CAN CHEW

The first key to building rituals is undertaking no more than one or two at a time. Given the limits of our willpower, the reason is obvious. It makes more sense to invest our limited willpower in creating one ritual that endures than to diffuse it across several new behaviors, increasing the likelihood that all of them will fail.

In most cases, it also makes sense to start small and build on success incrementally. If you've been almost completely sedentary, for example, you're more likely to be successful building a ritual around walking for fifteen minutes three days a week than you are trying to jog three miles a day five days a week. Success also tends to be self-reinforcing. If you stick with a ritual to walk three days a week, it's only a small leap to add another day to the regimen, and then two and three, and ultimately to begin jogging rather than walking.

Conventional wisdom suggests that it requires between twenty-one and thirty days to lock in a new behavior. We've found no credible research to support this assertion. Our own experience is that the time it takes to establish a ritual is highly variable and depends on the complexity of the new behavior, your level of motivation, and the frequency with which you practice it. Embedding a ritual can take anywhere from a couple of weeks to several months. Even then, it's possible to build several rituals over the course of a year, one at a time. Like many of our clients, we ourselves have built multiple rituals in our own lives, addressing each of the four sources of energy.

PRECISION AND SPECIFICITY

The second and perhaps most important key to building rituals is precision and specificity. Automaticity researchers have discovered the power of something they call "implementation intentions." In one study, a group of students was asked to write a report over the holidays describing what they had done on Christmas Eve. Half the group was asked to specify exactly when and where they'd do their writing; the other half weren't given any specific instructions. Only one-third of the latter group completed the assigned task. More than three-quarters of those who defined exactly when and where they'd write the report completed it. In another study, chronic procrastinators who set a specific time to complete a task were eight times as likely to follow through.

In a third study, a group of subjects was asked to exercise at least once for twenty minutes during the next week. That hardly seems like a daunting challenge, but based on the request itself, only 29 percent complied. A second group was given the same challenge, along with detailed information about the significant role exercise plays in reducing the risk of heart disease, an attempt to further motivate them. Compliance rose modestly, to 39 percent. A third group was asked to commit to exercising at a specific time, on a specific day, at a designated location. For this group, compliance more than doubled to an extraordinary 91 percent.

By defining precisely when we're going to undertake a behavior, we reduce the amount of energy we have to expend to get it done. Often, when we make a commitment to a new behavior such as exercising, we fail to recognize that unless we set aside a specific time to do it, it's unlikely we will. In part, that's because there is another behavior we're more accustomed to doing, out of habit; or because there is something easier and more pleasurable we could do. Each time we have to think about whether or not to do an activity—in the face of other temptations and potential distractions—we deplete our limited reservoir of will and discipline. If you have to consciously think for very long about doing something, it's unlikely you'll end up doing it for very long.

Exercise is a good example. Ask people who work out at a regular time on specific days whether they use a great deal of willpower to get to it, and the answer will almost always be no. The best evidence that a ritual has taken hold is the feeling of being pulled to it rather than having to push yourself to get it done. "On the days I miss my workout, I feel terrible," clients often tell us.

The more challenging the ritual—physically, mentally, or emotionally—the greater the need to be precise in implementing it. Robert, a senior leader at Sony Europe, created a ritual in which he set aside an hour once a week to think creatively and strategically. The demands at work were so intense that he found he otherwise didn't get around to a part of his job he considered important and that he felt added significant value.

At first Robert wasn't exacting about the time for his new ritual. If it got to the appointed hour for brainstorming and he had a quick phone call to make or an e-mail to write, he did those first. Before too long, the starting time he had established for his ritual began to slip, until one day he found himself coming up with an excuse for skipping it altogether. "I really don't have enough time left today to make it worthwhile," he told himself, "so I'm going to put it off." That's when he recognized something wasn't working. The seduction of attending to the urgent, along with the pull of his old habits, was overpowering him.

The solution, we helped Robert to see, was to give himself no leeway in the start time for his ritual. If a call or a conversation in his office began to run late, he took to telling the person "Look, I'm really sorry, but I have another appointment. We'll have to continue this later." Over time, he began setting expectations with others. When he got involved in something that had the potential to interfere with his brainstorming ritual, he made it explicit to his colleagues that he had a hard stop time to meet his next obligation. Once he established a time, he noticed that the business somehow always got done—a kind of reverse Parkinson's Law. Work not only expands to fill the time allotted to it, but also contracts to fit within the time allotted to it.

Inspired by his experience setting precise boundaries, Robert eventually created a second ritual. He reduced the length of most meetings he called from an hour to thirty minutes, and he also let participants know that all his meetings would start and end right on time. "The results were amazing," Robert told us. "Wasted time vanished. We got right to it. People loved knowing they wouldn't be kept waiting when they arrived or held late at the end. We've gotten more focused, and we get far more done at our meetings, in half the time."

WHAT WE RESIST PERSISTS

The third key to building rituals is to focus on something we do rather than something we continually try to resist doing. A diet, for example, works far better when you choose in advance exactly what you're going to eat rather than simply resisting tempting foods all day long. The power of a ritual is partly the fact that it's clearly defined, affirmative act. Baumeister's chocolate chip cookie study showed that trying to resist a behavior rapidly depletes our limited reserves of willpower. "It is probably easier and more effective to avoid temptation," Baumeister says, "than to resist it."

Many of our clients buy healthy snacks, put them into their desk drawers, and eat them at designated times, so they don't find themselves feeling hungry when they encounter food in the office or walk by a vending machine filled with sugary and salty snacks. "It matters whether we can shield an ongoing goal pursuit from distractions," explains psychologist Peter Gollwitzer, who has studied the power of implementation intentions. "Predeciding should help a person protect goal pursuit from tempting distractions, bad habits, or competing goals." Or, as David Besio, a professor and researcher at UCSF, puts it, "When you go into a day that's unplanned, then you're just faced with whatever hits you. If you have a plan, then you don't let the unplanned things get in your way."

The same principle applies to other, more complex behaviors. Imagine, for example, that your goal is to be more patient with others and not to interrupt them. If you simply define that as an intention—something you *won't* do anymore—it will almost certainly give way over time to your established habit of doing exactly what you always did in the past. Instead, a positive ritual might be to take a deep breath each time you notice yourself about to interrupt a colleague. That gives you an alternative behavior, which can become automatic over time. It's sometimes referred to as "If, then" behavior, as in 'When situation *X* arises, I will choose response *Y*.' By creating that intention, Gollwitzer concludes, "people can strategically switch from conscious and effortful control . . . to being automatically controlled by situational cues."

WHAT DO YOU WANT, AND WHAT WILL YOU DO TO AVOID GETTING IT?

The fourth and perhaps most paradoxical key to building rituals is to expect resistance to implementing them to arise along the way. The developmental psychologist William Perry put it wryly: "When someone comes to me for help," he said, "I listen very hard and ask myself, 'What does this person really want—and what will they do to keep from getting it?' " Homeostasis, derived from the Greek word for "standing still," allows us, biologically, to maintain a stable internal environment despite challenges ranging from viruses to changes in temperature. Our automatic internal processes make this possible, but they also help explain why we resist change.

We derive a sense of safety from doing what we've always done, even if it's suboptimal and even if it has the potential to damage us in the long run. Smoking, overeating, micromanaging, and constantly checking e-mail can all serve as ways to manage feelings of anxiety. In the short term, these behaviors provide a source of comfort and relief. If they're helping to get us through our days and nights, we don't give them up easily, even when we recognize rationally that they're costly and dysfunctional in the long run.

Harvard's Robert Kegan and his colleague Lisa Lahey, influenced in part by their mentor William Perry, have done pioneering work in defining something they call "immunity to change." Working with both individuals and organizations, they've demonstrated how even the most passionate commitment to a given change is invariably counterbalanced by an equally powerful but often unseen commitment *not* to change. "What is the commitment we make, often unconsciously," they ask, "to maintain the status quo and keep the very thing we say we want to happen from happening—because we are afraid of the consequences if it does happen?"

Imagine, for example, that you feel forever distracted and hurried in your life, a complaint we hear so commonly in the workplace that it seems nearly universal. Your primary commitment is to invest more time focused single-mindedly on your most important priorities. The next step, say Kegan and Lahey, is to ask yourself what you're currently doing (or not doing) to undermine that commitment. The answers might include constantly checking your e-mail; trying to do several activities at the same time; interrupting people in the middle of sentences; and not deciding in advance which tasks on your plate are likely to generate the greatest value.

The third step is to ask, "What is my competing commitment here?" The answers in this case might include "Feeling on top of things," "Being in control," "Getting a lot of things done," and even, perhaps, "Avoiding really difficult work for as long as I can." The final step is defining something that Kegan and Lahey call the "Big Assumption" behind each competing commitment. By that they mean the fear of what might happen if you actually followed through on your primary commitment and changed your behavior. In this instance, the big assumptions might range from "I'll be overwhelmed by all the tasks that will pile up when I'm not paying attention to them" to "People will make decisions without consulting me" to "I won't be there for my clients" to "I won't be able to stay focused, and I'll feel like a failure."

Because we mostly fail to recognize the fears that are inevitably associated with change, we often end up unconsciously sabotaging our own efforts to change. Bringing our competing commitments to light gives us a chance to assess whether the fears we have around a specific change are truly realistic. Often, they're not. For that reason, we next encourage our clients to ask themselves a simple question: "How can I design this ritual so I enjoy its intended benefits but also minimize the costs I fear it will prompt?"

A CULTURE THAT COOPERATES

The next key to successfully establishing rituals is to enlist the support of others. When you make a commitment to someone else to change a specific behavior, it creates a higher level of accountability. Success rates go up dramatically when we pair our clients with a partner—or even better, create a group of three or four—and ask them to check in with one another once a week to report on how they're doing. It's not just that most of us feel a desire to live up to our public commitments but also that others can help us see how we're getting in our own way. It's also positively reinforcing to be recognized by others for what we've accomplished.

When we first began doing this work, we focused mostly on helping individuals make changes. We paid very little attention to organizations. The consequence was that clients enthusiastically built new rituals, only to return to the workplace and discover that their bosses—and the cultures they worked in—had no interest in their changes and often resisted them. Perhaps no new behavior is more challenging to organizations, for example, than rituals focused on renewal. Powerful as the evidence is that intermittent renewal drives increased productivity (see chapter 6), the "more, bigger, faster" paradigm is deeply ingrained in most corporate cultures. So is the notion that any downtime is wasted time. Today, we work with senior leaders to develop organizational practices that support the work we are doing at the individual level, including promoting regular renewal during the workday. People can succeed at building rituals regardless of what's going on around them, but broad culture change depends on buy-in from the top.

"The leader must be more than a mere supporter," Kegan and Lahey have written about their work with organizations, echoing our own experience. "We cannot succeed if the leader is only authorizing our participation, if he or she is merely a sponsor or work being led by outsiders. We rely on the leaders we work with to be genuine partners, and when the resistance mounts, as it nearly always does, it is the leader . . . who must help the group renew its commitment to the journey."

KEEPING IT FRESH

The final key to building effective rituals is not to let them become so automatic that you lose track of whether they're still serving your intended goals. That requires a delicate dance between awareness and automaticity, another set of entailed opposites. Without ongoing self-awareness, the risk is that rituals eventually grow stale and become obsolete. Honest self-observation is the antidote to unwitting self-deception. Building new rituals can transform our behavior, but our instinctive resistance to change, our appetite for instant gratification, and our capacity to kid ourselves will never disappear. Inevitably, we lose our way and fall back at times. So long as we're willing to intermittently shine a light on ourselves and ask "How am I doing?"—hold ourselves accountable when we fall short—we each have the power to keep learning and growing.

CHAPTER THREE ACTION STEPS

- Reflect on a time when you have successfully made a change in your life or adopted a new behavior. What made doing so possible? Now think about a change you've tried but failed to make. What was the difference between success and failure?
- Identify a new behavior that you would like to build into your life. On what days and at what times could you engage in it? We know that people are exponentially more successful making changes when they undertake them at precise, scheduled times. What would you have to change in order to open up that time?
- When you think about launching a new behavior, what is most likely to get in the way of your success in adopting it? What might you have to give up? What do you fear will get in your way? Given the potential obstacles, what could you do to increase your chances of success?

PART II

SUSTAINABILITY/PHYSICAL

CHAPTER FOUR

Feeling the Pulse

All the systems in our body pulse rhythmically when we're healthy—heart rate, brain waves, body temperature, blood pressure, hormone levels. "It would be reasonable to say," explains the chronobiologist Josephine Arendt, "that everything that happens in our bodies is rhythmic until proven otherwise." Our most fundamental need is to spend and renew energy. We breathe in, and we breathe out. We can't do one for very long without doing the other, and the more deeply we do

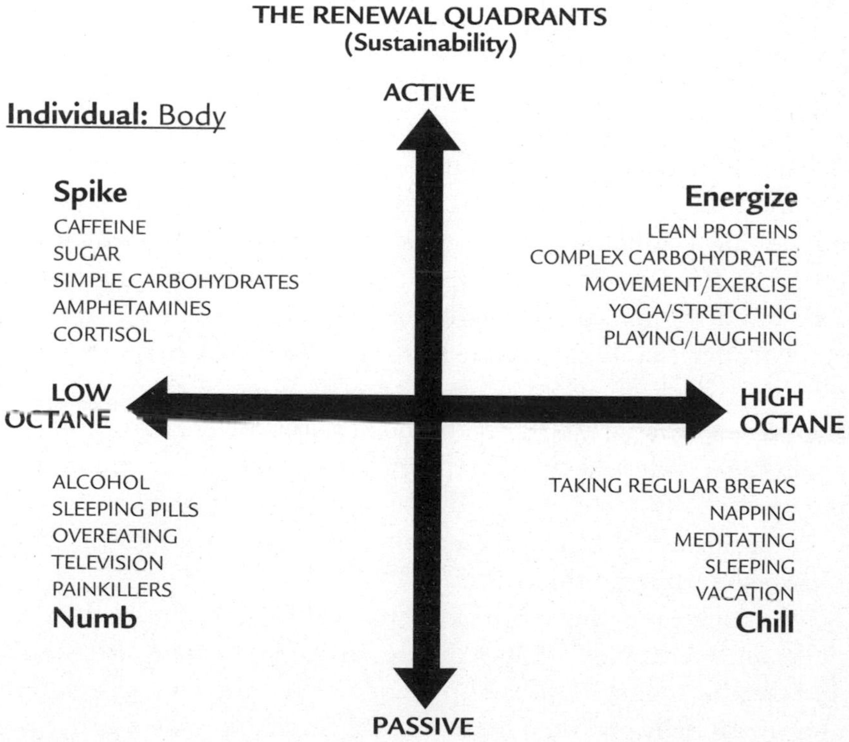

THE RENEWAL QUADRANTS
(Sustainability)

both, the better we operate, not just physically but also mentally and emotionally.

Obvious as it may seem to live in alignment with our inborn rhythms, we don't. The ethic of more, bigger, faster has prompted us to spend far more energy than we adequately renew, in a frenzied and largely futile effort to keep up with relentlessly rising demand. The quadrants on page 49 are a simple way to understand the rhythmic nature of optimal energy management at the physical level. The horizontal axis moves from the healthy, intentional behaviors on the right-hand side, which fuel and refuel physical energy, to the less healthy ones on the left-hand side. It's under intense demand, most commonly, that we default to the more expedient left-hand behaviors for a quick jolt of energy or to soothe and calm ourselves.

When we fail to get enough sleep and work for hours at a time without any breaks, we begin to rely more on caffeine, sugar, and other low-octane, short acting stimulants to keep us going during the day. As demands pile up, our body's own stress hormones—adrenaline, norephinephrine, cortisol—kick in, providing another source of speedy, short-term energy. The cost is that cortisol, in particular, becomes toxic to us when it circulates in our bodies for too long.

As our stress levels spike and our anxiety levels rise, we also often overeat—especially sugars and fats—in a misguided effort to calm and comfort ourselves. Alternatively, we fail to eat at all, which only fuels our edginess. When we get home, we may be physically exhausted, but we're often mentally and emotionally wired. We rely not just on food but also on alcohol to calm us down. Too tired to truly interact with our families, we turn instead to passive activities such as watching television, which is often a way to numb out rather than to truly renew or refuel. When we try to fall asleep, we begin ruminating about today's mistakes and tomorrow's demands and we end up relying on sleep medications to knock us out. Too tired to exercise when we wake up, we settle instead for a jolt of caffeine as the previous day's cycle begins to recapitulate itself.

We squeeze into our cars to commute to jobs in which we sit at our desks for hours at a time. By working for too long, too continuously, and sleeping too little, we end up spending too much energy mentally and emotionally, with too little renewal. By sitting too long and eating too much, we don't spend enough energy physically. The consequence is that we lose endurance and strength, and we put on weight.

It's a healthy pulse we're really after. Think for a moment about the Indianapolis 500. The driver who wins that race isn't the one who drives the fastest the longest and most continuously. The winner is the one who drives at the highest speeds when he's on the track but also makes the most efficient pit stops along the way to refuel, change the tires, and make mechanical adjustments and repairs. Maintenance and refueling are as critical to victory as racing itself. That's because the higher the demand, the greater and more frequent the need for renewal.

Much as that's true for machines, it's even more so for human beings. We're far more complex than any machine and we have vastly more moving parts. Still, most of us are more vigilant about refueling and maintaining our cars than we are about taking care of ourselves. When demand in our lives intensifies, our pattern is to hunker down and push harder, rather than to refuel more frequently. "We are usually unaware of [our] internal rhythms," writes Jennifer Ackerman in her book *Sex Sleep Eat Drink Dream,* "sensing them vividly only when we abuse them, during shift work, jet lag, or adjustment to daylight-savings time." In short, we're meant to pulse, but we lead increasingly linear lives, spending energy too continuously and renewing it too infrequently.

Consider Caleb, an accountant whose way of working is characteristic of many of our clients before we begin working with them. Caleb's job is always demanding, but between January and April, during the busy tax season, he switches into overdrive. His days can run as long as fifteen to sixteen hours, and it's rare that he takes a full day off.

Caleb likes to get to work early—no later than 7:30 A.M.—so he has some quiet time to himself before the office gets busy and the demands mount. His commute is an hour without traffic, so he typically awakens at 5:30 A.M., showers, dresses, and is out the door no later than 6:15 A.M. Neither his wife nor his two young children are up that early, and rather than eat breakfast alone, Caleb simply skips it. "I'm not really hungry that early anyway," he says. Instead, when he gets to his office, he treats himself to a grande latte at the Starbucks next to his firm's headquarters.

Much as Caleb would prefer to work out before heading for the office—he was a competitive athlete in both high school and college—he can't imagine waking up any earlier than he already does. Nor are the evenings an option. By the time he gets home, even on an early night, he feels far too exhausted to consider physical exercise. A dry martini or a glass of wine seems far more appealing. After the tax season subsides, Caleb tries to get at least one workout in on the weekend, or he plays pickup basketball at a nearby park. Even those activities make him feel a little guilty, given how little time he has with his children during the week.

In addition to his responsibilities to his primary client, a hedge fund, Caleb manages a team of just under a dozen more junior accountants. Caleb's day alternates between long hours in front of the computer at his desk and long meetings, often scheduled one after another, with no time in between. By 10 A.M. most days, he begins to feel hungry and typically orders out for a second coffee and a muffin or a bagel. He rarely leaves his desk for lunch, ordering in from the deli instead or rushing down to the company cafeteria to grab something that he can take back upstairs. On most days, someone in the office brings in some cake, candy, or cookies. To jump-start his energy at midafternoon, Caleb usually grabs a sweet, which he washes down with another cup of coffee. During busy season, it isn't uncommon for his team to order in pizza three nights in a row, simply because it's the simplest and quickest solution.

Outside the busy season, Caleb typically arrives home between 8 and 8:30 P.M. and tries to get to bed by 11 P.M. During busy season, he rarely gets home before 11 and sometimes even midnight. Even though he's physically exhausted on those evenings, he often finds himself tossing and turning in bed for an hour. "I've just learned to do without much sleep," he says.

From our perspective, Caleb lives a life with almost no waves. From the time he arrives at work until he leaves at night, he spends mental and emotional energy continuously. Physically, he's almost completely sedentary—sitting behind the wheel of his car, at his desk, in a conference room or splayed out on a couch at home, where he often falls asleep and spends the night. He eats at erratic intervals and gets his energy in fleeting bursts from the caffeine and sugar that are central to his diet, especially when he's feeling rushed and under stress.

Our first goal with clients is to establish a physical foundation that makes it possible for them to perform at their best. By shortchanging themselves physically, they're trying to perform at a high level on low-octane fuel, and sometimes with virtually no gas at all in their tanks. They fail to recognize that the way they take care of their bodies, day in and day out, directly influences how they feel, think and perform. Taking care of yourself physically won't turn you into a great performer—it's just one piece of a more complex puzzle—but failing to do so assures that you can't ever perform at your best.

John Weiser, forty-five, is the president for the Television Division of Sony Pictures Entertainment. As much as anyone with whom we've worked, Weiser has intentionally created a wavy, rhythmic way of life. He is asleep most nights by 10 P.M. at the latest, and he gets a minimum of seven hours of sleep. "If I get any less I've learned I'm not where I should be mentally the next day," he says. "Earlier in my career, there were times when I couldn't turn my mind off. I'd only get four or five hours of sleep, and I'd grind through the next day, but I knew I was operating at seventy percent."

Weiser wakes up at 5 A.M., before his wife and kids. "That's when I've chosen to have my alone time," he says. "It's when I take care of myself and build up my energy for the day ahead." By 5:30 A.M., he's at the gym on the Sony lot. He alternates among weight training, classes, and cardiovascular exercise for the next hour and a half. "Early morning in the gym is my foundation," he explains. "I feed off the positive energy I get from working out. It's how I get myself going, so when I'm done I can focus on everything else—clients, deals, the company, and the people who work for me.

"When someone walks up to me during the day smiling, looking healthy and happy and confident, it lifts me up and it lights up the room. That's what I try to do when I walk into a room. Getting my sleep and working out gives me good energy, and people respond to that in a really obvious way. They're energized by it."

Weiser also tries to build two twenty-minute meditation sessions into his workdays. "I've long since learned that I can handle more at work when I meditate," he explains. "I'm better with people, and I'm more focused and productive as a result. My assistant treats it as if I'm in a meeting that can't be disturbed." Weiser rarely misses a morning meditation, but given the unexpected demands that arise as the day wears on, he fits in his afternoon meditation only about half the time.

"When I miss it," he says, "I always wish I'd done it, because I feel a hundred percent better when I do, and I'm always calmer and more productive for the rest of the day."

Weiser is also a careful eater, and he focuses intentionally on foods that provide the most sustaining sources of energy, mostly proteins and complex carbohydrates. When he came to our first session, he brought along a jar of peanut butter, just to be certain that he'd have one of the staple foods he depends on to sustain his energy.

"People have a million different excuses why they don't eat the right food or why they skip meals," Weiser explains. "It's crazy to think the right kinds of food will be available to you 24/7. I think through where I'm going to be during the day and what I'm going to need to eat. It's no different than getting in a car for a trip from Los Angeles to Las Vegas and thinking in advance about where you're going to stop for gas along the way. If you don't, you're going to find yourself hitting empty, looking around and realizing you're in the desert." We urge our clients to pack food for any situation in which they're not sure what they'll find to eat, especially when they're traveling and find themselves in airports, surrounded only by junk food. Weiser's solution when he travels is to pack nuts, fruits, or even protein powder, which he can mix in a cup with water and drink wherever he is.

The final way that Weiser ensures that he balances energy expenditure with energy renewal is that he leaves work for home early enough to spend time with his family. Because he is highly focused, he gets a great deal done in the hours he is working. He almost never takes work home, nor does he look at e-mail there. Instead, he reserves the period between arriving home and bedtime for his wife and two young children. "I get time for myself in the morning," he says, "and the early evening is for my family. The truth is I need time for myself and time for them, and I get energized by both."

Weiser figured out intuitively what all of us need to do systematically. We're more effective at work when we regularly renew, and we're at our best when we alternate between active forms of renewal, such as exercise and play, and more passive forms, such as meditation and sleep.

CHAPTER FOUR ACTION STEPS

- Review the Renewal Quadrants on page 49. How well are you managing your physical energy? Do you spend more time on the right side of the quadrants or the left?
- Think about how you behave when demand is high. Do you tend to push yourself harder, eat more and worse, and sleep and exercise less? Do you work long hours without taking breaks? Each of these is a form of linear behavior. We're at our best when we pulse. How can you build a better balance between energy expenditure and energy renewal into your days?
- Identify what you currently do to recharge or refuel yourself during the course of your day at work. Based on what you've learned in this chapter, what can you do to better ensure that you get both active *and* passive forms of renewal over the course of the day?

CHAPTER FIVE

Sleep or Die

If physical energy is the foundation of all dimensions of energy, sleep is the foundation of physical energy. The circadian rhythm refers to the biological processes that occur over a twenty-four-hour cycle. We're genetically programmed to be awake during the day and to sleep at night. We operate best—physically, mentally, emotionally, and spiritually—when we align with that rhythm. For example, the hormone melatonin, which tends to induce sleep, is almost nonexistent in our bodies during daytime hours and reaches its peak between 11 P.M. and 3 A.M. The same is true for our core body temperature, which reaches its lowest level in the middle of the night and its highest level during the morning.

We challenge our circadian rhythms at our peril—whether by working during the night, traveling across time zones, or failing to sleep sufficiently. The consequences include extreme fatigue, compromised cognitive capacity, emotional instability, lower productivity, and greater susceptibility to illness.

No single behavior, we've come to believe, more fundamentally influences our effectiveness in waking life than sleep. In a famous series of experiments, the researcher Alan Rechtschaffen and his colleagues at the University of Chicago put a series of rats through the equivalent of hell by systematically depriving them of sleep. Within days, the rats began to eat significantly more than usual, perhaps as a way to get more energy to compensate for their lack of sleep. In less than a week, the rats lost control of their body temperature, began losing their hair, and developed lesions on their bodies that wouldn't heal. Within seventeen to twenty days, they were dead. William Dement, the widely acknowledged dean of sleep researchers, argues that sleep may well be more critical to our well-being than diet, exercise, and even heredity.

Among human beings, the record for continuous sleeplessness is just under nineteen days, during a rocking chair marathon. For the winner, outlasting his rivals proved to be a decidedly mixed blessing. By the end, he was suffering from slurred speech, blurred vision, significant lapses in memory and concentration, hallucinations, and paranoia. Amnesty International lists prolonged sleep deprivation as a form of torture, and it has been widely used as an interrogation tactic, including in the Iraq and Afghanistan wars. In his memoir *White Nights,* the late Israeli prime minister Menachem Begin vividly captured the experience of sleep deprivation when he was an inmate in a KGB prison: "In the head of the interrogated prisoner, a haze begins to form. His spirit is wearied to death, his legs are unsteady, and he has one sole desire: to sleep. . . . Anyone who has experienced this desire knows that not even hunger and thirst are comparable with it."

Nonetheless, sleep is also one of the first behaviors many of us are willing to sacrifice, on the mistaken assumption that doing so will allow us to be more productive. "We all think we have to stay awake to get more done," says Matthew Walker, the director of the sleep and neuroimaging lab at UC Berkeley. "I think that's simply not true. In fact, if you have a good night of sleep, what you'll find is that you can get more done than if you simply stay awake."

So how much sleep do we need? The National Sleep Foundation recommends between seven and nine hours. When researchers test subjects in environments without clocks or windows and ask them to sleep whenever they feel tired, approximately 95 percent of them sleep between seven and eight hours out of every twenty-four. Precious few of us can function well on much less. As Thomas Roth of the Henry Ford Sleep Disorders and Research Center says, "The percentage of the population who need less than five hours of sleep per night, rounded to a whole number, is zero."

Based on their own estimates, Americans average 6½ hours of sleep a night. Even that may be overstated. In a study led by Diane Lauderdale at the University of Chicago, 669 middle-aged adults reported that they slept an average of 7.5 hours a night. But they also wore wrist monitors that allowed the researchers to determine precisely when they actually fell asleep. The average turned out to be 6.1 hours.

In our own experience, working mostly with upper-level leaders and managers, a substantial percentage tell us they get six or fewer hours of sleep a night, and the majority of those say they simply don't need any more. The research strongly suggests otherwise. One explanation is that people who are sleep-deprived often don't recognize their own limitations. "It's convenient to say, 'I've learned to live without sleep,' " explains David Dinges, a sleep researcher at the University of Pennsylvania. "But you bring them into the laboratory and we don't see this adaptation." Charles Czeisler, another renowned sleep researcher and chronobiologist at Harvard Medical School, puts it more bluntly: "Like a drunk, a person who is sleep-deprived has no idea how functionally impaired he or she truly is. Most of us have forgotten what it really feels like to be awake." Thomas Wehr, the chief of the Section on Biological Rhythms at the NIH, takes it a step further. "Perhaps," he says, "we modern humans have never really known what it is to be fully awake."

Numerous studies of great performers suggest they sleep more than the rest of us, not less. That's true of the top violinists in Anders Ericsson's study, who slept an hour a night more than their less accomplished counterparts. As Berkeley's Matthew Walker puts it, "Practice does not quite make perfect. It's practice with a night of sleep that makes perfect." Two recent studies of athletes at Stanford University suggest a powerful correlation between sleep time and performance. In one study, members of the swim team maintained their usual sleep-waking pattern for two weeks and then increased to ten hours of sleep a day for six to seven weeks. Once they were sleeping longer hours, they began to report higher energy and improved mood. They also significantly improved their quickness off the starting block, as well as their turn times, sprint times, and kick-stroke rate.

"While this study focused specifically on collegiate swimmers," reported the lead author, Cherie Mah, of the Stanford Sleep Disorders Clinic and Research Laboratory, "it agrees with data from my other studies of different sports and suggests that athletes across all sports can greatly benefit from extra sleep." In an earlier study that Mah conducted among six players on the Stanford men's basketball team, more sleep led to improvements in alertness and mood, as well as in sprint times and free-throw accuracy. Mah and her colleagues have seen comparable gains among athletes on Stanford's football, tennis, golf, cross-country, and track and field teams.

FATTER, DUMBER, AND MORE DANGEROUS

Overwhelming evidence suggests that sleep deprivation takes a toll in nearly every aspect of our lives, including performance. In *Dream On: Sleep in the 24/7 Society,* Charles Leadbeater summed up the costs this way: "Lack of sleep makes us more inefficient at work and more dangerous behind the wheel of a car. It undermines the quality of our lives and makes us more vulnerable to illness. It is also responsible for making us less able to respond creatively to problems and opportunities, and less original, flexible and divergent in our thinking and thus less likely to generate new ideas."

At the most basic level, prolonged sleep deprivation has a negative impact on our health. Several studies have shown that immune response drops significantly among people who sleep less than seven to eight hours a night. Eve Van Cauter, a University of Chicago sleep researcher, found that subjects who slept four hours a night for six consecutive nights demonstrated not only a lower immune response but also diminished ability to regulate blood sugar, a risk factor for diabetes, and unusually high levels of circulating cortisol, a risk factor for high blood pressure. Among Van Cauter's most significant findings was that significant sleep deprivation dramatically lowers levels of leptin, the hormone that signals satiety, and helps us control how much we eat.

Subjects sleeping four hours a night for six nights produced 18 percent less leptin than those sleeping seven to eight hours. This finding, Van Cauter and others believe, goes a long way toward explaining the connection between obesity and sleep patterns. For example, a study of nearly 10,000 people found that subjects who slept five or fewer hours a night were 60 percent more likely to be obese than those who slept seven hours or more.

The Harvard Nurses' Health Study, which followed nearly 80,000 nurses over twenty-five years, uncovered a strong link between chronic sleep deprivation and increased risk of a range of diseases, including breast cancer, colon cancer, and coronary heart disease. Nurses who averaged five hours of sleep a night, for example, were significantly more likely to develop heart disease than those who got six hours.

They, in turn, were at greater risk than those who slept seven hours a night.

Nurses in the same study who regularly worked the night shift over many years were an astonishing 60 percent more likely to develop breast cancer. Numerous other studies have confirmed this link between shift work and breast cancer. The explanation, researchers have speculated, is that working during the night precludes exposure to the highest levels of the hormone melatonin, which is believed to restrain tumor growth.

At the cognitive level, we don't think well when we're tired. David Dinges found that subjects who slept less than six hours a night over a two-week period demonstrated a decrease in performance that was equivalent to that experienced after forty-eight continuous hours of sleep deprivation. More striking still, Harvard's Charles Czeisler found that averaging four hours a sleep for five consecutive nights has an impact on our memory, attention, and speed of thinking that is equivalent to being legally intoxicated.

Sleep is not simply cognitively restorative but also a time during which considerable learning occurs. Although the acquisition of knowledge occurs only during waking life, there is evidence that we process, consolidate, and stabilize memory during sleep. In one clever and fascinating study, subjects were asked to transform a string of eight digits into a different string by applying two simple rules. The more comfortable they got with the sequence, the faster they became.

None of the participants was told about a third hidden rule, which had the potential to provide a shortcut to the answer. Two groups were trained for the task in the evening. One went to sleep for the eight hours following the training. A second remained awake through the night. A third group was trained the morning of the next day and then remained awake for the next eight hours before being tested again. The group that went to sleep directly after the training demonstrated more than twice the likelihood of gaining insight into the hidden rule than either of the two groups that remained awake during the training.

Different kinds of learning occur during different stages of sleep. We sleep in five stages, which progress from lighter to deeper as our brain wave activity slows progressively and then speeds back up nearly to waking over the course of approximately ninety minutes. William Dement and Nathaniel Kleitman made this discovery in 1957, and Kleitman named it the "basic rest activity cycle" (BRAC).

It is during slow-wave sleep (SWS), the deepest of the five cycles, that we appear to process and consolidate fact-based information, such as a new language or the capitals of states. The processing and acquisition of more complex and emotionally charged information more commonly occurs in rapid eye movement (REM) sleep, the lightest stage of the cycle. REM sleep also appears to play a key role in remembering how to do an activity, such as typing or driving a car. Motor learning is consolidated during the middle stages of sleep. Visual learning is processed in both slow-wave and REM sleep. The practical implication of these findings is that uninterrupted ninety-minute cycles of sleep are essential not just for their restorative value but also to maximize our acquisition of knowledge.

The impact of sleep deprivation is also pernicious on the job, both because it prompts cognitive deficits and because it negatively influences our mood, a combination that undermines our judgment, especially under pressure. Many of the most devastating human-caused disasters during the past fifty years have taken place in the middle of the night or were connected to insufficient sleep or both. When the assistant captain at the helm of the *Exxon Valdez* ran his ship into a reef shortly after midnight on March 24, 1989, he had slept less than six hours during the previous forty-eight. Eleven million gallons of crude oil spilled into the sea. NASA officials in charge of the space shuttle *Challenger* had worked twenty-four consecutive hours before the shuttle launch that resulted in its explosion on January 28, 1986. On April 26 of the same year, a reactor exploded at the Chernobyl nuclear power plant in Ukraine at 1:23 A.M., releasing massive amounts of radiation. At the nuclear power plant on Three Mile Island, Pennsylvania, plant operators working under high stress in the middle of the night made a series of mistakes and poor judgment calls that prompted the core reactor's meltdown beginning at 4 A.M. on March 28, 1979.

Similar, if less broadly catastrophic accidents, occur in hospitals with frightening regularity every night. A 2004 Work Hours, Health and Safety Group study at Harvard, overseen by Charles Czeisler and his research team, found that medical interns working twenty-four-hour shifts made 36 percent more medical errors than those working sixteen-hour shifts and five times the number of diagnostic errors. Interns working twenty-four-hour shifts also had a 61 percent greater risk of stabbing themselves with a needle or scalpel while working, almost twice the risk of crashing their cars when they drove home, and five times the risk of a near-miss accident.

None of this should come as a great surprise. Study after study shows that people who work night shifts make more errors, suffer more injuries and health problems, and perform at lower levels than those who work normal daytime hours. So powerful are the body's natural rhythms that it's virtually impossible to fully adjust to working at night and sleeping during the day. "Ours is the only species," writes Jennifer Ackerman in *Sex Eat Sleep Drink Dream,* "that lights up its biological night, that overrides its own rhythms, crosses time zones, and works and sleeps at times that run counter to its internal clocks. We ignore what our clocks remember at our own peril." As just one example, shift workers who have no choice but to sleep in the daytime get an average of three to four hours a day less sleep than the rest of us and sleep less deeply.

THE SIMPLEST SOLUTION

Awareness is half the battle when it comes to sleep, both because most of us underestimate the costs of getting too little and because of the extraordinary value of getting enough. This recognition is the first step in making more sleep a priority.

If you're not getting enough sleep, you almost certainly need to go to bed earlier, given that you likely don't have the option of waking up later than you already do. The key to sleep is to be relaxed, something that is increasingly difficult to achieve given the pressure of our daily lives. One obvious alternative is to use sleep aids. Every form of sleep medication has its drawbacks, from limited hours of effectiveness, to leaving us feeling groggy in the morning, to being addictive. Alcohol, the most common form of self-medication when it comes to sleep, is likewise a double-edged sword. Because it acts initially as a sedative, it does induce asleep, and nearly 30 percent of insomniacs use alcohol at least occasionally to help them fall asleep. But alcohol is also metabolized rapidly by the body, which can lead to physiological withdrawal symptoms in the middle of the night, including frequent awakenings, shallow sleep, and less overall sleep time. In simple terms, the less alcohol you drink and the earlier you drink it, the more deeply you're likely to sleep through the night.

The best way to fall asleep naturally is to begin quieting down at least thirty to sixty minutes before you turn out the lights. That means avoiding anything stimulating as you get closer to your bedtime—e-mailing and the Internet, mystery novels, highly charged conversations—in favor of whatever you find relaxing: drinking a glass of milk or herbal tea, taking a bath or a shower, listening to music, or even reading a dull book.

Because feeling relaxed is so critical to sleep, it can also be helpful to intentionally "park" your anxieties before you turn out the lights. This simple technique involves writing down what you're worrying about in a notebook or on a piece of paper. For many of our clients, this strategy has proven to be a surprisingly powerful means of temporarily setting aside concerns that otherwise keep them awake. By writing down what's on your mind, you effectively give your brain permission to release it from conscious awareness. The same technique can be used when you wake up in the middle of the night, begin to ruminate, and have trouble getting back to sleep.

Setting a specific bedtime is especially critical, because without one, we tend to default back quickly to whatever time we're used to going to sleep or simply stay up until we feel tired. Once the lights are out, one effective way to relax is deep breathing and progressive relaxation—tightening and releasing muscles throughout your body, starting with your toes and working your way up. For obvious reasons, we sleep better in environments that are dark and quiet. It also helps to sleep in a cool room, which allows the body temperature to drop, as it's meant to do during sleep. If you have any doubt about the value of a cool room, think about what it's like to try to sleep on a hot summer night.

Peter Goettler, who headed investment banking at Barclays Capital until 2008, spent most of his working life feeling sleep-deprived. When that's the case, it's nearly always where we begin our work. Goettler went to sleep most nights between 11 P.M. and midnight and awoke around 5 A.M., scarcely an unusual sleep pattern for many of our clients. When Goettler got out of bed, he had the first of several cups of coffee to jack himself up. During the day, he often yo-yoed between feeling jittery and tired, especially in the late afternoons.

After working with us, Goettler decided to build a ritual in which he went to bed at 10 P.M., got up a half hour later in the morning, and stopped drinking coffee altogether. Almost immediately, he was successful at going to bed earlier. At first, he reported that he found himself waking up earlier and therefore sleeping the same number of hours he always had. It's a pattern we've often seen: the body can become deeply habituated even to sleeping patterns that leave us feeling tired.

We suggested that when he woke up, Goettler simply lie quietly in bed, relaxing as best he could and effectively giving his body permission to sleep longer. Even if it didn't work immediately, he'd be getting more rest. After a week or so, he did begin sleeping longer. The extended sleep was transformative for him. "I was more rested, I felt better, I thought more clearly, I got less tired as the day wore on, and I had more energy when I got home," he told us. "I never would have believed an hour more of sleep could make such a difference." Adequate sleep, we're convinced, sets the stage for taking more control of every other part of our lives.

CHAPTER FIVE ACTION STEPS

- Take a few moments to create a sleep log to determine how much sleep you are actually getting. (To download a template, go to www.theenergyproject.com/sleeplog.)
- How many hours of sleep have you averaged during the past week? Ninety-five percent of us require at least seven to eight hours of sleep a night to be fully rested. If you're not getting that much, you're probably working at a suboptimal level.
- Reflect on the activities you engage in during the hour prior to going to bed. The best way to fall asleep quickly and easily is to begin to quiet down at least thirty to sixty minutes before you turn out the lights. Choose activities that are relaxing rather than stimulating or demanding.
- If you wake up in the middle of the night and then struggle to fall back asleep because you're ruminating, put a pad of paper and a pen beside your bad. Before you go to sleep, write down anything you're feeling worried about. You can do the same thing if you tend to wake up in the middle of the night. It's called "parking your anxieties," and it is a powerful way to calm your mind and get a better night's sleep.

CHAPTER SIX

Making Waves

We're not meant to rest solely at night. A decade after Nathaniel Kleitman gave the name "basic rest activity cycle" to the ninety-minute period during which we move through the five stages of sleep, he suggested that we experience a parallel ninety-minute cycle in our waking life. At night we move from light to deep sleep. During the day we oscillate every ninety minutes or so from higher to lower alertness. We call these "ultradian" cycles, which literally means "less than a day."

In effect, our bodies are asking us for a break every ninety minutes or so. More often than not, and especially in the face of high demand, we ignore signals such as physical restlessness, wandering attention, and greater irritability. Instead, we grab a cup of coffee or unconsciously call up our emergency reserves, in the form of stress hormones such as adrenaline and cortisol. These hormones generate energy, but they also prompt a higher level of anxiety and reactivity, which ultimately undermine our effectiveness.

The Israeli sleep researcher Peretz Lavie found fascinating evidence for the ultradian rhythm in a series of experiments he conducted. Groups of subjects were asked to come into his lab during the evening, so that he could keep them awake throughout the night. The next morning at 7 A.M., the subjects were taken into bedrooms and given an opportunity to go to sleep for seven minutes at a time. Whether or not they succeeded, they were then asked to get out of bed and spend the next thirteen minutes awake. Over the subsequent twenty-four hours, the bedraggled subjects repeated this pattern every twenty minutes, or seventy-two times in all.

Having been kept up all of the previous night, it wouldn't have been surprising if the exhausted subjects found it easy to fall asleep each time they put their heads on a pillow. That *was* the case during the afternoons and from 10 P.M. on. At those times, it was far harder to wake subjects at the end of seven minutes. The surprising finding was a pattern that emerged throughout the day. Every ninety minutes or so, something that Lavie termed a "sleep gate" opened. During the subsequent half hour, his subjects were significantly more likely to fall asleep than at other times, clear evidence of the ultradian rhythm and the cyclical nature of our alertness and fatigue throughout the day.

Great performers intuitively understand their own cycles. That helps explain why the top violinists in the Ericsson study practiced for periods no longer than ninety minutes and why other researchers have found that top performers in fields ranging from chess to sports to scientific research tend to work in approximately ninety-minute cycles and then take a break. Meanwhile, most people continue to wrongly assume that working more continuously—hunkering down, staying the course, burning the midnight oil—is the best way to generate more productivity.

I spent my early career as a journalist, and I long operated from the assumption that when it came to writing, the longer I worked, the more I would accomplish. After learning about the ultradian rhythm a decade ago, I redesigned my workday, especially when I was writing books.

For years, my approach had been to sit down to work at seven A.M. and essentially remain there until seven P.M. It was like being chained to my desk. Like most writers, I found countless ways to avoid writing along the way, including taking phone calls, reading and responding to e-mails, sorting through the papers on my desk, and simply daydreaming. Without realizing it, I was pacing myself, and rarely fully engaging, because at some level I recognized I couldn't do so indefinitely. It was when I learned about the value of moving between intense effort and purposeful rest that I created a new schedule. I continued to begin my writing day at seven A.M. But instead of simply staying there as long as possible, I wrote in three or four separate periods of exactly ninety minutes and framed them as ultradian 'sprints.'

While I was writing, I turned off my e-mail, took no phone calls, and tried to focus as single-mindedly as possible. During my first renewal break I had breakfast. For my second I took a thirty- or forty-minute run, and for my third I had lunch and read the newspaper or a book for pleasure. If I did a fourth writing sprint, I lifted weights or meditated afterward. Then I spent the afternoon on phone calls and other work that didn't require such high concentration.

We derive recovery not only by literally stopping whatever it is we're doing, but also by simply changing channels. After ninety minutes sitting in front of a computer, running is a way to build physical capacity, but it is also a reliable way to prompt mental and emotional recovery. That's partly because running prompts the release of endorphins, which generate a sense of well-being, but also because running tends to move us out of conscious analytical thinking, facilitating mental and emotional renewal.

On this writing schedule, I rarely spent more than four and a half hours a day writing at my desk, compared to more than double that number of hours for my previous books. By limiting each writing cycle to ninety minutes and building in periods of renewal, I was able to focus far more intensely. The result was that I accomplished significantly more in fewer hours and was able to complete my two most recent books, including this one, in far less time than I had my earlier ones.

RESISTANCE TO RENEWAL

From an early age, many of us are programmed to believe that rest is for slackers. Time spent "not doing" is time wasted. Building intermittent breaks into the workday is not only counterintuitive, it's also countercultural in the vast majority of organizations. That's why we work not only with individuals, to help them experience the value of renewal, but also at the organizational level, to change cultures.

When we first introduced the concept of taking intermittent breaks to traders at financial institutions, they looked at us as if we'd gone off the deep end. "Get real," they told us. "Do you have any idea what our lives are like? We sit down in front of our screens at eight-thirty in the morning, and we stay there until four P.M., when the market closes. We barely have time to stand up, much less to take a break." The implicit assumption was that effective renewal requires significant periods of time. In fact, the value of renewal depends less on how much time we devote to it than on how effectively we do it, just as our productivity is less a function of how many hours we put in than of how productive we are during the hours we're working.

Because most of us neither value nor intentionally practice intermittent renewal, it's often something we don't do very well. But, we can systematically build our capacity to recover more efficiently. Professional tennis players, for example, build meticulous recovery rituals that allow them to drop as much as one heartbeat per second in the twenty to thirty seconds between points. That can mean a reduction in heart rate of 150 or 160 at the end of a point down to 120 or 130 before the next point, a powerful wave of recovery. Think of the advantage to a player who recovers that way throughout a match, playing against an opponent who doesn't understand the value of recovery.

In the workplace, we've helped our clients develop a variety of techniques for renewing themselves in very short periods of time. It's possible, for example, to significantly relax the body, quiet the mind, and calm the emotions simply by breathing more deeply and rhythmically. Breathing in through your nose to a count of three and out through your mouth to a count of six prompts a significant feeling of relaxation in as few as thirty to sixty seconds.

Meditators have understood this phenomenon for thousands of years. Hundreds of studies have confirmed meditation's broad-based benefits. At the most basic level, it's simply a means of relaxation and an antidote to stress. In one study conducted by Jon Kabat-Zinn, a leading meditation researcher, a group of twenty-two subjects who met the criteria for anxiety disorder or panic disorder participated in an eight-week group stress reduction program based on "mindfulness meditation." In repeated follow-up measures, twenty of the subjects—more than 90 percent—demonstrated significant reductions in anxiety. A substantial number also experienced diminished panic symptoms.

Breathing deeply, meditating, listening to music, and reading a novel are all forms of "passive" renewal, which involves lowering physiological arousal. "Active" renewal requires creating the opposite kind of physiological wave by raising the heart rate and arousal levels through aerobic exercise, weight lifting, or more strenuous forms of yoga.

It's always challenging to convince people who are facing intense demand that they'd be more productive if they renewed more frequently. Mark, for example, is the CFO of a large manufacturing company that was experiencing severe financial stress when we met him. "Renewal sounds great," he told us at our first session together, "but with all the demands on my time, it just feels like I'm better off working another hour, rather than sleeping an extra hour or taking time to work out. Maybe the consequence is that I won't be as efficient in the twelfth hour of the day as I was in the second or the third, but I still feel like I'll get more accomplished than if I didn't work that twelfth hour at all."

No research we cite to the contrary is ever as convincing as getting clients to experiment for themselves. We suggested to Mark that he schedule one significant break a day, in the afternoon, and then monitor the impact on his energy and focus over the rest of the day.

"I decided to really put the idea to the test," Mark told us. "I put a thirty-minute break into my calendar at two thirty every afternoon, and I asked my assistant to protect the time and to remind me if I started to run over into it. My ritual was to take a walk by myself, outside, and to intentionally think about something other than work. The truth is, I don't succeed every day, but I do most days. I enjoy being outside, and the unexpected bonus is that I get lot of creative ideas when I am out walking.

"When I return to my office, I make it a point to purposely focus on something challenging—say, reading a dense document or writing a complicated memo or even having a difficult conversation. I choose the sort of things that I would have previously avoided in the afternoons, because I didn't have the energy for them. What's happened is undeniable: I've discovered I can concentrate far better in the hour or two following my walks than at any other time of the day besides the first couple of hours in the morning. I was a huge skeptic going in, but now it takes a true crisis to make me miss my afternoon walk. It's given me a whole second half to my workday which just wasn't there before. I've also added a shorter break most mornings when I walk around the office and stop in to talk to one or two people about something other than work."

Another obstacle to renewing intermittently is that it isn't culturally acceptable in many organizations, and in some cases it's explicitly discouraged. Even then, it's possible to find ways to rest under the radar. One trader we worked with, who sat in a large open room, cheek by jowl with his colleagues, made it a practice to quietly slip away to the bathroom at least twice a day. There, he closeted himself in a stall, closed his eyes, and spent five minutes breathing quietly. Other clients, working in their own offices and with fewer peers watching over their shoulders, take a walk the way Mark does, close their office doors and sit quietly for a few minutes, or put on a pair of headphones and listen to music.

THE UNDERVALUED POWER OF NAPS

Perhaps no single daytime renewal behavior more reliably influences performance—and is less common in the workplace—than taking a nap. "Our circadian clocks are programmed for long sleep during the night and short sleep during the day," says Sara Mednick, formerly a researcher at UC San Diego and the author of *Take a Nap! Change Your Life.* As far back as the first century B.C., the Romans divided their days into separate periods for activities, prayers, meals, and a midday rest, which they named the "Sexta" because it took place six hours after dawn, at noon. This short nap was eventually renamed a "siesta," and it became commonplace, first in Spain and Italy, and then in many Latin American countries, where the heat was especially intense during the middle of the day. Winston Churchill, a daily napper, instinctively understood what scientists would eventually confirm about the value of naps. "We were not made by Nature to work, or even to play, from eight o'clock in the morning till midnight," he said. "We ought to break our days and our marches into two."

Evidence for the circadian influence on naps first emerged from sleep research conducted by Jürgen Aschoff during the early 1950s in abandoned World War II German bunkers. He chose the bunkers—effectively small apartments—because they had no windows and therefore no natural light. Aschoff had his subjects move into the bunkers for days at a time, without access to watches or clocks. Told to sleep whenever they felt tired, he found that they typically slept for seven to eight hours out of every twenty-four. He also found that they slept in two separate segments: one long period of six to seven hours, followed approximately twelve hours later by a shorter sleep of an hour or less.

Sara Mednick grew interested in naps as a graduate student at Harvard, when she took a course with Robert Stickgold, a professor of psychiatry who had extensively studied the effect of sleep on memory consolidation and various other kinds of learning. When Stickgold gave two sets of subjects the same memory challenge, he found that those who were permitted to sleep through the night improved in their performance the next day, while those who were kept awake did not. He also found that subjects who got eight hours of sleep significantly outperformed those who got only six hours and that those who got less than six hours showed no improvement in performing the task at all.

Mednick's simple but ingenious idea was to see if daytime naps prompted any comparable performance improvements on the same kind of task. Amazingly, she found that a sixty- to ninety-minute nap led to just as much improvement on the memory task as did eight full hours of sleep. Indeed, a daytime nap proved to be additive, so that when subjects took an afternoon nap following a full night of sleep, they did twice the amount of learning. In another experiment, Mednick gave subjects a visual task to practice on a computer screen at four intervals over the course of a day. The subjects who didn't nap along the way performed increasingly poorly as the day wore on. The subjects who were permitted to take a thirty-minute nap following the second session sustained the same level of performance for the third and fourth sessions.

Perhaps the most striking study was one conducted by NASA and the Federal Aviation Administration to study the effect of short naps on pilots flying long distances through the night. These pilots not only put in extended hours on duty but also cross multiple time zones and had a tendency to fall into frequent, brief "microsleeps" lasting a few seconds. The pilots were randomly divided into two groups. One group was instructed to take a midflight forty-minute nap, during which their copilots took over for them. A control group of pilots was allowed no nap at all. The nonnapping pilots demonstrated reduced performance on night flights, at the end of flights, and following consecutive flights. The napping pilots got an average of twenty-six minutes of sleep and maintained consistent performance both during the day and night and after consecutive flight legs. In vigilance tests following a nap, for example, their median reaction time improved by 16 percent. Tested at a similar point in the flight, the nonnapping pilots demonstrated a 34 percent deterioration in reaction time. During the critical final thirty minutes of the flight, the nonnapping pilots had an average of twenty-two "microsleeps" lasting between three and ten seconds. The nappers had none at all.

Mednick has taken this research a step further and developed a protocol for what she calls "the optimized napping formula." It's based on the notion that we can adjust the timing and length of naps to meet specific performance aims. It is during REM sleep, for example, that we embed complex learning and creativity appears to be enhanced. Perceptual skills also improve with increased REM sleep. To improve any of these capacities, Mednick concluded, it is best to nap earlier in the day, when REM activity is higher than it is as the day wears on.

By contrast, it is during slow-wave sleep (SWS) that the body most actively repairs itself. Cortisol, the catabolic hormone that breaks down tissue to make it available as energy for the body, is completely turned off during slow-wave sleep. Conversely, growth hormone, which builds and stimulates cell growth, is released during slow-wave sleep. If your goal is to get a deeper level of repair and restoration—say, after strenuous physical activity—it's better to nap in the later afternoon, when slow-wave cycles predominate. Because both the SWS and REM phases occur well into each ninety-minute sleep cycle, it's possible to derive their value only by napping for at least forty-five to sixty minutes.

The most powerful nap of all is one taken for ninety minutes between 1 and 3 P.M.—traditional siesta time—which is when the body most craves sleep. A ninety-minute nap also represents a full Basic Rest Activity Cycle, which guarantees the napper the benefits of all four sleep stages. In practical terms, few of us have the freedom to take such a long nap during workdays. In addition to the time longer naps require, a second drawback is the "sleep inertia" they can induce—the groggy feeling we sometimes feel upon awakening from them, which can persist for up to thirty minutes. The ninety-minute nap is likely a weekend option, when it can be used, among other things, as a way to make up for sleep deprivation during the week.

The best option for a nap at work is one limited to stages 1 and 2 sleep. Mednick and other researchers have found that we begin to experience a nap's restorative effects after just ten minutes. Stage 1, the lightest, typically lasts just five minutes, while stage 2 takes a minimum of seventeen minutes. By napping for less than thirty minutes—the so-called Power Nap—we avoid going into the deeper sleep of stages 3 and 4. The result is that we tend to be alert almost as soon as we awaken, both refreshed and better able to focus. The evidence is inconclusive about whether insomniacs sleep better or worse at night if they nap during the day, but if you are one, you have little to lose by experimenting with a fifteen- to thirty-minute daytime nap. If doing so results in your staying up even later at night or waking up more frequently, you can simply abandon the nap.

THE VACATION EFFECT

Much as we perform better with several short cycles of rest during the day and an extended period of sleep every night, so we are more productive when we regularly take vacations. But much as we are sleeping less, we're also taking less time off. On average, Americans now fail to use 439 million paid vacation days a year. In 2008, one-third of Americans said they intended to take no vacation at all. Another 33 percent planned a vacation of seven days or less. Only 14 percent scheduled a vacation of at least two weeks during 2008. "The idea of somebody going away for two weeks is really becoming a thing of the past," says a spokesman for the American Automobile Association. A congressional bill that would require companies with fifteen employees or more to provide at least seven paid sick days a year has languished in Congress for more than five years.

Europeans continue to enjoy far more vacation time than Americans, not least because European governments mandate companies to provide it. The European Union requires members to offer a minimum of four weeks paid vacation, plus holidays. Workers in countries such as Finland and France are entitled to six weeks of vacation, although in an increasingly global economy, workers at multinational companies across Europe increasingly feel the pressure to work more hours and vacation less.

The health costs from too little vacation are comparable to those from inadequate sleep. As part of the Framingham Heart Study, 750 women with no previous heart disease were tracked over twenty years. Those who took the fewest vacations proved to be twice as likely to get a heart attack as those who took the most vacations. A comparable study of 12,000 men in the Multiple Risk Factor Intervention Trial found that infrequent vacationers were 50 percent more likely to die of a heart attack than frequent vacationers. Overall, infrequent vacationers had a 20 percent higher risk of dying from any cause over the nine-year period of the study. Emotional health is similarly influenced by length of vacation. A 2005 study of 1,500 women found that the risk of depression diminished as they took more vacation. Those who took vacations twice a year were half as likely to be depressed as those who took a vacation once every two to five years.

There is also accumulating evidence that performance itself is closely correlated with vacation time. A 2006 study of employees at Ernst & Young, the accounting firm, found that for each ten hours of vacation employees took each month, their performance reviews were 8 percent higher the following year. The more vacation they took, the more their performance reviews improved and the more likely they were to stay at the firm.

Even tiny increments of time off seem to have very positive effects. Two Harvard Business School professors recently undertook a project among consultants at Boston Consulting Group. Consultants were asked to take off one evening a week—not one day but one evening—from all work. It's a measure of how out of control work has become in some professions that such a project was even possible. Amazingly, the experiment actually met with considerable resistance from the consultants themselves. The notion of not checking their BlackBerrys, and not making themselves available to clients even one night a week provoked concern and anxiety. But six months later, the consultants who managed to take the evening off reported higher job satisfaction, more open communication, better work/life balance, and a greater likelihood that they'd stay at the firm than the consultants who continued to work as they always had.

Whether it's evenings and weekends truly off, longer and more regular vacations, brief breaks during the day at ninety-minute intervals, short afternoon naps, or a minimum of seven to eight hours of sleep a night, the overwhelming evidence is that our health and productivity are enhanced by a rhythmic movement between work and rest. The best model for how we ought to be operating as adults may be the way we did as young children: alternating time spent actively learning with naps, playtime and gym periods, recesses and snacks—as well as with long periods of sleep at night. A recent study of 11,000 children ages eight and nine, published in the journal *Pediatrics,* found that children who were given at least fifteen minutes of recess a day behaved significantly better in class than those who had little or no recess time. "We should understand that kids need that break because the brain needs that break," said Dr. Romina M. Barros, a pediatrician and assistant clinical professor at Albert Einstein College of Medicine.

Unfortunately, recess and time allotted to renewal and play are diminishing in schools. The ethic of more, bigger, faster is increasingly being applied even to very young children. Thirty percent of schools now provide little or no daily recess. Many others are cutting out gym periods. At more than a dozen Achievement First charter schools in New York and Connecticut, the academic day is ninety minutes longer than at traditional schools, an attempt to close what the school's founders refer to as the "achievement gap" for disadvantaged kids. Kindergarteners at Achievement First work straight through from 7:30 in the morning until 1:45 in the afternoon. They're drilled in grammar, phonics and arithmetic, they learn to work on computers, and they even play vocabulary challenge games when they're waiting in lines for the bathroom. In the afternoons they take music and other classes until 4:30 P.M. and at night, these six-year-olds have homework to do.

The test scores of these children have increased significantly. But two questions remain unanswered, not just for them but for anyone who is being asked to work more and more hours and spend less and less time recovering and renewing. The first question is, what long-term toll does working in this way take on satisfaction and productivity? The second is, how much happier and more effective might we all become if we were taught how to effectively balance intense effort with deep renewal and became better at both?

CHAPTER SIX ACTION STEPS

- Reflect on how you work over the course of a typical day. We operate best when we make waves—focusing for ninety- to 120-minute cycles and then taking a break. How often do you build intermittent recovery into your day? What would give you the most efficient form of renewal?
- Is there any way you could take a twenty- to thirty-minute nap between 1 and 4 P.M., especially on days when you work very intensely during the mornings? You'll discover a remarkable impact on your ability to focus later in the afternoon. If it's not practical or permissible to take a nap, try simply leaning back in your chair with your eyes closed for five to ten minutes. That's still an effective form of renewal.
- When was the last time you completely disconnected from work, including checking e-mail, for any extended period of time? Designate at least one night a week to totally let go of the office from the time you leave work until you get up the following morning.

CHAPTER SEVEN

Use It or Lose It

Movement is sleep's opposite partner, the high side of a wave that fuels our health but whose value we underappreciate. Too little movement, like too little sleep, weakens and diminishes us in all dimensions of our lives. Intense movement, balanced by deep recovery, dramatically increases our capacity, not just physically but also mentally and emotionally.

"How much you move," explains Eric Heiden, an orthopedic surgeon and five-time Olympic speed-skating champion, "affects your strength, your power, your balance, how you look, how you think, how well you withstand the high winds and rain showers of life and how long you will stand. Everyone needs concentrated doses of several kinds of movement to remain fully functional."

Because our behaviors are so interdependent, the failure to exercise tends to prompt a vicious cycle. The more sedentary we become, the more we begin to avoid exercise. When we move less, we burn fewer calories, gain weight, lose strength, endurance and flexibility, and find it increasingly difficult and uncomfortable to move.

When we first met Steve Wanner, a young partner at Ernst & Young, he was working twelve- to fourteen-hour days, felt perpetually exhausted, slept poorly, and made no time to exercise. Although there is no evidence that being more fit reduces the need for sleep—elite performers typically get more sleep than average—there is considerable evidence that regular exercise makes it easier to get to sleep and leads to a higher quality of rest.

One of the first changes Wanner instituted was to go to sleep earlier and wake up in time to take an early-morning run before his wife and four children woke up. Running rejuvenated him, not just because it made him feel better physically but also because it made him feel better about himself. When Wanner got to work, he felt more positive and alert, and when he arrived home, he felt less tired and more able to engage with his family. Success at building a workout ritual eventually emboldened him to launch a number of other positive rituals around the way he organized his day. Whenever he did fall out of his routines during the busiest work periods, he felt the consequences on his mood and his productivity almost immediately.

Simon Ashby, a vice president at Sony Europe, also launched a series of changes in his life by adding an exercise routine. "I was always a halfhearted runner," he told us, "and I wanted to ritualize running more effectively. I don't have time to run in the early morning and I'm too tired in the evening, so it had to be at lunchtime. As I worked through this ritual, I realized there was a powerful story I told myself that was getting in my way, which went all the way back to high school. I hated changing in the dark, dirty locker room, and now I found myself imagining a moment when my colleagues would see me walking down the halls in my running kit and start laughing at me. But I decided to give it a go anyway, and instead of laughing at me, people did quite the opposite. My running gave *them* permission to exercise over lunch. After a quick jog over the motorway, I would find myself in beautiful countryside. It was relaxing and inspiring, and I came back feeling great and fully fueled for the afternoon ahead."

MOVE AND THRIVE

What makes exercise uniquely powerful is that it's simultaneously a way to build capacity physically and to reliably renew energy mentally and emotionally. The impact can also be experienced quickly and it is easily measurable.

In a study of 15,000 same-sex twins conducted in Finland, for example, the sibling who exercised regularly had a 55 percent lower risk of early death compared to the twin who did not. Nor was the exercise bar set very high. On average, the physically active twins exercised at moderate intensity—a brisk walking pace an average of six times a month, for thirty minutes at a time. In short, they invested just three hours a month on exercise. In another study, older adults who exercised just once a week were 40 percent less likely to die over the twelve years of the study than those who did nothing at all. Frequency of exercise can make an even more significant difference. In a third study, men who exercised at least five times a week were one-seventh as likely to get heart disease as those who exercised just once a week. "Regular exercise," a study in *The Journal of the American Medical Association* concluded, "acts like a vaccine on the immune system."

There is also broad and compelling evidence that fitness improves cognitive capacity and emotional well-being, two factors that powerfully influence performance and productivity. In a meta-analysis of some one hundred studies, a team of researchers in London concluded that "exercise improves mental health and well-being, reduces depression and anxiety and enhances cognitive functioning." The study also found that exercising regularly is more effective than doing so occasionally and that high-intensity exercise is better than low-intensity.

In a study aptly named SMILE (Standard Medical Intervention and Long-term Exercise) Duke researchers found that vigorous exercise for thirty to forty-five minutes per session three times a week was at least as effective as antidepressant drugs in reducing symptoms of depression. Scores of studies have shown that exercise also significantly reduces symptoms of anxiety. Regular exercise has also been shown to significantly slow shrinkage of the frontal cortex, where our capacity for conscious, purposeful thinking resides. This may help explain why regular exercisers in middle age have proven to be one-third as likely to get Alzheimer's disease in their seventies as those who didn't exercise at all.

Increasingly, the research suggests that we are best served by training both our cardiovascular capacity and our strength. In both cases, we get a high return from a relatively low investment of time. While nearly all of us require seven to eight hours of sleep a night to function optimally, we can thrive on only a fraction as much exercise. Agencies ranging from the American College of Sports Medicine to the American Heart Association suggest at least three and up to six days a week of moderate-intensity physical activity for twenty to forty-five minutes a day. Even that amount of time, most researchers now agree, can be split between two or three sessions over the course of a day, so long as each one is at least ten minutes long.

Modest as this seems for the richness of rewards it provides, a remarkable percentage of us remain sedentary. In the two most recent government reports, a paltry 15 percent of U.S. citizens regularly engaged in vigorous activity for twenty minutes a day at least three times a week. Twenty-five percent of Americans are almost completely sedentary, while 60 percent are only sporadically active. The more educated and more affluent people are, the more they exercise, but not as dramatically as you might suspect. Fifteen percent of those with a high school degree are physically active, for example, but even among adults with an advanced degree, the number rises to only 25 percent. Overall, the World Health Organization has found that between 60 and 85 percent of adults worldwide, including both developing and developed nations, are inactive. Two million deaths every day can be attributed to a sedentary lifestyle.

THE HEART WAVE

Although nearly every system in our body operates rhythmically when it's healthy, most are part of our autonomic nervous system and we have little or no control over them. Digestion, body temperature, and hormone levels all oscillate on their own clocks, mostly outside our awareness unless something goes wrong. Our heart rate is one of the few rhythms we can intentionally influence.

The greater our cardiovascular capacity, the more efficiently we can move oxygen throughout our bodies. The best way to build cardiovascular capacity is to regularly make waves—exerting ourselves for periods of time to drive up our heart rates and then recovering back to a resting rate. In the process we increase our heart rate *range.* The greater our range, the more flexibly we can respond to varying kinds of physiological and emotional demands. As we get older, our maximum heart rate decreases and so, therefore, does our range.

That isn't good news. A study published in *The New England Journal of Medicine* found that heart rate range strongly predicts mortality. Men whose resting heart rate was high (75 or above) or whose heart rate remained unusually low during exercise (lower than 89 beats), were four times as likely to die as men with normal heart rate ranges.

The good news is that exercise expands our heart rate range and can also significantly slow its decline over time.

If moving flexibly between lower and higher heart rates contributes to our overall health and effectiveness, what does the ideal wave look like? In the absence of regular exercise, the heart's ability to pump efficiently drops approximately 30 percent between ages thirty and seventy—nearly 1 percent a year—and faster after that. Through steady-state aerobic exercise, we train endurance, which is a reflection of the ability to consume oxygen more efficiently. Typically, that requires raising our heart rate into a certain range and holding it there for twenty, thirty, or even forty-five minutes. Marathon runners can do so for two or three hours at a time. They become virtual exhaling machines, washing out large amounts of carbon dioxide with each breath.

Aerobic exercise is good not only for the heart and lungs but also for the brain. Give a lab mouse the opportunity to run as freely as it likes, and researchers have found that its brainpower improves. Push the mouse to run even harder than it would choose to run by itself, and its cognitive power increases even more. The same seems to be true for human beings. Taiwanese researchers have found that cardiovascular exercise actually prompts us to produce new brain cells. In one study at the University of Illinois, a group of students was asked to memorize a string of letters and then pick them out from a list flashed at them. Next, they were asked to do one of three things for thirty minutes: sit quietly, run on a treadmill, or lift weights—in all cases followed by a thirty-minute "cool down." Then they were retested. The aerobic exercisers did best. In another study, the same proved true for brisk walkers compared to stretchers on before-and-after tests of cognition. While researchers aren't certain of the explanation they believe it may be that aerobic exercise increases blood flow to the brain.

INTERVAL TRAINING

Aerobic exercise creates a "long" wave by pushing our heart rate considerably above the range we maintain when we're sedentary—which most of us are the vast majority of the time. Creating a wave is vastly

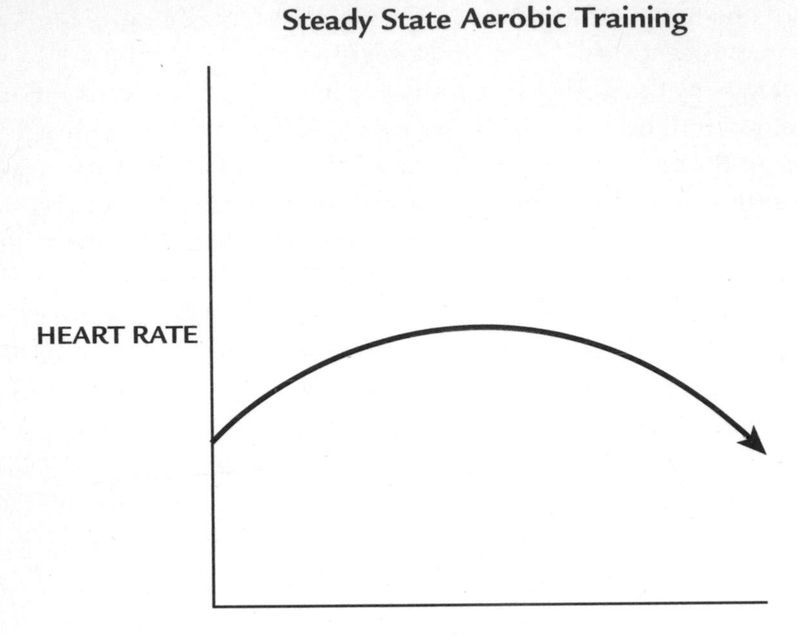

preferable to not moving and prompts a broad range of benefits. The aerobic wave is depicted in the diagram above.

In most aerobic activity, we move from one form of linear energy expenditure to another. The limit of steady-state aerobic exercise is that the body adapts relatively quickly to any level of continuous challenge. The consequence is that we cease building further cardiovascular capacity once we've reached a certain level of fitness.

Interval training operates on the premise that the value we derive from exercise has less to do with the time we invest in it than with the intensity of energy we expend for short periods of time, followed by full recovery. This training process is sometimes referred to as periodization, or the managing of work/rest ratios. It's the same principle that applies to increasing effectiveness in other disciplines, the way Ericsson's violinists did, by practicing at high intensity and focus for seventy-five to ninety minutes at a time and then taking a rest.

Interval training is *anaerobic,* meaning that it doesn't rely on oxygen but instead on lactic acid drawn from the muscles. Rather than continuous expenditure of energy, an "interval" typically lasts between thirty seconds and two minutes, during which you push considerably past your comfort zone. The wave is more spiky and looks like the diagram below.

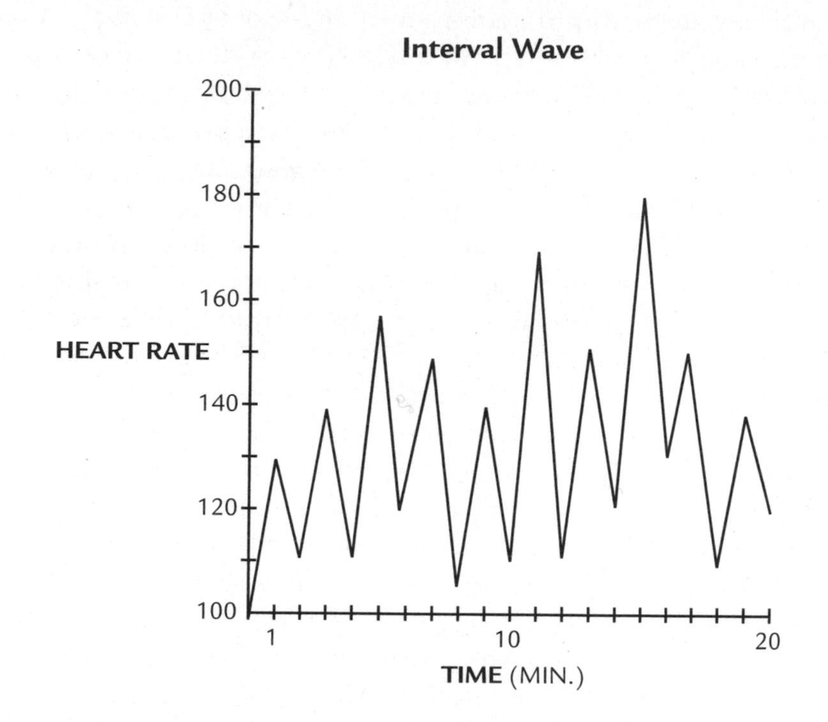

The notion of maximizing physical performance by alternating periods of intense activity with rest dates back to ancient Greece, when an author named Flavius Philostratus wrote about it in *Gymnasticus,* essentially a training manual for Greek Olympic athletes. Russian sports scientists began systematically applying the precepts to their Olympic athletes in the 1960s, with extraordinary success, and today interval training is common among athletes all over the world.

During the interval, lactic acid builds up, pushing you toward oxygen debt and ultimately forcing you to stop and rest. Each time you can motivate yourself to push a little longer or harder, you're effectively setting the body's limit higher. That's because during recovery, we all experience a phenomenon known as "supercompensation." In response to the higher demand the body has just experienced, it adapts—in this case by building more capillaries. Over time the heart becomes able to tolerate higher levels of lactic acid and therefore can pump more blood and oxygen to the rest of the body.

The effects of interval training can be extraordinary. In one study, subjects were asked to sprint for thirty seconds on a stationary bicycle and then pedal lightly for four minutes, in a series of intervals. After a total of just fifteen minutes of intense cycles—thirty intervals performed over two weeks—three-quarters of the subjects doubled the amount of time they could ride at a moderate level of intensity before exhaustion. More extraordinary still, the subjects had all been active and reasonably fit before the experiment.

Far more than steady-state aerobic exercise, interval training works both sides of the wave, extending our range at the top but also increasing the speed of our recovery back to a resting state. Fitness is simply a reflection of the speed of recovery. The fitter we are, the faster we recover. When we move too little—i.e., "undertrain"—we weaken, atrophy, and struggle to recover even from modest exertion. That doesn't mean we should challenge ourselves at the highest level every day. Push too hard, too frequently, and the result will eventually be breakdown and burnout, or what athletes call "overtraining." For that reason, interval training typically makes sense no more than twice a week.

In an experiment known as the Dallas Bed Rest and Training Study, researchers at Southwestern Medical School in Dallas recruited six college students to literally spend their summer in bed. The goal was to test the effect on their overall health, most notably their cardiovascular and pulmonary function. After just three weeks in bed, the subjects experienced a deterioration in cardiovascular fitness that was equivalent to twenty years of aging. It's hard to imagine more vivid proof of the adage "Use it or lose it."

Thirty years later, five of the six subjects were retested. Only two had continued to exercise with any regularity, and all had gained weight and body fat. Even so, the declines from thirty years of actually aging were less than those they had suffered during the original three weeks of bed rest. Immediately after being tested, the five men were put on an aerobic exercise program, which included regular walking, jogging, and cycling. In just six months, the declines they had suffered over the previous thirty years were completely reversed—extraordinary evidence that cardiovascular training has huge benefits, even late in life. We lose fitness very rapidly when we're sedentary, but we can also gain it back if we're willing to make the effort.

RESISTANCE TRAINING

In recent years, the research has made it increasingly clear that strength training—or resistance training, as it's sometimes called—is at least as important as training for endurance. Just as we lose approximately 1 percent of our cardiovascular capacity per year from the age of thirty on in the absence of training, so we lose an average of one-half pound of lean muscle mass every year. When it comes to strength, we've underestimated the costs to our everyday capacity, perhaps because for so long we tended to associate weight lifting with vanity and outsize bodybuilders. For example, the Dallas Bed Rest and Training Study, which was first conducted in 1966, focused exclusively on loss in cardiovascular capacity and didn't even look at loss of muscular strength.

Strength is arguably more fundamental than endurance, simply because we require strength to move at all. Building greater strength increases everything from metabolism to coordination to flexibility to bone density to balance. The average ninety-year-old who doesn't weight train must contract his thigh muscles at maximum capacity just to get out of a car or stand up from a sitting position. The leading cause of both injuries and death among people aged sixty-five or older in the United States is falls. A vast number of them are influenced by muscle weakness, declining coordination, and poor balance. Nearly one of every three people over age sixty-five suffers a fall annually. One-third of all women and one-sixth of all men suffer a hip fracture by the age of seventy. Between 18 and 33 percent of these patients die within a year of the fall, many from complications such as infection, blood clots, and pneumonia. As the baby boomer population continues to age, the number of falls, fractures, and deaths will likely increase dramatically.

But strength also serves us in our everyday lives. Because muscle burns calories so much more efficiently than fat, resistance training is an effective way to stay lean, even without losing weight, and also to fuel more sustainable high energy. We have one overall energy reservoir, and the more energy we expend physically just to accomplish everyday activities, the more fatigued we become, and the less energy we have available for everything else we do.

Surprisingly little investment is required to prevent loss of strength, even very late in life. In one of a series of studies of the elderly, a Tufts University researcher, Miriam Nelson, and her colleagues put a hundred residents of a nursing home on a ten-week resistance training program. The residents worked out three days a week for forty-five minutes a session, with plenty of rest between sets. The youngest subject in the study was seventy-two, the oldest was ninety-eight, and subjects had a mean age of eighty-seven. Nearly all of them required walkers, canes, or wheelchairs to get around. Over ten weeks, they more than doubled their strength on average and improved their "gait velocity" by 12 percent and their stair-climbing power by nearly 30 percent. The lesson is clear: it's not too late to gain significant strength until it's literally too late.

Building strength is by its nature an interval exercise, meaning it is characterized by successive waves of energy expenditure and energy renewal. Even though lifting weights is so strenuous that it can't be done for longer than a couple of minutes without rest, almost no deaths have been attributed to it. By contrast, there have been a good number attributed to steady-state aerobic exercise—perhaps most famously that of the running guru Jim Fixx at the age of fifty-two, directly following his daily run.

Strength training is an especially vivid example of how stress—and the attendant discomfort—is essential to our growth. As the Dallas Bed Rest and Training Study makes clear, if we fail to challenge our bodies regularly, they quickly atrophy. At the same time, when the stress we subject ourselves to is linear and continuous, damage is the inevitable outcome. The obstacle to increasing our capacity across all dimensions of our lives is not the stress caused by high demand but rather the absence of intermittent recovery. It's during renewal—not exertion—that growth occurs.

Above all, resistance training provides a vivid example of the value of intensity over volume. Arthur Jones was the inventor of Nautilus weight equipment and also a proponent of something he called "high-intensity training." The best way to build strength, he began arguing in the 1960s, is through workouts that are brief, intense, and relatively widely spaced. Jones suggested performing just one set of eight to twelve repetitions for any given muscle group, and only one time a week, or at most twice. Each set of repetitions, he argued, should be done to the point of failure, meaning total fatigue of the muscle. In practical terms, that meant training sessions as short as thirty minutes. "SuperSlow" refers to an even shorter and more intense version of the original Jones protocol, in which practitioners lift and lower a weight to strengthen a specific muscle group at a very slow speed—ten seconds up and ten seconds down. An entire workout requires twenty minutes or less and can produce remarkable gains.

Although there is still some disagreement about the ideal number of sets to perform for each muscle group, the preponderance of scientific evidence suggests that a single set for each muscle produces results at least as good as multiple sets and with less chance of injury. There is virtually unanimous agreement that after intensely training a given muscle group, at least two days of rest (and up to seven) are required to ensure maximum repair and growth.

Among the small percentage of clients who were doing strength training regularly when we began working with them, almost none trained their muscles to complete exhaustion. That's hardly surprising, even though most of them were aware that doing so is considered the best and most efficient way to build strength. It's difficult and counterintuitive to push ourselves to the very limits of our capacity. Doing so is not just physically uncomfortable but also tends to prompt primitive survival fears.

In defining the ideal way to train, our point is not that we should all be lifting the greatest possible weight to the point of complete muscle failure or running intervals at the highest possible heart rate. Rather, it's to illustrate three principles that we believe are fundamental to sustainable high performance. The first is that we cannot expect growth or improvement in any dimension of our lives without intentionally and regularly challenging our current capacity. The second is that intense effort for short periods, followed by intentional rest and recovery, is more efficient, more satisfying, and ultimately more productive than moderate, continuous effort for longer periods of time. The third principle is that Aesop had it wrong in his classic fable about the tortoise and the hare. It isn't the tortoise, slow and steady, that wins the race. Rather, it's the hare, who balances intense bursts of energy with intermittent periods of recovery.

CHAPTER SEVEN ACTION STEPS

- Take a few moments to create an exercise log. (To download a template, go to www.theenergyproject.com/exerciselog.) Write down exactly what exercise you got during the past seven days, including walking, and how long you engaged in it. Experts say we need twenty to forty-five minutes of exercise three to six days a week, including two weight training sessions. How well are you doing?
- If you're struggling to find the time or the motivation to start an exercise routine, buy a pedometer and record the number of steps you take every day. Shoot for 10,000. Look for ways to increase your number of steps by taking the stairs, parking your car farther away from your office, taking a walk as a recovery break during the day, or even holding walking meetings with colleagues.
- At least once a week, do an interval workout. Buy a heart rate monitor to better gauge your efforts and push past your comfort zone for an interval of thirty seconds to a minute. Then take thirty seconds to a minute to allow your heart to recover to a comfortable resting rate. (For more information, go to www.theenergyproject.com/intervaltraining.)

CHAPTER EIGHT

Less Is More

What a hornet's nest nutrition is. How to possibly navigate the endless stream of contradictory studies, conflicting advice, and confusing data?

This much we know for sure: the more we eat, the fatter we get, the more energy we expend, and the less healthy we become. And we are undeniably eating more.

Much as the ethic of more, bigger, faster dominates the workplace, so it has come to define the way we eat—with similar costs to our productivity and sustainability. Many of the foods that fuel us in the short term exact a damaging toll over time.

Consider this: Between 1960 and 2000, the average weight of American men between the ages of twenty-one and twenty-nine jumped from 163 to 191 pounds. During the same period, the average woman went from 140 to 164. That's a heavy burden we're carrying around.

Body mass index (BMI) is the standard measure for determining whether we are overweight or obese. A BMI between 18 and 25 is considered normal. A BMI above 25 is overweight, and above 30 is obese. On the one hand, the body mass index is a crude, inexact measurement that fails to sufficiently account for differences in gender, body type, and percentage of body fat versus lean muscle mass. Based on BMI, for example, most professional basketball players would be considered overweight or obese, which is hardly the case. For the vast majority of us, however, a BMI over 30—say, a woman five feet, five inches tall weighing 180 pounds or a man five feet, ten inches tall at 210 pounds—would be undeniably obese.

In response to similar increases around the globe, the World Health Organization coined the term "globesity" in 1998 to describe what they concluded is a global epidemic. During the past decade, it has only gotten worse. More than 550 million people around the world are now considered obese, while another 1.6 billion are overweight. In the United States, one-third of Americans are overweight, and another one-third are obese—the highest rates in the developed world. But even in countries with traditionally slim populations, the numbers have risen dramatically. In France, for example, the percentage of those who are overweight has increased by 50 percent during the past decade and is now 42 percent, including 12 percent who are obese.

Obesity is close to overtaking smoking as the most preventable cause of death and today accounts for more than 100,000 deaths a year. In a National Cancer Institute study of more than a half-million Americans, an obese fifty-year-old was more than twice as likely to die as a fifty-year-old at a normal weight, controlling for other risk factors. Even a slightly overweight fifty-year-old ran a 20 to 40 percent higher risk of dying prematurely. Being overweight or obese also puts us at far greater risk of developing chronic diseases such as hypertension, heart disease, stroke, arthritis, several forms of cancer, and diabetes, the disease most clearly associated with weight gain.

For every pound of excess weight, the risk of developing diabetes increases by 4 percent. The incidence of type 2, or adult-onset, diabetes has doubled during the past thirty years and is expected to nearly double again by 2025. Equally striking is the fact that the disease is almost completely preventable simply through lifestyle changes. A National Institutes of Health study of more than 3,000 adults at high risk for type 2 diabetes found that their likelihood of developing the disease could be reduced by nearly 60 percent simply through a program aimed at modest weight loss—5 to 7 percent—and thirty minutes of exercise five days a week. For employers, the expense associated with overweight and obesity—an estimated $150 billion a year—shows up not just in the form of higher health insurance premiums but also in absenteeism and disability claims, as well as in more indirect ways, such as lower energy and stamina and a significantly higher incidence of depression among employees.

The immediate influence of the food we eat is on our energy levels. Along with oxygen, food is our most essential form of fuel, but most of us struggle to eat in a way that is at once healthy, energizing, and pleasurable. Instead, we're constantly skittering between one or another of those goals, often in the course of a single day, without ever feeling we're getting the sustenance and satisfaction we're seeking.

From an energy perspective, the key to nutrition is maintaining a stable, steady level of blood sugar. Food is our primary source of glucose, and it fuels our brains and the rest of the cells in our body. When our blood glucose levels spike too high or drop too low for too long, we function less efficiently, and eventually we become sick. Insulin is the hormone that regulates our blood sugar, both by helping it get into our cells and by removing excess amounts of it from our blood. Chronically high blood sugar levels are referred to as hyperglycemia. When we're unable to produce insulin at all, the result is type 1 or juvenile-onset diabetes. The treatment is to inject insulin directly into the bloodstream at regular intervals every day and to monitor blood sugar levels closely. When we eat too many foods high in sugar, our blood glucose levels rise and insulin eventually becomes less efficient at taking up excess amounts in the blood. The result can be type 2 diabetes. The American Heart Association now recommends that women consume no more than six teaspoons or 100 calories of refined sugar a day and men no more than nine teaspoons or 150 calories.

By contrast, when our blood sugar levels are too low—after a long period of not eating—we experience hypoglycemia and its accompanying symptoms, including lethargy, unsteadiness, distractibility, irritability, and even fainting. All foods influence our blood sugar levels, but they do so at different speeds, for varying durations and at greater or lesser cost to our health and alertness. The good news is that we have the power to regulate and stabilize our blood glucose levels and therefore our energy levels and our long-term health. The key is not just the food we choose to eat but also how much of it we consume and at what intervals.

THE SUMO WRESTLER DIET

The first problem many of our clients have, fueled by the rising demands in their lives, is that they often go for long periods without eating at all. The result is that their blood glucose levels drop, and so does their alertness as the day wears on. By the time they finally get around to eating—often not until lunch, sometimes not until dinner—they're feeling famished. At that point, they end up eating much more than their bodies need. It's a yo-yo effect, in which they find themselves feeling either hungry or stuffed but rarely just well fed and satisfied. We refer to this as the sumo wrestler diet, because in order to gain as much weight as possible, these huge 600-pound athletes have discovered it is best to skip breakfast, never eat before noon, consume one or two meals at most—always huge ones—and sleep immediately after eating in order to increase their fat storage.

But we're not sumo wrestlers, and what we're after is a steady source of energy all day long. Breakfast is especially critical to regulating our blood sugar levels because it typically follows the longest period we go at any one time without eating. Metabolism is the rate at which we burn calories, and eating breakfast stokes it and also gives us energy for the day ahead.

The best studies of the consequences of skipping breakfast have been conducted among children, but the same principles apply to all of us. Hunger at any time has been shown to reduce a child's ability to pay attention, absorb information, and respond appropriately to the environment. Sound familiar? In a study titled Energizing the Classroom, conducted among elementary school children in a Minnesota school district, those who were provided a free breakfast demonstrated better attention in class, fewer behavior problems, and increases in math and reading scores. In a second study, children who ate breakfast evidenced better speed and accuracy in retrieving information, made fewer errors on standardized achievement tests, and exhibited increased vigilance on tasks. We should never allow ourselves to get too hungry, not just because it makes us less effective but also because it makes us more likely to eventually eat too much.

The Hunger Scale makes this easy to visualize:

THE HUNGER SCALE

10. Feel sick; hate the thought of food; post-Thanksgiving dinner.
9. Stuffed; headaches, lethargy, ready to sleep.
8. Uncomfortable; bloated; change into sweats.
7. Sluggish; ate too much; loosen belt, unbutton pants.
6. Full; but still have room for a good dessert.
5. Satisfied; don't feel food in stomach; lasts two to three hours.
4. Mildly hungry; stomach is beginning to stir.
3. Hungry; stomach growling, light-headed.
2. Famished; irritable, nauseated, preoccupied.
1. Beyond hungry: so hungry you aren't hungry anymore.

The aim should be to always operate between 4 and 6—a gentle wave—so that you eat when you begin to feel hungry but never so much that you feel stuffed. For many of our clients, this requires re-awakening an awareness of what the stirrings of hunger feel like *before* they're overwhelming. It's well documented and scarcely surprising that the hungrier we are, the more we eat. The prescription that best serves sustainable energy is to eat something at least every three hours, which effectively means five to six times a day. It's the equivalent of intermittently adding logs to a fire, but not so many at any one time that the fire gets snuffed out. A series of researchers have found that subjects who eat small portions frequently, rather than just two or three meals a day, experienced benefits including lower appetite and fewer overall calories consumed, better insulin sensitivity, lower body fat percentages and even higher energy levels.

Mark Fields is the president of the Americas for the Ford Motor Company, where we've done our work for a number of years. It's difficult to overstate the demands of Fields' job during a period when Ford has struggled mightily for its survival. He works long hours, not least because his family lives in Florida, to which he commutes over the weekend. During the week, he lives alone in Detroit. When we first met Fields, his eating habits weren't much different from those of many of our clients.

Fields was accustomed to waking up very early each morning, around 5 A.M. He didn't feel especially hungry at that hour, so he skipped breakfast altogether and usually arrived at the office before 7 A.M. Mornings typically consisted of one meeting after another, and his only sustenance was a large cup of coffee, sometimes two. At noon he ate lunch, which consisted of either a salad or a sandwich. Fields rarely ate anything during the afternoon, even as his energy began to flag. When he arrived home, his favorite indulgence was M&M's, after which he typically ate his biggest meal of the day. Like so many of our clients, he had only two eating gears: all or nothing.

The problem, from an energy perspective, is that Fields was underfueling himself throughout the day, when he needed the most energy, and overfueling himself at night, when he least needed energy. One of the first changes we had him make was to eat a high-energy breakfast every day—in his case a whey protein drink mixed with skim milk and fruit. He also began eating a small snack at midmorning and a second one in the midafternoon. Almost immediately, he noticed a significant improvement in his energy level. In the morning, he felt less need for coffee to keep him fueled, and in the afternoon, the combination of a snack and his new ritual of taking a fifteen-minute walk outdoors gave him an energy lift for the last several hours of his workday. When he got home, he no longer felt intensely hungry, was able to give up the M&M's altogether, and he ate a smaller dinner.

Within several weeks, Fields shifted from eating two meals a day to eating five separate times. On its face, that sounds like a great formula for gaining weight. He didn't, nor do the vast majority of our clients. One factor may be that eating more frequently keeps our metabolism high and therefore burning calories more efficiently. The more significant reason is that Fields ate less at any given meal. We ordinarily suggest a breakfast of 300 to 400 calories and a midmorning and midafternoon snack of no more than 150 calories. In practical terms, that could mean anything from an apple to a small handful of nuts to a cup of low-fat yogurt.

PORTION DISTORTION

It's obviously easier to eat less at primary meals if you've had small snacks in between. But easier doesn't mean easy. The world we live in is forever encouraging us to eat more, bigger, faster. Part of our challenge is the extraordinary increase in the portion sizes at restaurants and in supermarkets. "People eat in units," the dietician Lisa Young writes in *The Portion Teller*. "Whatever the unit is, most people will eat the entire unit, no matter how big or small."

Consider the beloved bagel. Its average size has doubled since 1960. Today, it typically has the same number of calories as five pieces of bread. The same doubling, tripling, and even quadrupling in size applies to the hamburgers, fries, and sodas you buy at McDonald's or Burger King; the package of trail mix or candy you grab off the shelf at an airport newsstand; the muffin you buy with your grande latte at Starbucks; the bottomless pasta bowl at Olive Garden; or the glass of wine you sip at your local bar.

It can also be shocking to discover how many calories there are even in what appear to be very small amounts of food. A handful of nuts the size of a golf ball is 200 calories. A three-ounce hamburger—the size of a deck of cards and smaller than we ordinarily eat—is nearly 400 calories. A shot glass of most salad dressings is 150 calories.

Part of the problem is that we're frequently unaware of how much we're eating, not least because we eat it so fast. Numerous experiments have shown that it takes twenty minutes for our brains and our bodies to recognize that we're full, but we often consume our meals on the run in considerably less than that. The average time we spend eating lunch alone at a fast-food restaurant is eleven minutes, less if we're on the run. At a cafeteria in the workplace, the average is twenty-three minutes. Even at a moderately priced sit-down restaurant, it's only twenty-eight minutes. More often than not, we're doing other things when we eat alone—working at a computer, watching television, reading a book, talking on the phone—all of which distract us from noticing how much we're consuming.

A second issue, argues Brian Wansink, a professor of nutritional science at Cornell, is that our stomachs have effectively developed just three settings. The first, he says, is "I'm starving," the second is "I'm stuffed," and the third is "I'm full, but I can still eat more." It's the last, he believes, that gets us into the most trouble. Our body sends us one signal and our minds override it. The classic example is eating a huge meal, feeling completely full, and then being offered a tempting dessert. Almost magically, we discover room in our bloated stomachs for more.

"Everyone—every single one of us—eats how much we eat largely because of what's around us," Wansink writes in *Mindless Eating.* "We overeat not because of hunger but because of family and friends, packages and plates, names and numbers, labels and lights, colors and candles, shapes and smells, distractions and distances, cupboards and containers. This list is almost as endless as it's invisible."

Wansink runs something called the Food and Brand Lab at Cornell University, where he and his colleagues have done a series of clever studies to demonstrate just how oblivious we are to how much we eat. In one study, they gave a group of moviegoers free buckets of either a medium-size or a large-size bucket of popcorn on entering the theater. The subjects weren't told that the popcorn was actually five days old, tasted like Styrofoam, and was so stale that it squeaked when it was eaten. At the end of the movie, the subjects were asked to return their buckets to the researchers and then respond to a brief survey. Here was one of the questions for the big-bucket eaters:

> Some people tonight were given medium-size buckets of popcorn, and others, like yourself, were given these large-size buckets. We have found that the average person who is given a large-size container eats more than if they are given a medium-size container. Do you think you ate more because you had the large size?

The majority of respondents confidently said they had not. In fact, the big-bucket group had eaten an average 53 percent more, which was the equivalent of 21 more handfuls, or an extra 173 calories, of *stale* popcorn. They kept eating and eating, Wansink concluded, not because the popcorn tasted good or even because they were hungry. Many had just eaten lunch. Instead, they were responding reflexively to a series of "hidden persuaders" or unconscious cues, including the expectation of eating popcorn in a movie theater, the distraction of the movie itself, and the sound of others eating the same squeaky, stale popcorn.

In another study, Wansink found that five minutes after leaving dinner at an Italian restaurant, the diners, who had been secretly observed while eating, couldn't accurately recall how much bread they'd eaten. On average, they estimated eating 28 percent less than they actually ate. Twelve percent of those who had eaten bread denied they'd had any at all. Even the size of the plates we use can have a dramatic impact on how much we eat. When Wansink gave subjects large bowls for ice cream, they dished out at least 30 percent more for themselves than those who were given smaller bowls. When he gave those with larger bowls a large scooper to dish out the ice cream, they dished out 57 percent more than those given smaller scoopers and smaller bowls.

In an even more elaborate experiment, Wansink and his collaborators designed a system that made it possible to secretly and continuously refill bowls of soup on a table by way of a rubber tube that came up through a hole drilled in the table and then through the bottom of the soup bowl. Subjects were seated at tables for four and invited in to sample free soup. Two people at each table received ordinary 18-ounce bowls of soup. The other two had 18-ounce bowls that continually refilled as they ate, but not to the top, so they would continue to believe they were making progress. To distract the group from what they were eating, the researchers generated a discussion about their summer plans.

After twenty minutes, the students were instructed to stop eating and asked to estimate how many calories they'd consumed. Interestingly, both groups estimated an average of about 125 calories. In reality, the group given a fixed amount of soup had consumed an average of 155 calories. The group with the constantly refilling bowls had consumed 268 calories—or nearly 75 percent more than their tablemates.

WHAT TO EAT?

Numerous forces over the past several decades have coalesced to dramatically increase how much food we eat. They include the growth in portion sizes, the variety of choices available, and the number of meals we eat out, especially fast food. One of the most powerful and invisible reasons we eat more is that the food we get in restaurants and purchase from grocery stores has been carefully designed to be ever more stimulating and alluring. Over time, in certain combinations, these foods overwhelm our body's natural instinct to resist excesses of any kind.

In his extraordinary book, *The End of Overeating*, former FDA commissioner David Kessler demonstrates that certain foods he terms "hyperpalatable" can be as addictive as drugs such as cocaine and heroin. Nor is it just sugar that seduces us. In a series of experiments beginning in the 1980s, a University of Washington researcher, Adam Drewnowski, demonstrated that we are even more drawn to sugar in combination with fat. "Fat," Drewnowski explains, "is "responsible for the characteristic texture, flavor, and aroma of many foods and largely determines the palatability of the diet."

Another researcher cited in Kessler's book, Anthony Sclafani at the University of Chicago, fed a group of rats a variety of ordinary supermarket foods such as chocolate, salami, peanut butter, bananas, and cheese. In just ten days, the supermarket-fed rats weighed twice as much as rats fed a more typical, blander diet. In another study, NIH researchers confined male subjects—human beings in this case—to a hospital ward. They were given easy access to a rich variety of foods twenty-four hours a day but also asked to stick as closely as possible to their typical eating patterns. The subjects ended up eating an average of 4,500 calories a day—50 percent more than they needed to maintain a stable weight.

"Hyperpalatable foods are hyperstimulants," writes Kessler. "And when a stimulant produces reward, we want more of it. Foods high in sugar, fat, and salt promote more of everything: more arousal . . . more thoughts of food . . . more urge to pursue food . . . more dopamine-stimulated approach behavior . . . more consumption . . . more opioid-driven reward . . . more overeating to feel better . . . more delay in feeling full . . . more loss of control . . . more preoccupation with food . . . more habit-driven behavior . . . and ultimately, more and more weight gain." Kessler terms this phenomenon "conditioned overeating."

Part of the explanation is that we're powerfully drawn to variety, which helps explain why diets that emphasize one kind of nutrient at a near-total expense to another—very-low-fat or low-carbohydrate diets, for example—eventually prompt feelings of deprivation and craving. It's definitely possible to control weight and stabilize blood sugar by eating at extremes. A raft of dueling studies and passionate advocates has made the case for both low-fat *and* low-carbohydrate diets. Mediating between viewpoints in these food wars is like trying to negotiate between the Israelis and the Palestinians: no one gives much ground. What's clear is that for most of us, it's both difficult and unappealing to eat at any extreme over the long term. The best way to maintain a diet that is healthy, energizing, satisfying, and sustainable, I believe, is to include all nutrients in modest portions and to eat frequently. As the incomparable food writer Michael Pollan pithily puts it, "Eat. Not too much. Mostly plants."

Just as it's undeniable that eating too much of any food is bad for us, so it's clear that foods high in sugar—cookies, muffins, cakes, candy, and sodas—and simple carbohydrates—pasta, potatoes, and breads—are what most powerfully drive up our blood sugar levels and increase the likelihood of developing diabetes. But the more immediate problem with sugars and simple carbohydrates is that they provide a poor source of enduring energy.

The foods that sustain us best are those that are released slowly into the blood stream, which keeps our energy steady. The glycemic index (GI) was developed in the early 1980s by researchers trying to help people with diabetes. The GI rates the effect of specific foods on our blood sugar levels. Foods that break down into glucose rapidly have a high GI, while those that are released into the bloodstream slowly have a low GI. Most fruits and vegetables, with the exception of potatoes, carrots, and watermelon, are low-GI foods. Foods including white rice, sweet potatoes, and whole wheat products have mid-range GIs. So do most milk chocolate bars and cookies, because their high sugar content is offset by fat, which is digested more slowly. The worst GI offenders are simple carbohydrates such as white bread, corn flakes, baked potatoes, French fries, potato chips, white bread, and beer.

Consider for a moment the consequences of eating a muffin at midmorning after skipping breakfast or a bag of potato chips as a snack in the late afternoon. The body breaks these foods down into glucose very quickly during digestion and releases the glucose into the bloodstream. We experience a surge of energy, which is precisely what we're after. But because the glucose is released all at once, the energy is short-lived, which only increases our desire to eat more of the food that gave us the energy in the first place.

Add fat and salt to sugar, in alluring combinations, and the centers of the brain associated with desire light up and release more dopamine, which drives our inclination to eat more. "When layer upon layer of complexity is built into food, the effect becomes more powerful," explains Kessler. The psychologist Walter Mischel refers to this phenomenon as a "hot stimulus." Foods highest in fat, sugar, and salt generate the hottest stimulus of all.

A Cinnabon, to take just one example, is the ubiquitous and fragrant warm cinnamon roll slathered with frosting and sold in airports and shopping centers around the world. A Cinnabon roll, it turns out, contains three different kinds of sugar, including granulated white sugar, brown sugar in the sticky filling, and powdered sugar applied on top, along with cinnamon syrup, cream cheese, vanilla, lemon, and salt. A single Caramel Pecanbon—all of the above, plus nuts—contains 1,100 calories, 56 grams of fat, 600 milligrams of salt, 114 grams of carbohydrate, and 47 grams of sugar.

THE DEPRIVATION TRAP

Daunting as those numbers are, what you may be thinking is how delicious that Caramel Pecanbon would taste right now. If that's so, it's hardly surprising. The reason diets so rarely result in long-term weight loss is that they're based on actively avoiding the most desirable foods. We squander vast amounts of energy resisting certain foods until we can't stand it anymore, at which point we give in and eat too much of them. The speed with which we lose weight rarely matches the speed with which we regain it. Along the way, we run our blood sugar levels up and down, which costs us energy in the short term and wreaks havoc on our bodies over the long term.

We cannot make changes that last by resisting temptation. "Focusing single-mindedly on *not* eating eventually pushes us to eat more," explains Kessler. "Feeling deprived only increases the reward of food and then usually gives way to indulgence and often to abandon." The cycle is self-reinforcing. "The emotional drivers of wanting," Kessler explains,

> struggle with the desperate desire to resist temptation. Behavior-activating messages that urge pursuit clash with internal messages demanding control. Our brains become battlegrounds. Ultimately our decision to reach for that food—to relax our struggle for restraint, to give in to consumption—becomes the only possible relief from the anxiety of a war within. But the satisfaction doesn't last. By responding to a salient cue with action that generates immediate reward, we only strengthen the association between the cue and its reward.

Saying "no" to a temptation very quickly invokes the limits of our conscious will and discipline. Wansink and his colleague Jim Painter did a study in which they put dishes full of Hershey's Kisses on the desks of a series of secretaries in office locations that got minimal foot traffic, to minimize the risk that passersby would eat the Kisses. Half the secretaries were given dishes with clear glass lids that were transparent, and half were given dishes with opaque lids. The secretaries who could see the chocolates all day long ate 71 percent more than those who could not. "If we see that temptress of a candy jar every five minutes," Wansink concluded, "it means needing to say no 12 times the first hour, 12 times the second hour, and so on. Eventually some of those no's turn into yes's."

Wansink is referring to our limited reservoir of will and discipline, which is depleted by each act of self-regulation. In addition, the more energy we expend resisting tempting foods, the less we have left over for the more important tasks in our lives. Or, as Russell Fazio, a psychology professor at Ohio State, explained it to Kessler: "Many times our resources are sufficiently taxed in day-to-day life that we just can't engage in that kind of motivated overriding of our impulses." Deprivation, Kessler concluded, is our real enemy. "When you use all of your emotional energy to void a behavior, you can become anxious and tense. . . . We can't sustain a change in behavior if it leaves us hungry, unhappy, angry, or resentful."

PLEASURE MATTERS

The final key to eating smart is not to relentlessly resist pleasure. That means including the sugary, fat foods that many of us love most as part of our regular diet, but in portions that are intentionally limited and modest. To make that possible, we must replace our bad habits and impulsive behaviors with greater awareness and positive rituals.

We first met Gary Farro back in 2004, when he was a young banker at Wachovia. A former all-state football player, Farro was ambitious and hardworking, but he had allowed his weight to climb steadily to 265, far more than he needed on his six foot frame. He told himself that working out would only take time away from his job, and he was so busy that eating became almost an afterthought.

"I ran out of the house each morning without breakfast," he explains, "and I got into the habit of not eating at all until I remembered I had to eat, which could easily be two P.M. or later. I just wasn't really paying attention to what I was doing or how I felt or what the impact was. By the time I did get around to eating, I was so hungry I almost always gorged. I didn't think twice about eating something that wasn't good for me, because it was just easier to grab whatever was there."

The first breakthrough for Farro occurred when we helped him make the connection between the way he was eating and his energy level at work, especially in the afternoon, when he invariably found himself crashing. The second key was building rituals to define precisely what he was going to eat. He began eating a breakfast of either an apple, a banana with a cup of yogurt or a granola bar every morning. He also started taking a break at work approximately every two hours and eating a handful of almonds or another piece of fruit. At his main meals, he began eating less. Unhappy to discover how much stamina he'd lost as he got heavier, he also started working out regularly. In less than a year, without ever consciously dieting or depriving himself, he lost nearly sixty pounds, and he's kept them off for four years, through changes that included getting married, the birth of his first daughter, and moving to a new banking job in the midst of the economic meltdown.

"It was mostly about wanting to feel better," Farro told us. "I just realized I had a lot more energy and I was a lot more effective when I changed the way I ate. It used to be that I'd get home at the end of the day and just collapse. Now I've got a two-year-old daughter, and the last thing I want is to be so tired that I can't spend quality time with her when I get home. I work twelve-hour days, but I never crash. When I get home, I have time with my daughter, and after she goes to sleep, I go to the gym at least three days a week, or I head down to my basement and get on the treadmill for thirty minutes."

The key to gaining control of our eating, as Farro discovered, is deciding in advance what we're going to eat, in what portions, and at what intervals. Only then can we circumvent the endless temptations, unconscious cues, and alluring surprises that override our self-discipline and cause us to go off track. "When you go into a day that's unplanned, then you're just faced with whatever hits you," says the clinical dietician David Besio. "If you have a plan and you know what you're going to be eating that day, then you don't let the unplanned things get in your way."

CHAPTER EIGHT ACTION STEPS

- If you find you're eating too much or you are skipping meals too often, initiate a food log for one week. (To download a template, go to www.theenergyproject.com/foodlog.) Tracking what you eat, how much you eat, and when you eat it is the first step on the road to changing your eating habits. Are you following the sumo wrestler diet—going for long periods of time without eating and then eating a large meal in the evening? What one step can you take to get a more stable source of energy from the food you eat?
- Strive to eat small meals every three to four hours throughout the day, starting with breakfast. A high-protein, low-carbohydrate breakfast is especially critical to jump-starting our metabolism and keeping us from overeating later in the morning.
- Download a copy of the hunger scale at www.theenergyproject.com/hungerscale. Use it to increase your awareness of when you need to eat and when you've had enough to eat. Experiment with eating more slowly than you normally do by putting your utensils down after each bite of food. Research shows that it takes twenty minutes for our brains and our bodies to recognize that we are full.

CHAPTER NINE

Creating a Culture That Pulses

THE RENEWAL QUADRANTS

REFUEL

Organizational: Sustainability

ENCOURAGE MARATHON, NOT SPRINT
PROVIDE POOR FOOD CHOICES
BUILD COFFEE AND SWEETS CULTURE
DISCOURAGE/PROHIBIT DAYTIME EXERCISE
EAT AT DESK AND KEEP WORKING

STRESS INTERMITTENTLY
PROVIDE AND REWARD USE OF FITNESS FACILITIES
OFFER HEALTHFUL FOOD AT DISCOUNTED PRICES/FREE
ENCOURAGE MOVEMENT THROUGHOUT DAY
EDUCATE ABOUT MANAGING ENERGY

HIGH OCTANE

EXPECT WORK ON EVENINGS/WEEKENDS
ENCOURAGE SHORT "WORKING" VACATIONS
PROHIBIT FLEXIBLE HOURS
MINIMIZE TIME FOR EATING
REWARD MAXIMUM FACE TIME OVER OUTPUT

INSTITUTIONAL RENEWAL BREAKS/ROOMS
CREATE RENEWAL ROOMS
MAXIMIZE FLEXIBLE HOURS
ENCOURAGE NAPPING
LIMIT LENGTH AND FREQUENCY OF MEETINGS
MANDATE VACATIONS/OFFER SABBATICALS

REST

We were thrilled, five years ago, when we convinced executives at Wachovia bank to build a renewal room on a busy floor populated mostly by senior executives. The small, windowless office they chose wasn't ideal, but it was a start—and a statement. The furnishings included a comfortable couch and a couple of reclining chairs. All things considered, it was a pleasant enough place to hang out. The problem was that no one would go near it. It was as if the room had been designated a toxic waste site. Spending time in the renewal room was the equivalent of walking around the office with a sandwich board that read "Look at me, I'm not working."

The creation of a space in which people might go to relax for a few minutes didn't fool anyone into believing the company culture was changing. It didn't go unnoticed that the president of the company wasn't slipping in to catch a few winks. Despite our efforts, long hours tethered to a desk were still widely viewed as a key sign of commitment and a prerequisite to career advancement. The renewal room sat fallow for two or three months until someone decided to put an end to the pretense. The chairs and couch were replaced by a desk and chair, and a rising young executive moved in.

At most organizations, the unspoken expectations come through loud and clear: arrive early and work late; hunker down in front of your computer; take as few breaks as possible; eat lunch at your desk; refuel your energy between meals with caffeine and sugary snacks from the vending machines; and take your work home in the evenings and on the weekend. If you feel you must take a vacation, please keep it short, and be sure to check your BlackBerry wherever you are at least several times a day.

We've talked in previous chapters about how to take on these challenges individually. If you are a leader or a manager, creating a new way of working begins with recognizing that renewal serves performance. At a personal level, you must be willing not just to support but also to model new behaviors and to help those you manage to build their own energy management rituals. Finally, your organization must create policies, practices, and services that will support a new way of working.

The first key shift is to stop evaluating performance by the number of hours employees put in and instead measure it by the value they produce. That means not just permitting intermittent renewal but actively encouraging it as a key to sustainable high performance. It also means treating employees like adults by giving them freedom to decide how best to get their work done and holding them accountable for their results, not the hours they work.

The second shift in leader mind-set is from a singular focus on the competency of employees—the skills they need to get their jobs done—to an equal emphasis on capacity—the quantity and quality of fuel in their tanks. Capacity is something we've all taken for granted, because for so long we were accustomed to having more of it than we needed. As the demands in our lives have increased, our energy reserves have inexorably run down. Much as the pressure on the planet's finite natural resources is compelling us, for the first time, to develop renewable resources, so organizations must help employees find new ways to renew their own resources. Systematically investing in people's capacity, beginning at the physical level, is the key to fueling *sustainable* high performance.

An increasing number of organizations focus some attention on how employees take care of themselves physically, but typically as part of an effort to control health care costs or provide a perk, rather than as a way to drive higher performance. Most organizational initiatives are housed in wellness programs that rarely command the attention of senior leaders. Most leaders still don't actively take into account that the way employees manage their physical energy is critical to both their productivity and their satisfaction.

Periodization refers to the way athletes train in cycles—alternating intense work with periods of recovery daily, weekly, yearly—in an effort to marshal the highest energy for key competitive events. We believe leaders and their companies need to think in similar terms. Several researchers have studied the way work is typically done in organizations. The chart on the next page reflects the patterns of energy that the vast majority of us typically experience over the course of a week.

On Monday, just back from the weekend, it takes most of us time to warm up mentally, much the way athletes do by stretching and jogging before competing. McGill University researcher Debbie Moskowitz has found that Monday is the best day for low-demand administrative tasks, including setting goals, organizing, and planning. By Tuesday, most of us are fully ramped up. Over the next two days, our capacity for focus and engagement is at a peak. It makes sense, both individually and organizationally, to tackle the most challenging work: addressing the most difficult problems, taking on writing assignments, working through strategy, and doing creative brainstorming.

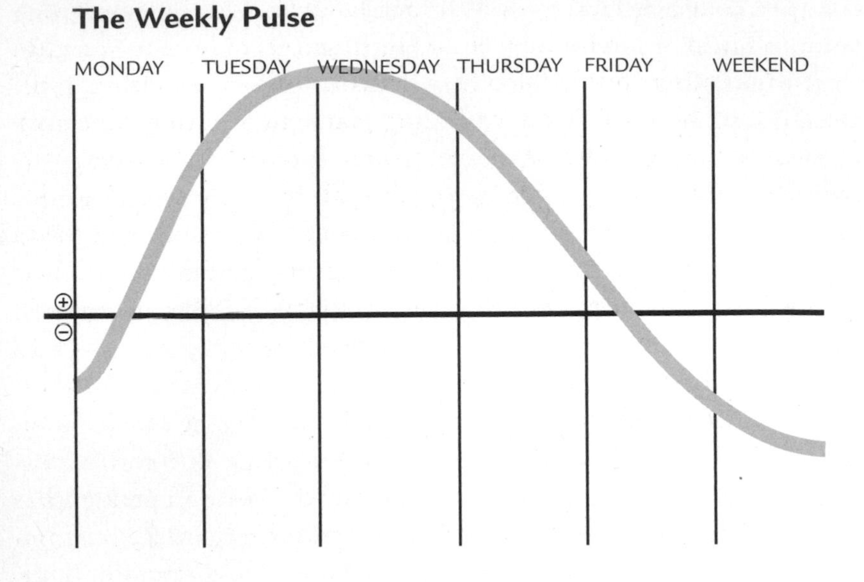

By Thursday afternoon, Moskowitz has found, our energy often begins to ebb. This can be a good day for meetings in which reaching consensus is important. By Friday, we're usually at the lowest level of energy for the week, especially in the afternoon. This can be a good day for more open-ended work, such as brainstorming, long-range planning, and relationship building. Designing the work flow for yourself and your team with these rhythms in mind means you're taking advantage of the natural flow of your energy and theirs.

SETTING A NEW RHYTHM

Among all of the companies with whom we've worked, none has taken the importance of working rhythmically more to heart than Sony Europe. "When I began to see the world in terms of energy, I realized that it waves up and down," says Roy White, the vice president of human resources for the division. An athlete himself, White recognized the potential power of periodization at the organizational level, especially in dealing with periods of highest demand.

The busiest season for Sony is the fall, heading into Christmas. This intense push is followed almost immediately by meetings that

Sony UK holds with its key dealers each January. A nearly monthlong event, it's held in a relatively remote setting to ensure that Sony has the full attention of its customers. Historically, the month is built around long hours sharing marketing plans, negotiating contracts, and socializing with dealer partners, often into the wee hours of the morning. The pattern repeats itself day after day for several weeks. When we began working with Sony, many of the salespeople told us they'd come to dread the toll these meetings took on them and their families, both because they were away for so long and because it took so much time to recover when they returned home.

To help them better manage their energy, we created a Survival Guide, grounded in the core principle that the greater the demand, the greater the need for regular renewal. With that in mind, we encouraged the managers to focus on reducing their alcohol intake during their evening meetings, ritualize morning exercise, eat more often and more lightly, and go to sleep at a designated and reasonable hour. "The results were incredible," Andy Benson, Sony UK's commercial director, told us. "Not only did people come through in better shape, our dealer partners also noticed a sharper and more focused Sony."

Sony UK's team also changed the way they managed their days at the office. The annual budget and planning meetings had long been another dreaded event. They typically lasted all day and went on well into the night. Attention wandered, tempers flared, and frustration grew as people became more and more exhausted. As the Sony leaders began to embrace the concept of intermittent recovery, they decided to divide the meetings into ninety-minute sessions, with breaks in between each one. Today, among the 2,000 employees who have been through our work at Sony Electronics, 90 percent report that taking regular breaks away from their desks has significantly increased their energy and performance levels. Eighty percent say their work/life balance has improved.

FROM THE TOP DOWN

Fujio Nishida, the president of Sony Europe, models the importance of renewal. Nishida was won over to its importance during the work we did with him and his senior team beginning in 2006. "That was when I made the link between eating, sleep, rest, exercise, and business performance," he told us. "One of the things it led to was my giving up smoking, which I realized I had been using as a form of recovery, stepping outside for a smoke when I was feeling a lot of stress. Who would have believed it, but I replaced it with a ritual around breathing. It worked just as well, and I haven't smoked since.

"I had never seen recovery as a means to improving my performance, but it has. At the same time, the story about my giving up smoking spread all around the organization. I think it gave people a kind of permission around recovery they hadn't felt before. I started seeing more people in the gym. Instead of feeling guilty, as they would have before, they now could say, 'This is great, I'm doing something for me that also benefits the organization.' "

Simon Ashby, who is responsible for operations, information systems, and logistics at Sony, had long struggled with the fact that his best project managers were always in the highest demand and therefore the most vulnerable to burning out. "Before, they would be fried in the bang, bang, bang of delivery and given no recovery at all," Ashby explains. "Now we build downtime into their schedules so they're recovering regularly. Even in a terrible economy and under incredible pressure, we're sticking by our commitment to recovery. We view it as a means of getting the highest performance, and it's working."

Andreas Ditter, former vice president of Sony Audio in Europe and now managing director for Sony Home Pictures Entertainment in Germany, took every member of his team through our curriculum. "One of my takeaways was that the key to performance isn't how long people work," he told us. "I made it clear to my team that the key to getting better numbers wasn't more hours but more vitality, focus, passion, and positive emotion. I wanted people to believe that taking care of themselves wasn't a luxury but a necessity. This was not the Sony way of working, and I think it caused deep culture shock at first."

Like Nishida, Ditter made it a personal mission to model the new behaviors he expected from others. He began taking regular renewal breaks, whether it was breathing quietly for a few minutes, taking walks outside, or working out in the gym at midday. Despite an intense schedule, he made a commitment to himself to leave work at least several days a week at 5:30 P.M. "It was a leap of faith," he says, "and I think my senior team struggled at first to make the connection between their energy and their productivity. But we've been rewarded with tremendous results and a whole new sense of possibility." In Sony Europe's most recent employee satisfaction survey, Ditter's team had the greatest improvement in scores among all Sony Europe business units on measures of satisfaction, motivation, and loyalty.

The changes at Sony Europe have reached down to the factory floor. Steve Dalton is the managing director in charge of the Sony factory in south Wales, which manufactures cutting-edge camera systems and houses Sony UK's main customer market service operations. Like Nishida and Ditter, Dalton went through the program first as an individual. He made several changes in his life, beginning at the physical level, and they had a big impact on his energy levels. An erratic sleeper, he began ritualizing the time he went to bed each night to ensure he got eight hours of sleep. He put gym equipment in a room in his house and began exercising immediately after waking up. During the day, he made it a practice to eat something healthy at least every two to three hours.

Energized by his own experience, Dalton decided to take all 270 employees at his factory through the program. There was already a gym on-site, but it sat empty most of the time. With Dalton's support, the gym is now widely used, especially at the beginning and end of the day. As part of their bonus for hitting specific business targets, factory workers were also given a card that allowed them free access to local leisure and fitness facilities. Words such as "recovery" and "managing energy" became a part of the language on the factory floor.

There was also measurable impact on the factory's bottom line. Overtime hours have dropped in half since workers went through the program. "Previously, in order to achieve our targets, it was a given that people would stay late in the evenings and come in on Saturdays," Dalton told us. "That's not the norm anymore, because people are more productive when they are here and because they see the value of taking their recovery time." Days lost to sickness have dropped by 40 percent, and turnover among staff is down from 8.2 to 3.2 percent. At 91 percent, overall employee satisfaction is among the highest of any division at Sony Electronics, factory or nonfactory.

Sony Europe also made a significant investment in building "chill-out rooms" across the company, including massage chairs, comfortable sofas, low natural lights, and a rule prohibiting the use of cell phones and PDAs. In contrast to our experience at Wachovia, the rooms at Sony are widely used. Sony's leadership has also created more shared spaces in which people can meet and hang out, including a playroom at the central office in Basingstoke, with table and computer games. "These facilities," explains Trevor Johnson, the corporate services manager responsible for building them, "are a recognition that while our business is about machines, it depends on people. We work in a fast-moving competitive sector, and occasionally you just need to take a break to clear your mind."

Leaders at Britain's National Policing Improvement Agency, charged with leading change across U.K. police forces, had a similar epiphany about the power of renewal after we took them through our curriculum. "By reframing our work as a series of sprints, we've turned the team around," explains Derek Mann, head of workforce modernization at the agency. "We were on the brink of burnout. Now we have a common language around recovery and the means to sustain our energy in the face of huge challenges."

THE NAP GAP

Only an estimated 1 percent of companies permit employees to nap at work. A handful of forward-thinking organizations, such as Google, Cisco Apple, and Pixar, do officially sanction naps. "You get tunnel vision when you're hammering away at a problem," Mark Holmes, an art director at Pixar, told a reporter. "You keep going down this same path, again and again, just tweaking, making incremental changes at best. Sleep erases that. It resets you. You wake up and realize—wait a minute!—there is another way to do this."

Google offers napping pods in a range of public spaces at its Mountain View headquarters. The pods are leather recliners with egg-shaped hoods that can be closed, making it possible to shut out light and noise. Nonetheless, our experience in working at Google is that the pods don't get much use during the regular workday, suggesting how much of a leap it is to publicly acknowledge that you're going to take a nap in the workplace.

To drive home the power of naps, we've introduced into some of our own workshops a point during the midafternoon when we ask all participants to take a nap. We literally re-create nursery school, putting mats down on the floor and turning off the lights for twenty to thirty minutes. Some people fall asleep and others don't, but nearly everyone gets a significant dose of midday rest. The payback in productivity is often immediately clear to the nappers. Whereas their attention may have begun to flag, they find themselves reenergized for the rest of the afternoon.

Napping will take hold in organizations, we believe, only when it is viewed as part of a broader and more systematic effort to build cultures that recognize renewal as a crucial component of performance. In the meantime, providing employees more flexibility in their work schedules effectively gives them the freedom to take charge of managing their own energy throughout the day.

Take, for example, the cost of commuting to employers and employees alike. More than 11 million Americans now spend more than two hours a day traveling to and from work, many using energy to no productive purpose during that time. Much of this travel occurs in the morning, when people are typically most energized and alert. In many cases, they arrive at work feeling frustrated and worn out by their commute. If it's not absolutely necessary for the job, how does it make sense to require employees to invest precious energy just getting to work at a specific time? Why not allow them to travel outside rush hour or to work from home at least some of the time? In addition to reducing unproductive time, this sort of flexibility also has the potential to give people more opportunity to get sufficient sleep.

THE TIME TRAP

Exercise is one of the first sacrifices most of us make in the face of long rush hour commutes and long hours at work. If we're leaving home at dawn and returning after dark, who has the time or the energy to work out? Fitness improves the health of a company's employees and has been consistently shown to decrease overall health care costs. It's also a very reliable form of renewal during the workday. A significant and increasing percentage of large organizations now have fitness facilities on-site. Far fewer companies have cultures in which employees feel comfortable working out during the day, much less encouraged to do so.

We made midday exercise a focus of the work we did with a group of accountants at Ernst & Young just in advance of busy season. It's standard for accountants at these firms to put in twelve- to fourteen-hour days throughout the tax season, and they're measured in significant part by the total number of hours they bill every week. The irony is that many of them are working on jobs that are billed to the client for an overall fee, not at an hourly rate. If the job can be completed in fewer hours, it actually generates more profit for the firm. Why, then, would a company measure its employees by their hours? The answer, we've been told over and over, is that it's always been done that way and no one has yet found a better way to measure individual productivity.

The system serves no one well, not at accounting firms, law firms, advertising firms, or any other personal service organizations that charge clients by the hour. Employees, knowing they're rewarded for putting in the maximum number of hours, have no incentive to work more efficiently. If they do get their assigned work done, they're typically given more work to do. Those working the greatest number of hours consistently tell us they get less and less productive the more hours they work. In addition, the greater the number of hours they bill on a given day, the more likely the quality of their work suffers. Firms that bill by the hour operate in a system that ensures that neither they nor their employees are rewarded for working more efficiently. Clients, in turn, may not get the best quality of work they could.

SPRINT AND RECOVER

The key to the success of any of our interventions is the degree to which senior leaders, led by the CEO, actively endorse it. In the case of Ernst & Young Arthur Tulley, the managing partner responsible for the EY team that went through our program was an enthusiastic and engaged supporter of the work. He attended all of the sessions himself and made it clear to employees that he wasn't concerned about the number of hours they worked each day. On the contrary, he urged them to get their work done as efficiently as possible, without sacrificing quality, and then to go home. Tulley recognized that the earlier people left, the more time they'd have at home, the more sleep they'd be likely to get, and the better they'd feel both the next day and over the long haul.

With that in mind, we taught Tulley's team members to work in ninety-minute sprints, focusing without distraction, followed by true renewal breaks so that they could truly refuel themselves. Most important, we encouraged them to take one longer break in the afternoon at 3 or 4 P.M., when their energy was flagging anyway. A nap would have been ideal, but that was still a bit much for the traditional culture of an accounting firm. Many participants elected to go to a nearby gym and work out for an hour. Feeling refreshed and more alert afterward, they found they were able to focus much more efficiently when they returned to the office. The result was that they got more work done in the later part of the day and were often able to leave earlier than they had in the past.

Many participants reported that the busy season that followed our work with them was the least stressful they'd ever experienced. By the end of it, the team as a whole had managed to get more overall work accomplished in fewer hours—a good outcome both for EY and its employees. We're convinced that the first large accounting firm that moves to billing all its clients by the job rather than by the hour will gain a significant competitive advantage. The result, we believe, will be not only higher productivity but a huge advantage in attracting and retaining the best performers.

WE ARE WHAT WE EAT

The final potential source of increased physical energy in the workplace is the food we eat. The key issue for large organizations is the kind of food they offer in vending machines, cafeterias, dining rooms, and at meetings. The staple foods in most vending machines and at most offsites are candy, cookies, and chips, filled with sugar, salt, and fat. These foods provide a quick and short-lived buzz when people's energy is flagging, but they take a toll on their health and productivity over time. At Google, there is just a single vending machine on its main campus, and it's there to make a point. The machine is filled with candy and other junk food, but items are priced in inverse proportion to their nutritional value. The worst foods cost the most. You can buy a bag of Famous Amos cookies for $4.55 or shortbread cookies for $3.40 if that's your thing, but they're going to cost you an arm and a leg.

Most cafeterias and dining rooms we've visited at large companies offer a range of food choices, including healthy ones. It's relatively rare, however, to find companies that explicitly emphasize and promote healthier, energy-rich foods. One of the simplest ways to do so is to offer such choices at subsidized lower prices. The main dining room at Sony Pictures in Los Angeles, where all employees have gone through our work, now offers a healthy meal and a salad bar each day at a reduced rate.

No company we've encountered comes close to the kind of investment Google makes in feeding its employees or treats food as a more integral part of its overall culture. In their initial public offering, co-CEOs Sergey Brin and Larry Page were explicit about their intentions. "We provide many unusual benefits for our employees, including meals free of charge," they wrote. "We are careful to consider the long-term advantages to the company of these benefits."

At its Mountain View headquarters, Google has eleven different restaurants that offer breakfast, lunch, and dinner to employees at no cost. Many of the chefs have been recruited from high-end Bay Area restaurants, and we can vouchsafe from our own experience that the food is extraordinary: fresh, varied, healthy, and bountiful. The cafés are packed at mealtimes, and employees are encouraged to intermingle. There are also "microkitchens" throughout the campus, which offer healthy snacks all day long.

From our perspective, Google's policy creates a more rhythmic and productive way of working on several levels. It encourages people to leave their desks intermittently, especially at lunch. It gets them to move physically, especially in Mountain View, where the cafés are spread all over the campus. The dining rooms themselves, furnished with long tables, prompt employees to sit together. As long as you don't overeat, a meal at Google leaves you feeling better.

Over time, nearly all of us grow accustomed to even the greatest luxuries. Even so, our strong sense from nearly all the employees we've worked with at Google is that free meals and unlimited snacks are a perk they value and appreciate every day. Whatever else it does, offering three high-quality meals a day almost certainly serves an aim any company ought to share: to energize its employees every day with high-octane fuel.

CHAPTER NINE ACTION STEPS

- As a leader, your first responsibility when it comes to renewal is to practice it yourself. Next, speak to the people who work for you about how effectively they're renewing their energy physically. Emphasize the relationship between great performance and regular renewal. Encourage them to work out at midday as a way to increase their energy and focus better in the afternoons. Permit them to take short naps and periodic breaks. Never hold a meeting for more than ninety minutes at a time.
- Do you measure people's performance at least in part by their willingness to put in long hours? It isn't the number of hours they work that matters most but the value they produce. Can you make that paradigm shift in your mind and then in your behavior? Are you prepared to have a conversation with every person who works for you about what schedule would allow each of them to work most effectively—and then do your best to make that possible? If not, what's standing in the way?
- Review the Weekly Pulse chart on page 110 and share it with your team. Lead a discussion with them about the optimal days to take on different tasks. What changes should you make, individually and collectively, to be more productive?

PART III

SECURITY/EMOTIONAL

CHAPTER TEN

The War Between the States

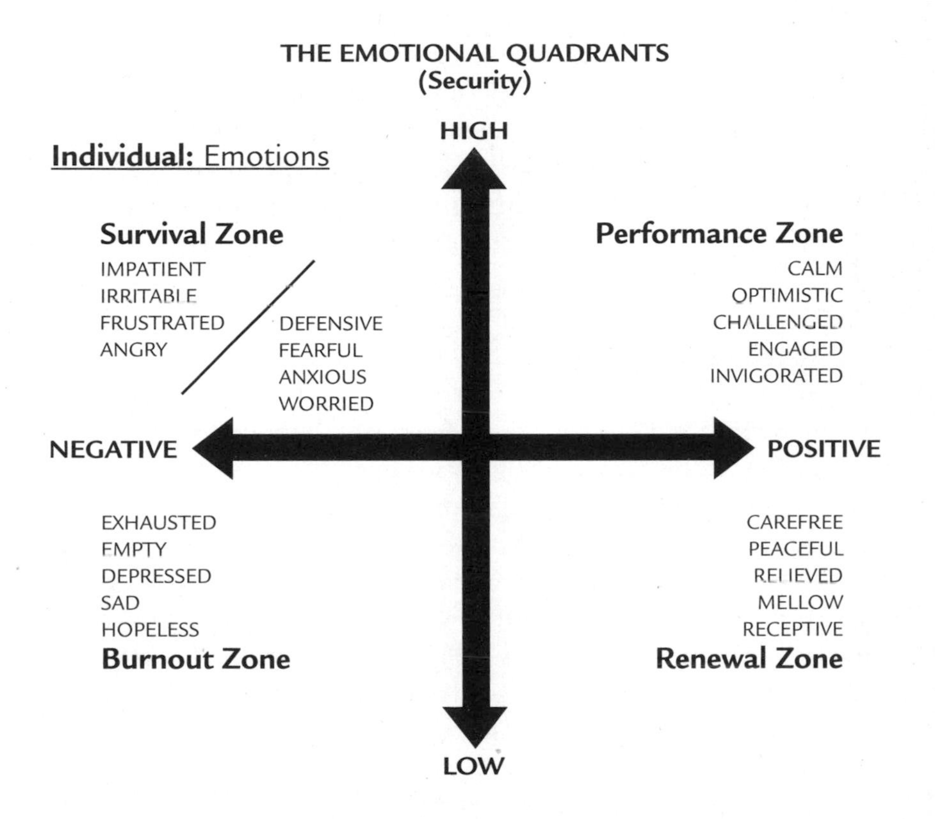

How we feel profoundly influences how we perform. The problem is that much of the time, we're not even aware of how we're feeling, nor what impact those emotions are having on our effectiveness and on the people with whom we work.

Although "emotional intelligence" is now part of the vocabulary in most organizations, few leaders we've worked with are fully comfortable engaging their own emotions or managing the emotions of others. For many of them, emotions remain messy, complicated, and often discomfiting. In too many companies, the unspoken expectation is that employees will park their emotions at the door when they arrive for work each morning. The most common mode of interaction is polite, bland, conflict-avoidant and often inauthentic. When strong emotions are expressed at all, they tend to be the reactive and negative ones that arise under stress, and they're usually tamped back down as quickly as possible.

But emotions influence us, and those around us, whether we consciously recognize them or not. The more aware we are of what we're feeling at any given moment, the more power we have to influence how we're feeling. Skillful management of our emotions creates the potential for better relationships and for greater effectiveness at work.

There are four basic ways we can feel over the course of the day. They're depicted in the Emotional Quadrants, on the previous page. The vertical axis refers to the quantity of our energy, from low to high. The horizontal axis refers to the quality of our energy, from negative to positive. The result is four zones that describe in broad terms how we're feeling at any given time. There are subtler gradations of each emotional state across both axes, but for most of our clients, the four states are readily recognizable.

Take a few moments before reading any further to think about how you feel when you're performing at your best. What adjectives come to mind? Now write them down. How would you characterize what they have in common? Over the years, we've asked this same question of thousands of people—athletes and artists, heart surgeons and ICU nurses, teachers and students, cops and corporate executives. With very few exceptions, they describe feelings associated with high positive energy: upper-right quadrant.

We call this the Performance Zone, and it's the best place to be when you're working toward a specific goal, whether that means sitting in front of a computer, leading a meeting, competing on an athletic field, performing a heart transplant operation, or taking an exam. It's no big news that positive emotions are associated with performing at your best. In all likelihood, you came up with a list of adjectives close to those in the upper-right quadrant above.

What's less obvious is that we can't perform at our best when we're not in the Performance Zone. Put another way, any time you're not feeling optimistic, engaged, upbeat, focused, enthusiastic, and committed, you're suboptimal. For most of us, there are significant periods of time when we're not feeling high positive energy. That prompts a second question: "When you're not in the Performance Zone, where are you, and what are the consequences?"

In terms of the quadrants, there are three other possibilities. Only a tiny percentage of our clients say that they spend any significant time at work in the lower-right quadrant, feeling relaxed, peaceful, laid back and serene. Despite what we've said about the power of intermittent renewal, it remains both counterintuitive at a personal level and countercultural in the vast majority of organizations.

That leaves the left-hand quadrants, both of which are characterized by negative emotions. Many of us find ourselves in the Burnout Zone—lower left—after intense periods of stressful work. But typically it's not a place people stay in for long. On the most obvious level, it's the worst zone from which to work. If you spend much time there, it's likely to put your job in jeopardy. It's also hard to imagine an employee telling a boss, "I'm feeling kind of hopeless and depressed today." The vast majority of clients tell us that when they're not in the Performance Zone at work, it's because they've fallen into the Survival Zone: upper left. Unlike the Renewal Zone and the Burnout Zone, the Survival Zone is an acceptable place in which to operate in most organizations. Expressing anger, fear, frustration, and impatience—the characteristic emotions of the Survival Zone—is all too common in the workplace. Anger, frustration, and impatience fuel fear, after all, and fear fuels action. Many leaders still rely heavily on negative emotions to generate the results they're after.

FEAR CENTRAL

Few of us intentionally choose to work from the Survival Zone. Instead, we move there reactively and instinctively when we perceive a sense of threat or danger—a conflict that arises with a client, colleague, or boss or an external event such as a sudden deadline or a disappointing outcome. At the physiological level, the Survival Zone represents a fight-or-flight response. It's triggered by the amygdala, a small, almond-shaped region in the midbrain below the cortex that processes emotion and that the neuroscientist Joseph LeDoux has termed "fear central." Among other things, the amygdala prompts activation of the sympathetic nervous system, which responds by flooding adrenaline, noradrenaline, and cortisol into our bloodstream. These stress hormones prompt a series of physiological responses, including increased heart rate, narrowing of vision, muscle contraction, and the flow of blood from the brain into our extremities. Each of these responses increases our ability to either fight or flee.

In physiological terms, we have two distinct selves, and they operate with very different agendas and often at cross-purposes. We refer to the conflict between our parasympathetic nervous system, which calms us down, and our sympathetic nervous system, which arouses us, as "the war between the states." In parasympathetic arousal, the self we're aware of operates under the aegis of our prefrontal cortex. It has a limitless ability to learn and grow. In this state, we're capable of making rational choices based on a careful consideration of the costs and benefits. Our second, more primitive self, run by our sympathetic nervous system, falls under the province of our limbic system—emotions, impulses, instincts, and habits. This self runs automatically and reactively, mostly outside our conscious control, and is designed to ensure our immediate survival and safety. It's incapable of reflective thinking.

"Remove the convoluted frontal cortex from a human brain," writes the psychiatrist Ian McCallum, "and you will be faced with an individual who is both disturbed and disturbing, grossly lacking in insight and without any sense of consequence. . . . Without the frontal lobe, we lose what is arguably the most important ability of human socialization—the capacity to deliberately inhibit our actions. We lose our ability to regulate our behavior."

A hardwired response to danger was especially useful to us thousands of years ago, when we faced life-or-death threats from predators every day. Today, we rarely face such dangers. Our bodies, however, don't make the distinction between a real threat to our survival and our more everyday fears. An angry boss, a conflict with a colleague, a difficult deadline, a dissatisfied client, an imposing workload or an unreturned phone call can all prompt our fight-or-flight response. The problem is that when our survival isn't literally at stake, the benefits of fight-or-flight are often far outweighed by the costs.

The first ones are to our health. Cortisol, for example, is a catabolic hormone, and its function is to break things down. That serves us well in many situations. For example, cortisol breaks down fats and carbohydrates and increases glucose in the bloodstream, which gives us greater energy. But when cortisol circulates in our bodies for too long, too continuously, it effectively turns into a poison. It can undermine our ability to learn by damaging the hippocampus, the seat of memory in the brain. It can also severely weaken the immune system by interfering with normal T-cell production, and it has been linked to a range of illnesses, including diabetes and heart disease. "It's vital to our health that we pay very close attention to how much time we spend hooked into the circuitry of anger, or the depths of despair," explains the neuroanatomist Jill Bolte Taylor, who wrote the best-selling book *My Stroke of Insight.*

The second cost of the fight-or-flight reaction is that it inhibits the activity of our prefrontal cortex, which largely shuts down when the sympathetic nervous system takes over. That's for good reason: conscious thinking actually slows the speed of our reaction to life-threatening danger. It takes our prefrontal cortex as much as two full seconds to register and respond to an imminent danger. The amygdala can recognize and react to a perceived threat in as few as two-hundredths of second, something the psychologist Jonathan Haidt refers to aptly as "a neural shortcut." But this instant reactivity doesn't serve us well when the challenges are complex but not life-threatening. In fight or flight, we lose the capacity to calmly and clearly think through the best possible response to the situation at hand.

At the most basic level, we sacrifice reasoning power. With reduced cognitive capacity, we also tend to become more concrete and to think less creatively and strategically. More broadly, we lose the capacity to take into account the long-term consequences of any given behavior, not least because our vision in fight or flight literally narrows to home in on the immediate threat. Fear also begets fear. When the amygdala is chronically aroused, the brain becomes hypervigilant, often sensing danger even where it doesn't truly exist. The classic example is the posttraumatic stress disorder many soldiers experience when they return from fighting in Iraq and Afghanistan. What served them well in war makes their everyday lives dysfunctional. Their fear of attack can become so heightened that any sharp noise may prompt behaviors ranging from paralyzing panic, an extreme form of flight, to unprovoked violence, an extreme version of fight.

Fear and fury may be a fuel for action, but in most situations they undermine our performance. Imagine for a moment that someone you love is about to undergo brain surgery, or that a pilot has to land the plane you're on in the midst of a heavy storm, or that your child's teacher must figure out how best to respond in an emergency. Would you rather the person in charge of these situations be feeling frustrated, angry and terrified, or calm, composed and clear-thinking? The answer is self-evident. It's no different when *you* are the person facing a crisis.

The same is true at the organizational level. The revered management guru W. Edwards Deming grounded his work in the attempt to drive fear out of organizations. "It is unbelievable what happens when you unloose fear," he said. "Fear takes a horrible toll." After surveying the research, Daniel Goleman concluded that "The more intense the pressure, the more our performance and thinking will suffer. . . . The greater the anxiety we feel, the more impaired is the brain's cognitive efficiency."

THE CHIEF ENERGY OFFICER

The third problem with negative emotions is their impact on others. The research is increasingly clear that all emotions are contagious, for better or for worse. We often ask our clients to describe the qualities of a leader they've especially admired or viewed as a role model or a mentor. Think about this yourself. Who would you choose, and what adjectives would apply? Again, take a few moments to write down your answers before continuing.

We've asked this question hundreds of times, and here are the ten most common answers:

- Encouraging
- Inspiring
- Kind
- Positive

- Calm
- Smart
- Visionary
- Supportive
- Decisive
- Fair

No one has ever said to us, "What I loved about my boss is how angry he got. It showed me how much he cared." Or: "I loved his impatience. It really kept me on my toes." Negative emotions may fuel action, but they don't inspire people. To the contrary, the research suggests that leaders who operate from anger and negativity literally have the power to make their employees sick.

One study examined health care workers who had two supervisors, one they liked and the other whom they couldn't stand. On the days the bad boss worked, the average blood pressure of the workers jumped from 113/75 to 126/81, an increase from normal to nearly hypertensive. In another study, workers who felt unfairly criticized by a boss or felt they had a boss who didn't listen to their concerns had a 30 percent higher rate of coronary disease than those with bosses they felt treated them fairly and were concerned with their welfare.

We think of leaders as "chief energy officers." The core challenge for leaders, we believe, is to recruit, mobilize, inspire, focus, and refuel the energy of those they lead—to nudge them toward high positive. In a metareview of more than two hundred leadership studies, the researchers Bruce Avolio and Fred Luthans found only one quality among leaders who consistently had a positive impact on others. The best leaders were able to see in others capacities these employees didn't yet fully recognize in themselves. But how often do leaders play this role—raising the confidence of those they lead—especially when they themselves are feeling under pressure? Leaders are no less vulnerable than the rest of us to feeling threatened and overwhelmed or to reacting from fight or flight. What sets leaders apart is their disproportionate influence on those they lead, by virtue of their position and power. Whatever they're feeling reverberates through the workplaces they oversee.

"I'd always assumed it was perfectly reasonable for me to get upset with someone who screwed up or wasn't pulling his weight," explained Fred, a senior leader at a leading financial institution. "How else was I going to get the person to change? What I came to understand is that if I had a tough conversation with someone and he left my office feeling fearful or angry or put down, he wasn't going to be capable of going back and doing his best work. The conversation was actually counterproductive. I still believe you have to use high negative sometimes to get a person's attention, when nothing else is working. What I try to do now is be sure I'm making a choice to use negative emotions. When I do have a tough conversation with someone, I try to end it with that person knowing I believe in him and I'm confident he can get the job done. If I ever stop believing that—and communicating that—it's probably time to let the person go."

The final cost of high negative emotions is that they quickly deplete our energy. If you spend too much time in the Survival Zone, you'll eventually end up in the Burnout Zone, which is plainly the worst place from which to perform. Athletes understand this phenomenon at a visceral level. In his autobiography, John McEnroe discusses the toll that getting angry took on his performance. "My shtick, of course, was getting upset," he writes. "Did it help me more than it hurt me? I don't think so. Ultimately my father was right—I probably would have done better if I hadn't ever gotten into that." Great as he was, McEnroe won his final grand slam tournament at the age of twenty-five. Anger took an insidious toll on the length of his career.

The energy cost of negative emotions may not be as obvious for those who work in jobs with minimal physical demands, but the toll shows up in subtler ways. Think about a day during which you're feeling anxious, and the impact that has on your ability to focus. How much does an angry confrontation take out of you? What's the cost to your commitment and your productivity if you have a boss you actively dislike?

EMOTIONAL RENEWAL

The antidote to falling reactively into the Survival Zone is to intentionally spend more time in the Renewal Zone. If fitness physically is defined as the speed of recovery, resilience is the speed of recovery emotionally. At a physiological level, the issue is not how high the level of cortisol spikes in our system during the fight-or-flight response but how quickly it returns to normal levels. "It takes less than ninety seconds for limbic system programs to be triggered, surge throughout the body, and then be completely flushed out of our systems," explains Jill Bolte Taylor. "If you stay angry after ninety seconds, it's because you've chosen to stay angry."

Regularly accessing positive emotions is the key to avoiding the Survival Zone. Much as our reservoir of physical energy is drawn down inexorably over the course of the day, so the more difficult challenges we encounter at work deplete our reservoir of positive emotion. Physical and emotional energy are inextricably connected. The way we take care of ourselves physically has a profound influence on our emotions. We feel better after a good night's sleep, and we're emotionally rejuvenated after a run or a good workout. Indeed, the simplest way to regenerate positive emotion is to challenge yourself physically, especially after you've been sitting in front of a desk for several hours, or to rest or sleep when you're truly exhausted. Conversely, succeeding at a difficult task at work, having a great conversation with a colleague, or doing something you deeply enjoy during a break not only lifts your spirits but also energizes you physically.

It's in our self-interest to cultivate positive emotions, not just because they make us feel good but also because they fuel more productivity and effectiveness across all dimensions of our lives. We allow ourselves to be pulled into the Survival Zone by the people around us and by the events that occur over the course of the day. But even in the face of the most stressful demands, we have the power to profoundly influence how we feel. What that requires is learning how to pulse rhythmically between the Performance Zone and the Renewal Zone, so we're capable of responding resiliently to any challenge that arises.

CHAPTER TEN ACTION STEPS

- The more aware we are of what we're feeling, the more we have the power to influence those feelings. Set aside two to three specific times during the day when you ask yourself what emotional quadrant you're in. If it's one of the negative left-hand quadrants, take a few moments to try to understand what put you there.
- The antidote to falling reactively into the Survival Zone is to intentionally spend more time in the Renewal Zone. Make a list of activities that you enjoy most and which make you feel best. Intentionally schedule at least one of these activities into your life each week.
- Energy is contagious. What effect does your energy have on those around you? If you're a leader, the effect of your energy is higher by virtue of your position. After any conversation you're in, take a moment to ask yourself whether the person you were talking to walked away feeling better or worse than when the conversation began. Either way, how did you contribute?

CHAPTER ELEVEN

If You Ain't Got Pride, You Ain't Got Nothin'

A trigger is an event, behavior, or circumstance that consistently prompts negative emotions and propels us into fight or flight—the Survival Zone. We experience triggers every day, to greater and lesser degrees. Mostly they're annoyances, akin to a bee landing on your arm or a leg. You're distracted for a moment until you swat it away. Occasionally you do get stung, the discomfort lingers, and the pain becomes preoccupying. On other occasions, it seems as if we're being triggered all day long. One event after another drives us to impatience, fear, frustration, or anger.

Though it's certainly possible to be triggered positively—by a beautiful sunset, an unexpected compliment, a happy memory—we're biologically wired to sense danger. The result is that we notice what's wrong with our lives far more readily than we do what's right. In a paper entitled "Bad Is Stronger than Good," Roy Baumeister and his colleagues reviewed dozens of studies on the subject and summarized them this way:

> Bad emotions, bad parents, and bad feedback have more impact than good ones, and bad information is processed more thoroughly than good. The self is more motivated to avoid bad self-definitions than to pursue good ones. Bad impressions and bad stereotypes are quicker to form and more resistant to disconfirmation than good ones.

This phenomenon has also been called "negativity bias." "Over and over," explains Jonathan Haidt, "psychologists find that the human mind reacts to bad things more quickly, strongly, and persistently than to equivalent good things." When you receive a performance review of some kind at work, do you focus more on the positive comments or the negative ones? Do you spend more time savoring your gains from investments you make, or worrying about your losses? Numerous studies suggest that losing something makes us far unhappier than acquiring the same thing makes us happier. Conversely, when we have to give something up, we're much more upset than we were happy to have acquired the same thing in the first place.

"It is evolutionarily adaptive for bad to be stronger than good," argues Baumeister. "Survival requires urgent attention to possible bad outcomes, but it is less urgent with regard to good ones." Although such vigilance is no longer as critical to our survival as it was thousands of years ago, we're still highly attuned to perceived threats to our everyday well-being.

As we've discussed, we each react to the perception of threat or danger with either fight or flight. Consider the following example: the strong likelihood, based on my experience, is that you're not reading this book with much focus or retention. Your mind is wandering frequently, and you're easily distracted by whatever is going on around you. The consequence is that you're missing much of the argument we're making. I'm also willing to bet that you rarely read with much focus, which is why most of your knowledge is superficial and you end up spending a lot of time winging it, without truly understanding what you're talking about.

How does that strike you? Have I got it pretty much right? My strong suspicion is that I do, even if you feel compelled to deny it.

Okay, now take a moment to scan your body. How are you feeling at this moment? Are you breathing any faster than usual? Do you sense any anxiety in your stomach or your chest? Are you feeling flushed or perhaps slightly uneasy? Perhaps instead you're feeling irritated and annoyed by what I just told you about yourself.

If so, fair enough. My *aim* was to trigger you. In reality, of course, I have no evidence that what I just said about you has any basis in fact. Even so, if you're like most people I work with, the likelihood is that it *did* trigger you, at least to some extent, and perhaps so quickly that you might not even have noticed it was happening. That may have happened even if you suspected I was just trying to get a rise out of you.

Your amygdala—your early warning system—picked up the potential threat posed by my words even before your prefrontal cortex had a chance to evaluate whether the words had any reasonable validity. If your amygdala did take over, it sent a message to your brain stem, which, in a fraction of a second, engineered the release of stress hormones into your bloodstream, all to get you prepared to defend yourself. Those hormones are probably still coursing through your bloodstream, although the levels should be dropping now that your prefrontal cortex has gotten in on the act and figured out that this was all a ruse.

So how did you react to my insult? Was it in fight, so that you felt annoyed by our presumption? Perhaps you thought to yourself, "What an idiotic presumption. I *was* focused on what I was reading, and even if I hadn't been, it's not like what you're saying here is rocket science." Or did you react in flight, so that what you felt instead was a bit exposed or embarrassed or self-critical? As in "Boy, it's really true that I don't pay attention very well. I should definitely concentrate better. I wonder if people can tell when I'm not really listening to them." In fight, we react by turning our negative emotions against others. In flight, we turn negative emotions on ourselves. Neither response serves us very well for very long. We end up making ourselves feel bad or others feel bad or both, and rarely consciously. When we sense a threat, we simply react.

WHATEVER YOU FEEL COMPELLED TO DO, DON'T

The first place a trigger shows up is in our bodies. In fight or flight, you'll recall, the sympathetic nervous system takes over, prepares us to react quickly, and overrides our reflective capacity. It robs us, in short, of the chance to make an intentional decision. Your first challenge is to become aware of the feelings that arise when you're triggered, before you act on them. That may mean noticing your heart beating faster, a sense of tightness in your chest, or a feeling of frustration, anxiety, discomfort, or anger. When you begin to notice the negative feelings arising, the next step is to apply what we call the "Golden Rule" of triggers: "Whatever you feel compelled to do, don't."

The key word here is "compelled." Compulsions are not choices, and they rarely lead to a positive outcome. If your typical instinct is to strike out when you feel threatened, the best thing you can do is to hold your fire. If your instinct under threat is to pull back, the best thing you can do is to stay engaged. In either case, the key is to move from automatic to intentional mode, so you're capable of making a conscious decision about how to respond. Simply taking a deep breath and exhaling slowly can be helpful because it's a rapid and effective way of decreasing your physiological arousal and returning to a state of greater calm. Feeling your feet—your toes, then the balls of your feet, then your heels—is powerful because doing so pulls you back into your body and out of the visceral experience of threat.

For Jonathan, a senior executive we worked with at a large consumer products company, realizing precisely what most often pushed his buttons proved valuable. "I now realize that the times I get most triggered are when I'm feeling really pressed," he told us. "Either there's a lot of things on my plate, or I'm trying to meet a really tough deadline. In those situations, it's easy for me to feel like people are wasting my time. So let's say I get an e-mail asking for something that I think the person could have handled himself. I'm liable to dash off a short, sarcastic response. The moment I click 'Send,' I know I shouldn't have, but then it's too late. I end up having to clean up the mess I've created, which wastes my time and theirs. What I'm learning to do now is to take a deep breath and hit the 'Draft' key instead, so my e-mail automatically is saved rather than sent. By the time I get back to it later, I've calmed down, and I almost always end up either deleting the e-mail altogether or completely rewriting it."

OUR CORE EMOTIONAL NEED

If a trigger is a response to the experience of threat and danger, what exactly do we feel is at risk? Why, in short, do certain events and interactions predictably drive us into the high negative zone? This isn't the sort of question most of us think about very often, not least because we're rarely consciously aware that we've been triggered. Even when we do start to notice our negative emotions, we're usually more concerned with getting the unpleasantness behind us or blaming it on someone else than we are in figuring out what prompted it in the first place.

Still, because bad is stronger than good, triggers leaves a strong memory trace. When we ask people to recall a recent trigger, almost no one has a difficult time doing so. Over the years, our clients have shared literally thousands of examples with us. In the overwhelming majority of cases, the origin of the trigger can be traced to a feeling of having been devalued or diminished by someone else's words or behavior. Our core emotional need is to feel secure—to be valued—and challenges to our self-worth do just the opposite. They make us feel devalued and insecure, and most of us find such feelings uncomfortable at best and intolerable at worst.

James Gilligan, a professor of psychiatry at the University of Pennsylvania, has spent forty years studying violence. "In the course of that work," he writes, "I have been struck by the frequency with which I received the same answer when I asked prisoners, or mental patients, why they assaulted or even killed someone. Time after time, they would reply, 'because he disrespected me.' " Gilligan has found that gaining respect, even more than money, is often the motive for armed robbery. "When I actually sat down and spoke at length with men who had repeatedly committed such crimes, I would start to hear comments like 'I never got so much respect before in my life as I did when I pointed a gun at some dude's face.' "

Gilligan tells the story of working with an inmate in a prison who seemed uncontrollable. The inmate kept assaulting guards, despite increasingly severe punishments, until he was finally placed in solitary confinement twenty-four hours a day. Even then, whenever a guard opened the door to his cell, the inmate attacked. Gilligan was brought in to try to help. "What do you want so badly," he asked the inmate, "that you are willing to give up everything else in order to get it?" Ordinarily so inarticulate that it was difficult to understand anything he said, the inmate suddenly stood up tall and replied to Gilligan's question with absolute clarity: "Pride. Dignity. Self-esteem." Then he added, "And I'll kill every motherfucker in that cell block if I have to in order to get it. If you ain't got pride, you ain't got nothin.' "

This need for respect is primal and survival-based. Elijah Anderson, a sociologist at Yale, has spent many years studying violence, and specifically something he calls the "code of the streets" that emerges out of the cultures of poor inner city communities in which opportunities for social mobility are severely limited. "At the heart of the code," Anderson writes, "is the issue of respect—loosely defined as being treated 'right,' or granted the deference one deserves . . . respect is viewed as an entity that is hard-won but easily lost, and so must constantly be guarded." The street codes include "If someone disses you, you got to straighten them out" and "Don't punk out."

But the result is a classic zero-sum game: survival of the baddest. "The extent to which one person can raise himself up," says Anderson, "depends on his ability to put another person down. There is a generalized sense that very little respect is to be had, and therefore everyone competes to get what affirmation he can of the little that is available." Echoing Gilligan's experience with the violent inmate, Anderson has found that "Many inner-city young men in particular crave respect to such a degree that they will risk their lives to attain and maintain it."

The executives with whom we work plainly have more ways than inner-city kids do to gain the respect of others. But feeling valued is no less essential to them. Without a stable sense of value, after all, who are we? Much as we aspire to feel good about ourselves regardless of what others may say, our sense of self-worth is profoundly influenced by the degree to which others value us. "We want them to acknowledge our existence, take account of us, and react to us," explains William Irvine in his provocative book *On Desire*. "We might want them to love us, and if not love us then at least admire us. And if we can't have people's admiration, we seek their respect or recognition." Or, as Daniel Goleman puts it, "Threats to our standing in the eyes of others are remarkably potent biologically, almost as powerful as those to our very survival."

Above all other stresses, it's the feeling of being personally criticized that appears to take the greatest toll on our bodies, and on our ability to think clearly. In a meta-analysis of 208 stress-related studies, the researchers Margaret Kemeny and Sally Dickerson found that the highest rises in cortisol levels—the most extreme fight-or-flight responses—are prompted by "threats to one's social self, or threat to one's social acceptance, esteem, and status." An impersonal stressor such as an endlessly ringing alarm is obviously annoying, but it prompts a far less pernicious stress response. When people are subjected to an uncontrollable alarm, their cortisol levels rise but return to a baseline level within forty minutes. By contrast, a threat to their self-esteem prompts cortisol levels to remain elevated for more than an hour. That helps explains why even the most "constructive" criticism so rarely has much impact on us and is often counterproductive. To really take in and process critical feedback, it must be delivered by someone who makes us feel safe and who we truly believe has our best interests at heart. We're far less likely to feel inspired by someone who says "Here's what's wrong with what you did" than we are by a more forward-looking "Here's what works so far, and here's what I think you need to do to take this to the next level."

In another of his reviews of the literature, Baumeister and his colleague Mark Leary looked at the degree to which "the need to belong" is a fundamental human motivation. Abraham Maslow first gave the word "belongingness" currency in the 1960s, when he defined it as the most important need after safety in his hierarchy of needs. Baumeister and Leary were interested to see if the empirical evidence supported Maslow's hypothesis. "Much of what human beings do is done in the service of belongingness," they concluded, after looking at dozens of studies. "Belongingness can be almost as compelling a need as food." Or, as the UCLA neuroscientist Matthew Lieberman bluntly puts it, "To a mammal, being socially connected to caregivers is necessary to survival."

Positive connection with others underlies our sense of security, which is critical to our effectiveness. The more we feel our value is at risk, the more energy we spend defending it and the less energy we have available to create value. A trigger serves as an alarm, alerting us to a potential danger at hand. In our experiences with thousands of clients, the trigger almost always has something to do with the feeling of being devalued. Consider this list of the ten triggers we hear most frequently:

- Feeling spoken to with condescension and lack of respect
- Being treated unfairly
- Not feeling appreciated
- Not being listened to or feeling heard
- Someone else taking credit for my work
- Being kept waiting
- Someone else's sloppy work on a project I'm overseeing

- Feeling criticized or blamed
- Unrealistic deadlines
- People who think they know it all

A SECURE BASE

The need to feel cared for and secure has its origins at the earliest stages of our development, which makes biological sense. Without being cared for, we wouldn't survive. In a fascinating series of studies, Michael Meaney, a neuroendocrinologist at McGill University, found that the quality of nurturing a mother rat gives to her offspring literally alters the way the DNA in the offspring's genes are expressed. Exposed to stress, baby rats who've received a lot of licking and grooming from their mothers later produce fewer stress hormones than rats who receive less care. The more nurtured rats also grow up to be more alert, confident, and bold in their behaviors and more likely to nurture their own offspring. The same pattern is true, Meaney believes, of all species. More than any species, however, human beings carry this need for nurturing forward throughout their lives, at home and at work, the intensity depending on the degree to which it was met early in their lives.

The renowned physician and psychoanalyst John Bowlby spent a lifetime studying parent-child attachment in human beings, motivated in part by his own experience growing up in an emotionally chilly upper-class British family in the early 1900s. Like most such children at the time, he rarely saw his parents and was sent off to boarding school at the age of seven, an experience he found frightening and painful.

Bowlby's theories about attachment grew out of observing and treating children, many of them World War II orphans, as well as children who were hospitalized or institutionalized and therefore separated from a primary caretaker. The key to healthy emotional development, Bowlby came to believe, is what he termed "a secure base from which a child or an adolescent can make sorties into the outside world and to which he can return knowing for sure that he will be welcomed when he gets there, nourished physically and emotionally, comforted if distressed, reassured if frightened."

In Bowlby's formulation and that of his American disciple Mary Ainsworth, a secure base and a safe haven provide a reliable source of emotional renewal that makes it possible for a child to risk exploring the unknown. The more secure the child's base, the more confident she becomes and the more willing she is to venture into the world, for longer and longer periods of time. Margaret Mahler, a psychoanalyst and contemporary of Sigmund Freud, specifically described the "return to base" as an opportunity to "refuel." In short, feeling valued and secure is a basic form of stress inoculation.

Our early-childhood experiences leave an imprint that powerfully and predictably influences our security–and our vulnerability to triggers–throughout our lives. Even as adults, Baumeister concludes, the fear of aloneness and the absence of caring relationships are "worse than the pain of emotional or physical abuse." Over time, the source of a secure base typically evolves from a parent to a spouse or a partner. The extent to which this need is met profoundly influences not just the quality of our relationships, but also our effectiveness in the world. "A great deal of neurotic, maladaptive and destructive behavior," writes Baumeister, "seems to reflect either desperate attempts to establish or maintain relationships with other people or sheer frustration and purposelessness when one's own need to belong goes unmet."

Phillip Shaver, an attachment researcher and psychologist influenced by Bowlby and Ainsworth, estimates that just over half of Americans demonstrate "secure attachment," marked by the capacity for trusting relationships, good self-esteem, and comfort in sharing feelings with friends and partners. Approximately 20 percent of us are what Ainsworth originally termed "anxious," meaning we often worry that we're not getting enough love and are clingy and overly dependent as a consequence. The other quarter of us are "avoidant," meaning we're distrusting of others, struggle with closeness, and tend to be more emotionally remote, withholding, and detached.

Threatening events exacerbate our need for a secure base, even as adults. "To remain within easy access of a familiar individual known to be ready and willing to come to our aid in an emergency," Bowlby wrote, "is clearly a good insurance policy–whatever our age." The need for such a person helps to explain the intriguing Gallup Organization finding that one of the keys to high engagement and high performance is "having a best friend at work." A friend or trusted mentor at work creates a secure base—a source of continuing emotional nourishment, safety, and security in the face of everyday challenges. We frame this in energy terms: the greater the demand we face, the greater our need for renewal and recovery—not just physically but also emotionally.

Healthy emotional development—and the highest level of effectiveness—requires the ability to move freely and flexibly between autonomy and secure connection with others. Too little encouragement, love, and protection—on the job or off—leaves us feeling unsafe, insecure, fearful, and unprepared to function effectively. Paradoxically, narcissism—excessive self-regard and self-absorption—is one of the ways we defend against an underlying sense of inadequacy. "A common defense against the painful experience of deflated value is inflated value," explains psychologist Terrence Real.

Two behaviors are common among leaders and managers when their own basic emotional needs haven't been satisfied in nourishing, enduring ways. The first is insistently calling attention to their own value, often through the arbitrary exercise of power. The most obvious manifestations are a high need for control, poor listening skills, impatience, and self-aggrandizement. So long as leaders are unwilling to look honestly at themselves—to recognize their own fears and shortcomings—they can't grow or change. The people they lead or manage also pay a price. The second common deficit-driven behavior among leaders and managers is disparaging others to bolster themselves. This can take the form of relentless criticism of those they oversee and, more subtly, the withholding of any kind of positive feedback. The performance impact is clear: the less people feel valued and appreciated, the less engaged, loyal, and productive they tend to be.

In some cases, inflated self-regard is not a cover for insecurity but rather a genuine sense of entitlement, self-satisfaction, and superiority. In one study of 37,000 college students, narcissistic personality traits increased from the 1980s to the present at the same rate that obesity did. In a second study, 11,000 teenagers between fourteen and sixteen years of age filled out a 400-item questionnaire in either 1951 or in 1989. The most significant change came in response to the statement "I am an important person." Only 12 percent answered "yes" in 1951, while nearly 80 percent did so in 1989.

That could be perceived as good news, but the sense of superiority many of these self-important people feel is unwarranted. High self-esteem, for example, has not been correlated with better grades, test scores, or job performance. "College students with inflated views of themselves (who think they are better than they actually are) make poorer grades the longer they are in college [and] they are also more likely to drop out," say the researchers Jean M. Twenge and W. Keith Campbell. When narcissists are administered tests of their general competence, they're far more confident of their answers than their humbler counterparts but score no better. Nearly 40 percent of American eighth-graders report confidence in their math skills, compared to just 6 percent of South Koreans, but the South Koreans score far higher on actual tests. In another study, leaders who rated themselves high and also scored high on narcissistic traits were seen by their peers as below average. When employees view leaders as egotistical and self-absorbed, they also give them below average scores in interpersonal skills and integrity.

Whether inflated self-regard is a thin cover for inadequacy or an inflated and unwarranted confidence, it's at least as dysfunctional as insecurity. Excessive self-importance, self-absorption, high need for admiration, and sensitivity to criticism—common traits of the grandiose—all undermine our capacity to learn, grow and take responsibility for our shortcomings and missteps. Envy, lack of empathy, and quickness to anger all conspire to prevent narcissistic leaders from establishing and maintaining close relationships and working effectively with others. In short, high self-regard unbalanced by the capacity to value and appreciate others can be pernicious.

Even well short of these extremes, the vast majority of us struggle to varying degrees with not feeling sufficiently valued in the workplace and are guilty at times of devaluing others. We spend much of our lives feeling either "one up" or "one down"—better than or not as good as. Both positions separate us from others, and neither serves us well. "The paradox of the grandiose position," writes Terrence Real, "is that it solidifies the very relationship disconnections whose pain it seeks to soothe."

Because our core need for value is so rarely acknowledged or addressed in most organizations, we typically try to keep this hunger under wraps and invisible at work. Vulnerability, after all, makes all of us feel uncomfortable and at risk. At the same time, we go to great lengths and expend enormous energy to protect our sense of value when it's threatened—whether in the form of lashing out, blaming others, denying, rationalizing, or withdrawing.

The fight response to a feeling of insufficient value is to call attention to ourselves more aggressively. We see this in leaders who flaunt their power, hog credit for successes, blame others for failures, and brook no dissent. By contrast, humility is often a measure of a leader's true confidence. In *Good to Great,* Jim Collins identifies humility, along with fierce resolve, as one of the two key qualities of CEOs of the most enduringly successful companies. This makes sense from an energy perspective. The leader who is secure in his own value is free to invest energy in empowering others.

The flight response, when our value feels at risk, is a means of minimizing the threat by avoiding conflict with others altogether. At most organizations we've worked in, flight is more common than fight. But the impact on employees is at least as insidious. In one company, for example, the CEO simply refused to have conversations he felt would be upsetting to others and therefore difficult for him. He wanted to be liked, above all, but his behavior had the opposite impact. The CEO's most senior executives had no idea where they stood with him, learned over the years not to trust that he was telling them what he really felt, and felt destabilized as a result. The CEO's insistence on avoiding conflict prompted considerable enmity from his executives. They walked around feeling frustrated, insecure, and even angry but afraid to say anything about the problem, which undermined his own and the company's effectiveness.

Envy and greed are two of the other primary manifestations of our unmet needs for security and value. Money is a means by which we try to ensure our security but also to stoke our sense of value. What money buys is visible and concrete, but it's also limited and one-dimensional. Greed is a reflection of the experience that no amount of money is ever enough to fill our deeper needs. How else to explain the lust for ever-larger sums that led so many of those in the banking industry—already wealthy—to make the sort of reckless, shortsighted choices that led to the current financial crisis? Nor is money the only way we express our greed and our unmet need for value. Greed also shows up in everything from the unwillingness to delegate to the hoarding of information.

Envy is greed directed at what others have that we want. It prompts us not just to squander energy by comparing ourselves unfavorably with others, but also to seek value at their expense. Is it surprising that when we gossip, the stories we tell are ten times as likely to be negative as positive? As François de La Rochefoucauld gently and amusingly observed, "We all have strength enough to endure the trouble of others." Or, as the novelist Pete Dexter put it more bluntly, describing his reaction to the success of fellow writers: "Jealousy's the wrong word for what I usually feel. It's closer to hoping they get hit by a car."

When we try to build our value at the expense of others, through greed or envy, they typically respond as if their own survival is at stake. It's akin to two drowning people trying to save themselves by pushing the other one down. Nobody wins. Likewise, the attempt to prove our superiority over others ends up separating us from the intimate connections we so crave. Our well-being depends not just on building our own value, but also on actively valuing others.

CHAPTER ELEVEN ACTION STEPS

- Our core emotional need is to feel secure. In most cases, negative emotions can be traced to the experience of not feeling valued. Think of the most recent time you felt upset—angry, frustrated, anxious, even impatient. Can you trace it back to a perceived threat to your own value? Become more aware of how much energy you spend worrying about, or trying to restore, or asserting your value.
- Go back to page 139 and revisit the most common triggers. Triggers show up first in our bodies. Notice the next time you feel your heart beating faster, tightness in your chest, or queasiness in your stomach. You will have now identified a way of recognizing when you've been triggered, simply by the way you're feeling physically.
- When a trigger lands you in the "Survival Zone," the first key is to calm your physiology. That requires applying what we've called the Golden Rule of Triggers: whatever you feel compelled to do, don't. Instead take a deep breath, and then feel your feet. Buy time until your body calms down, so that you can make an intentional choice about how to best respond to the trigger.

CHAPTER TWELVE

The Facts and the Stories We Tell

Jake worked for a large technology company in Silicon Valley but hungered to launch his own business. He'd spent the past year trying to raise money for a Web-based approach to evaluating financial risk. Alan was a wealthy investor, based in Boston, whom Jake met through Susan, a mutual acquaintance. A month later, when Alan was visiting San Francisco, he invited Jake to meet him for breakfast. The scheduled hour stretched into three. By the time they parted, Jake was convinced he'd found his financing. Alan promised to be in touch within a few days. In the interim, he encouraged Jake to call or e-mail him about any further thoughts he had. "You can reach me anytime," Alan told him. "I'm always on my BlackBerry."

Over the weekend, Jake had a flood of new insights about the venture and on Monday morning he sent Alan an e-mail. When he hadn't heard back by the following morning, he called Alan but got his voice mail. Disappointed not to get a response, Jake didn't make too much of it. "Something must have come up," he told himself. "This is a busy guy."

Late in the day Wednesday, Jake tried again, phone and e-mail, but still got no response. He considered calling Susan but remembered she was out of the country on a mountain-climbing vacation. Wary of pushing Alan too hard, Jake let two more days go by before e-mailing him again on Friday. Again no response. At midafternoon, Jake happened to flip on CNBC in his office. There was Alan, talking on *Squawk Box* about some of his recent investments. So much for his being preoccupied by an emergency, Jake thought.

Feeling dissed and devalued, Jake angrily concluded that there was no point in continuing to pursue Alan. "Who wants to be involved with a guy like that anyway?" he said to himself. A week later, still simmering, he called Susan, who had just arrived home from vacation.

"What a phony jerk your friend is," he told her. "He tells me how great my idea is, encourages me to call him anytime, and then he doesn't even have the decency to respond to any of my messages."

"That's funny," Susan replied, "because I just got an e-mail from Alan telling me he sent you detailed comments on your business plan and never heard back from *you*." Jake felt his stomach lurch. Could he inadvertently have given Alan his *work* e-mail? He opened his computer and went straight to the spam file. Sure enough, there was the e-mail from Alan, dated the Monday after they met, with a long attachment that had never gotten through Jake's company firewall.

"Quite an adventure since our great meeting," the note began. "As I was about to board my flight, I reached into my jacket pocket and realized my BlackBerry was missing. By the time I landed in Boston, someone had opened an online bank account in my name. I had to close down every account I have. My new cell phone number is at the bottom of this page and I'm writing you from my new e-mail. The good news is I got time to do a revised business plan, which I've attached. Let's talk tomorrow. Alan."

So how exactly did Jake get it so wrong? In his mind, he made his judgment about Alan based on the facts. What he didn't recognize is that he chose to put the facts together to create a specific story.

A *fact* is something that can be objectively verified by any person. It is irrefutable. It was a fact that Jake made several calls and sent several e-mails to Alan. It was a fact that he received no phone messages back from Alan, nor any e-mails, at least not ones that landed in his inbox. It was also a fact that Alan appeared on CNBC.

A *story,* by contrast, is something we create to make sense of the facts. We do so because human beings are meaning-making animals. We seek to understand. The problem is that we often tell our stories so fast that we mistake them for the facts and then treat our stories as if they're irrefutably true. Also, because bad is stronger than good, we often instinctively tell negative stories.

Jake's story was that Alan's failure to return several phone calls and e-mails meant Alan was rude and disingenuous. Moreover, if

Alan had time to shoot the breeze on CNBC, that proved he obviously hadn't been deterred from responding to Jake by any emergency. Plausible as Jake's story seemed to him at the time—"I'm just telling you what happened," he said to Susan—it didn't reflect what had *really* happened. Not surprising, the fact that Alan received no reply to his e-mail prompted him to tell a similarly negative story about Jake. It didn't occur to either one of them that there might be a perfectly plausible explanation for the behavior of the other. Instead, each of them felt devalued, triggered, and angry. Each believed his feelings were justified by the facts, and neither got what he really wanted.

Awareness by itself can powerfully diminish our reactivity. By simply being curious about how we're responding, we move from the role of the person experiencing our feelings to that of self-observer. Rather than feeling rocked by the emotions our stories create—"I'm angry," "The guy is a jerk," "I wasn't treated fairly"—we stand apart, more dispassionately. Instead of acting on our feelings, we're free to coolly evaluate them. By shifting perspectives, we reintroduce the power of choice.

Plainly, we can't change the facts, but we do have a choice about what to make of them. We *can* take more control of the stories we choose to tell ourselves. We can also use our reflective capacity to see the world in subtler, more empowering ways, without rationalizing, minimizing, or denying the facts. To the degree that it serves us well, we can intentionally cultivate a positive bias to offset our evolutionary bias for the negative.

REALISTIC OPTIMISM

Positive thinking has long had a bad name in sophisticated circles. In *Candide,* written in the midst of the Enlightenment in 1759, Voltaire mocks the optimism of Candide's tutor, Dr. Pangloss, and his relentless belief that "all is for the best in the best of all possible worlds." Pollyanna, the title character in Eleanor Porter's early-twentieth-century children's books, was able to resourcefully find the good in any situation. Over time, a Pollyanna came to symbolize a fatuous person who is unreasonably or illogically optimistic. Books such as

Norman Vincent Peale's *The Power of Positive Thinking* and Dale Carnegie's *How to Win Friends and Influence People* have sold millions of copies, but they're often disparaged as simpleminded hype.

Optimism can indeed be a form of self-deception and denial—something Roy Baumeister calls "an exclusively confirmatory approach to information processing." Or, as the psychologist Christopher Peterson puts it, "Unrelenting optimism precludes the caution, sobriety, and conservation of resources that accompany sadness in a normal and presumably adaptive response to setback." In its extreme form, optimism is a reductionistic choosing up of sides. It may make us feel better in the short term, but it doesn't equip us to operate effectively in a complex world or to learn from our mistakes.

Relentless pessimism, on the other hand, is just as narrow and extreme and may be even more dysfunctional. The evidence is clear that persistent negative emotions take a toll on our health, our capacity to think clearly, and ultimately our effectiveness. "A healthy psychological immune system strikes a balance that allows us to feel good enough to cope with our situation but bad enough to do something about it," Daniel Gilbert writes in his wonderful book *Stumbling on Happiness.* What, then, might be a more nuanced perspective that includes both optimism and pessimism, positivity and negativity, without choosing up sides between them?

The psychologist Sandra Schneider has coined the term "realistic optimism," which she defines as "accepting the reality of the current situation and finding a satisfying meaning therein." In contrast to blind faith, false hope, and magical thinking, realistic optimism balances a hopeful and positive perspective with a recognition that the desired outcome may or may not occur. "Realistic optimism," Schneider explains, "involves being lenient in our evaluation of past events, actively appreciating the positive aspects of our current situation and routinely emphasizing possible opportunities for the future." If realism refers to the facts, optimism is the outgrowth of the story we choose to tell about those facts. Realistic optimism serves as a fuel for exerting the maximum effort on the right priorities in order to influence the best possible outcome.

Imagine that you're five feet, four inches tall and your single-minded goal is a career in the NBA. Optimism is likely to lead only to disappointment. If your more realistic goal is to be the best basketball player you're capable of being despite your height disadvantage, optimism may make you more resilient and willing to work harder to improve. Numerous studies have demonstrated that focusing on a positive outcome rather than avoiding a negative one typically leads to greater persistence, more flexibility in finding ways to reach a goal, increased creativity in solving problems, greater internal motivation, more satisfaction, and better results. Expecting to succeed, in short, makes us more likely to succeed. "Each of us can be considered an active player in the quality of our experiences," writes Schneider, "with at least partial control of whether good things happen. Realistically, having a good attitude is likely to pay off."

By contrast, denying reality—either by actively avoiding information you prefer not to know or by looking selectively for evidence that confirms what you already believe—doesn't make it go away. In *Good to Great,* Jim Collins finds the pitch-perfect example of realistic optimism in the story of James Stockdale, the highest-ranking naval officer held as a prisoner of war during Vietnam. Over the seven years he was held prisoner, Stockdale was tortured repeatedly, held in solitary confinement, and given no reason to believe he would ever make it out alive.

"I never lost faith in the end of the story," Stockdale told Collins. "I never doubted not only that I would get out, but also that I would prevail in the end and turn the event into the defining event of my life." The key was an ability to embrace both optimism and realism concurrently—something Collins named "the Stockdale Paradox." As Stockdale explained it, "You must never confuse faith that you will prevail in the end—which you can never afford to lose—with the discipline to confront the most brutal facts of your current reality, whatever they might be."

More common, and often unconsciously, we look to confirm what we already believe—by telling ourselves stories that match our preconceptions. "Over and over again," explains Jonathan Haidt, "studies show that people set out on a cognitive mission to bring back reasons to support their preferred belief or action. And because we are usually successful in this mission, we end up with the illusion of objectivity. We really believe that our position is rationally and objectively justified."

Think of the story Jake told himself when he believed that Alan wasn't responding to his e-mails and phone calls. Taking a stance of realistic optimism, rather than instantly assuming the worst, might well have prompted Jake to tell a different story than he did about Alan's seeming failure to respond. "He was genuinely enthusiastic," Jake might have said to himself. "I'm going to assume there's a good explanation for his not calling." Telling *that* story would have left Jake feeling better, rather than squandering his energy in anger and frustration. It also might have prompted him to pursue Alan more avidly, rather than writing him off.

BEYOND BLAME

When we default reactively to telling negative stories, we almost invariably assign ourselves the role of victim. That's what Jake did with Alan (and Alan likely did with Jake). Blaming others for what goes wrong in our lives is a form of self-protection. By off-loading responsibility, we feel better in the short term. It's a form of protection we learn very early in our lives. "It's not *my* fault," we protest defensively. The limitation of the victim role is that it undermines our power to influence our circumstances.

The alternative is taking responsibility. That doesn't mean blaming ourselves for everything bad that happens to us, because that's just substituting one extreme for another. Rather, it means intentionally looking for where our responsibility lies in any given situation—and how the story we choose to tell might influence the outcome. When we met Linda, a VP at a global advertising agency, she told us that her biggest trigger at work was that her boss often failed to respond to her requests for feedback on projects she was about to undertake. Linda concluded that he didn't consider her ideas worth his time and often worried that her days at the agency were numbered. She felt devalued by her boss, and it dawned on her that she often took out her frustration on the members of her own team.

As soon as we introduced Linda to the difference between facts and stories, she realized that she really had no idea if her story about her boss was accurate. The next time she met with him, she felt emboldened to pose the question directly. "I'm just wondering," she said, "why you don't ever seem to respond to my requests for feedback." He looked surprised. "You've always covered every angle, and there's no need," he said. "I only respond to those kinds of e-mails when I see a problem. I'm really sorry. I thought you knew."

The experience prompted Linda to build a ritual around a new way of responding when she found herself assuming the worst. "The story I'm telling myself," she would say to the person who had triggered her, and then she'd share what she was assuming. "Have I got it right," she'd conclude, "or is it just my story?" In most cases, she found that her worst fears weren't confirmed. In the rare instances when they were, the way she asked the question—taking responsibility for her assumption—allowed her to have a conversation about the situation rather than putting the other person on the defensive.

Paul, a team leader at a large oil company, often found himself triggered by the fact that Andrew, a member of his team in charge of strategic planning, didn't seem to spend much time at his desk. Paul became convinced that Andrew was slacking, even though Andrew remained one of the most creative and productive members of his team. We asked Paul to consider a simple question: "Might there be a more positive explanation for why Andrew isn't always at his desk?" On reflection, Paul concluded that perhaps Andrew was doing his work somewhere else at times. More important, he realized that, given Andrew's high productivity, it really didn't matter where he did his work.

When we're triggered—and the underlying explanation is that we feel devalued—we typically revert to telling our stories in black and white. It's right or wrong, good or bad, hero or villain. Neither of these extremes captures the richer, more complex reality of what goes on in most interactions. Instead, we set up a contest in which someone has to lose. If I'm right, you're wrong. If I'm the hero, you're the villain.

But what if each of these opposites were true about you? Right *and* wrong. Good *and* bad. Villain *and* hero. Take a moment to get a pen and a sheet of paper. Draw a line down the middle of the page. Now consider this question: What do you like best about yourself, and what is it that people most appreciate about you? On the left-hand side, write a list of your best qualities. Make it as complete as possible before you read any further. Don't stop until you've come up with at least a half-dozen qualities.

Okay, now think for a moment about what qualities you like

least in yourself and that you imagine others would most like to see change. On the right-hand side of the page, write down as comprehensive a list as you can. Don't read any further until you've completed both lists.

Now take a look at both columns. The person with the qualities on the left probably sounds attractive—someone you'd like and admire. The person on the right most likely seems unappealing—someone you'd be inclined to avoid, perhaps even at all costs.

So which one is *really* you?

The answer, of course, is both, but that's difficult for any of us to acknowledge. The negative qualities feel threatening—evidence of inadequacies and unworthiness that tend to offset the positive list. As usual, it's the negative that catches our attention. Carl Jung referred to these qualities as our *shadow*—the weaknesses, shortcomings, and unacceptable aspects of ourselves that we typically seek to disown.

"Everyone carries a shadow," Jung wrote, "and the less it is embodied in the individual's conscious life, the blacker and denser it is." Indeed, the more oblivious we are to our limitations, the more likely we are to unwittingly act them out or project them onto others. Here's how I put it in *The Power of Full Engagement,* "Frightened by an underlying feeling of powerlessness, the bully compensates by treating people harshly. Haunted by unacknowledged feelings of inadequacy, the successful executive forever parades his achievements and talks endlessly about the famous and important people he knows. Unable to face her own underlying envy, the polite and proper hostess finds subtle ways to disparage and dismiss everyone around her."

Parading our strengths and denying our shadow doesn't win friends or influence people, and it's an energy drain. "Healthy self-esteem," writes Terrence Real, "is the capacity to cherish oneself in the face of one's own imperfections." Frightening as it may be to acknowledge our shortcomings and admit our mistakes, the irony is that doing so tends to inspire greater respect, not less.

By accepting the whole of who we are, we no longer have to defend our value so vigilantly. What previously triggered us can instead become a source of learning and information. If we're honest self-observers, we acknowledge what is true, without losing value in the process, and we discard what is not true. Rather than defending ourselves against perceived threats and attacks, we use the best of the feedback we get to become more of who we're capable of being.

THE LENSES

Our identity is the sum of the stories we tell about ourselves. Our worldview is the sum of the stories we tell about others. We have an extraordinary capacity to shape our reality, for better or for worse. Each of us, however, has a default lens. We call this lens reality, because most of us believe we see things the way they are. In truth, each of us sees reality through a fixed lens that selectively filters our view of the world. To paraphrase Paul Simon in "The Boxer": "A man sees what he wants to see and disregards the rest." We must learn to look through a broader range of lenses.

The first new way of seeing is through the Reflective Lens. That requires asking two very simple questions when you feel yourself being triggered. The first is "What are the facts here?" The second is "What is the story I'm telling myself about those facts?" Making this distinction allows us to stand outside ourselves and observe our experience rather than simply reacting to it. It also opens us to the possibility that whatever story we're telling ourselves isn't necessarily true—or might not be the only one we could tell.

Triggers almost invariably prompt us to tell stories that leave us feeling devalued. The reflective lens gives us the chance to consider an alternative story. For Jake, with whom we began this chapter, the story could have been that other priorities had commanded Alan's attention but there was still every reason to believe Alan's initial enthusiasm was real. For Paul, who initially told himself that Andrew was a slacker because he wasn't reliably at his desk, a more realistically optimistic story was that Andrew was working elsewhere and, in any case, was getting his job done.

When we feel bruised by someone else's words, we typically assume the person intended to hurt us. If a boss or a colleague walks by without acknowledging us, we feel snubbed. But just as likely, she was preoccupied with an issue of her own—perhaps even something that triggered *her*—in which case what we experienced wasn't aimed at us at all. The reflective lens helps us not to settle on our stories so quickly and instead to remain curious, even to give the benefit of the doubt so long as there is any doubt. We derive benefit from that perspective. By remaining curious and even realistically optimistic, rather than reactive, we think better, perform better, and get along with others more easily.

A second more spacious way of viewing the world is through the Reverse Lens. That simply means looking at a given situation through the eyes of your perceived antagonist. It doesn't mean sacrificing your own point of view but rather widening your lens. Almost certainly, the person you feel triggered by sees the situation very differently than you do. The first question to ask yourself might be "What is he feeling, and how does that make sense?"

Fred, a banking executive with whom we worked, told us a story about asking Bianca, a Spanish-speaking member of his team, to handle a small transaction with a key Mexican client who was more comfortable negotiating in her native language. Bianca agreed, but several weeks later, Fred discovered that the transaction had never gotten done. Seething at Bianca but uneasy about confronting her, he simply avoided her instead.

When we asked Fred to try on the Reverse Lens, he found it difficult at first, as many of our clients do. "It just wasn't important to her," he said. We asked if there might be any other plausible explanation, from her perspective. "Well, yes," he acknowledged. Bianca had been working on a major deal of her own. Fred wasn't the only one who requested her help with Spanish-speaking clients. Perhaps, he speculated, Bianca felt resentful at being expected to serve as a translator every time someone on the team needed help. In a matter of minutes, Fred moved from feeling angry to feeling abashed.

The next day, Fred approached Bianca about the favor he'd asked. "It occurred to me," he told her, "that you're really busy and you've got a million requests like mine. Why don't I just deal with this myself?" Bianca was plainly relieved. "Wow, I really appreciate your saying that. No one else here seems to notice. The truth is, it just totally slipped my mind. I'm really sorry. Let me handle it right now."

Counterintuitively, one of the most powerful ways to reclaim your value when you're triggered is to find a way to value the person who triggered you. That may be by acknowledging your own role in the situation or by seeing it from the other person's perspective. Fred did both. Once Bianca felt understood, her reflexive response was to take care of Fred. You've likely had this same experience. You apologize to someone you know was upset with you about something, only to have the person suddenly seem more concerned about your welfare. "Oh, it was nothing," she says. "Don't worry about it." When our own value isn't at risk, we much prefer to be in connection with others than in conflict. We're also hardwired to reciprocate. Value another person, and that person is likely to value you back.

A third alternative way to view the world is through the Long Lens. Let's say that whatever triggered you feels threatening and devaluing, even after you've distinguished between the facts and your story about them, and even after you try to see it from the other person's perspective. In short, there's no way to tell a credibly positive story about your circumstances. Perhaps you're working fourteen-hour days on a project, you're exhausted, you barely have time to see your young children, and you can't see any way out. Or maybe you have a boss who is relentlessly critical of you for no good reason you can discern. Or you're stuck in a job you find boring and beneath you, but it's hard for you to imagine finding a better alternative in a bad economy.

Candide's Dr. Pangloss might be able to find "the best of all possible worlds" in such scenarios, but most of us can't. So what realistically optimistic story can you tell when things really *are* grim? The value of the Long Lens is that it provides a way to look out into the future, regardless of what's going on in the present. This can be useful because it turns out we're terrible predictors in the present of how we're going to feel tomorrow, much less six months from now.

"Most of us have a tough time imagining a tomorrow that is terribly different from today," writes Daniel Gilbert in *Stumbling on Happiness*. "We cannot feel good about an imaginary future when we are busy feeling bad about an actual present . . . [W]hen we try to overlook, ignore, or set aside our current gloomy state and make a forecast about how we will feel tomorrow, we find that it's a lot like trying to imagine the taste of marshmallow while chewing liver."

More than half the people in the United States, Gilbert points out, will experience a trauma such as rape, physical assault, or a natural disaster during their lifetimes. Is there any doubt these events are horrific when they happen and difficult to get past? Still, somehow most of us do, and we cope far better than we could have imagined possible at the time. A series of studies has shown, for example, that those who suffer permanently paralyzing spinal cord injuries ultimately return to levels of happiness nearly equal to those of similarly aged nondisabled people. "The fact is that negative events do affect us," explains Gilbert, "but they generally don't affect us as much or for as long as we expect them to."

The Long Lens is a means of looking past the narrow perspective of the present and being able to imagine a better future. After Lance Armstrong lay close to death from cancer that spread through his body and then miraculously recovered, he wrote these words: "If you asked me to choose between winning the Tour de France or having cancer, I would choose cancer . . . because of what it has done for me as a human being, a man, a husband, a son, and a father. . . . If there is a purpose to the suffering that is cancer, I think it must be this: it's meant to improve us."

In the face of facts that seem incontrovertibly grim, we encourage our clients to ask themselves this question: "Regardless of how I feel about what's happening right now, how can I learn and grow from this experience?" As Alan Mulally, the president and CEO of Ford, told us, referring to the challenge of taking over a company that was nearly bankrupt: "The expectation I tried to set is that you deal with whatever the current reality is, and then you say 'Okay, so how are we going to move forward?'"

Imagine you lose your job, as so many people have during the past several years. The impact is devastating financially and a harsh blow to your self-confidence. That's the reality when it happens—but it's not a permanent reality. The Long Lens may allow you to see the potential for learning, growth, and a better future, despite the current hardship. Forced to slow down, perhaps you take time to focus on what you *really* want for yourself and from your life. Or maybe you decide to try something entrepreneurial that you've long been interested in doing but never had the time to pursue. Or you choose to volunteer time to a cause you deeply believe in. Or you use the opportunity to connect more deeply with your family. Along the way, you discover that you *can* cope with severe adversity. Who is to say you won't emerge stronger and more resilient for what you've gone through? Can you think of an example in your life of something that seemed terrible when it happened but seems trivial in retrospect or actually led to an important opportunity or a positive new direction?

We have vastly more control over how we experience what happens to us—and how we behave as a result—than we ordinarily believe. When we feel threatened, we often weave the facts into stories that confirm our worst fears. But we also have the option to face the facts exactly as they are—to see reality unvarnished, in all its complexity—and then focus on making the most of the life we've been given.

CHAPTER TWELVE ACTION STEPS

- Think of a recent event or circumstance that triggered you. Write down the facts about what happened—only the facts. Now write down the story you're telling yourself about those facts. Making this distinction allows us to observe our experience rather than simply reacting to it.
- Using the same event or circumstance, challenge yourself to come up with a more empowering story that makes it possible for you to hold on to your value, despite what's happened. How, for example, would you respond in this situation from your best self?
- When we're triggered, we typically revert to telling our stories in terms of black and white, good and bad, hero and villain. These extremes fail to capture the complexity of what's usually happened. Go back to page 153 and complete the exercise there. Practice acknowledging a part of yourself that is imperfect, without allowing it to define all of who you are. Are you comfortable saying "I am that, but I'm not *only* that?"

CHAPTER THIRTEEN

A New Value Proposition

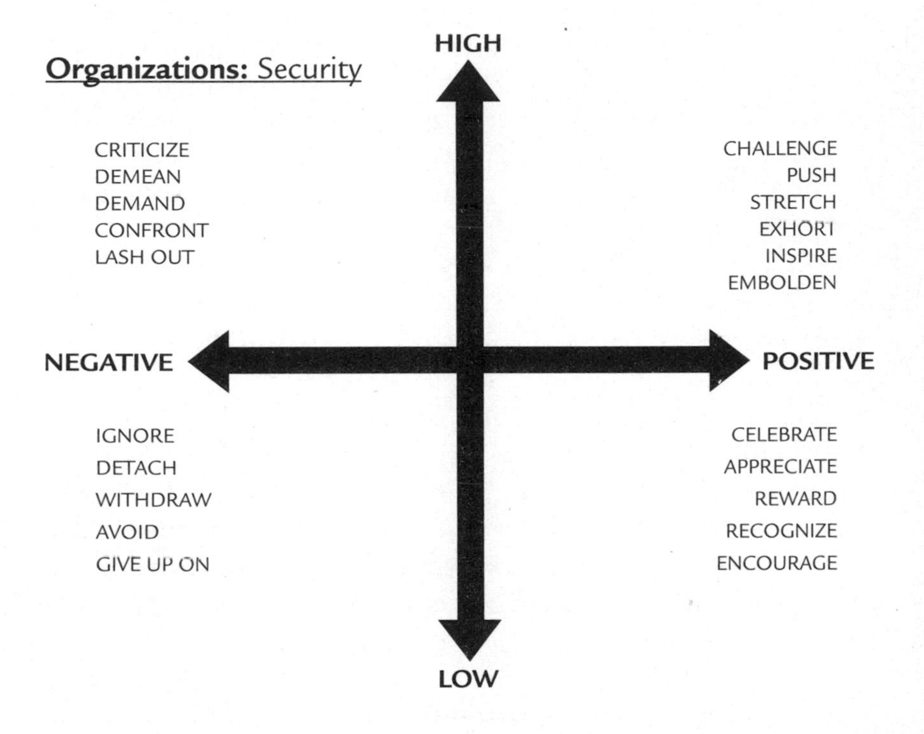

Every organization has a distinct emotional climate, and typically it's set at the top. That's why we refer to leaders as "chief energy officers." Energy, after all, is contagious. A leader's job is to mobilize, focus, inspire, and regularly renew the energy of those they lead. Just as individuals perform best when they move between expending and renewing energy, so leaders inspire the highest performance when they move between challenging people to exceed themselves—the right quadrant—and regularly recognizing and rewarding their plishments—the lower-right quadrant.

its 2007 study of 90,000 employees in eighteen countries, Towers Perrin found that the single highest driver of engagement was whether or not senior management was perceived to be sincerely interested in employees' well-being. An organization's reputation as a great place to work was the highest driver of retention; second was the satisfaction of employees with the organization's people decisions. The third was having a positive relationship with one's direct supervisor. The conclusion is inescapable: truly valuing people pays huge dividends.

The vast majority of employers don't do so very effectively. Only 38 percent of employees worldwide believe their senior managers are genuinely interested in their well-being. More than 50 percent feel they're treated as if they don't matter at all or that they're just another part of the organization to be managed. Only one out of every ten employees feel they're treated as vital corporate assets.

Building a culture that deeply values people doesn't preclude holding them to high standards. In the upper-right organizational quadrant depicted on the previous page, leaders inspire the highest performance by pushing those they lead beyond their comfort zones: challenging, stretching, exhorting, emboldening, and inspiring them to exceed their own limits. Stress is the means by which we expand capacity, as long as it's balanced by intermittent renewal. That means leaders and organizations must also intentionally spend time encouraging, recognizing, appreciating, rewarding, and celebrating people's accomplishments—the lower-right quadrant. Pushing people too relentlessly, even with the most positive intent, eventually runs them down. Pumping them up without good cause only encourages low-quality work. It's when leaders find the right balance between time spent in the upper-right and lower-right quadrants that they fuel the ideal performance pulse.

It's certainly possible to lead from the upper-left quadrant, using a blend of threats, bullying, and criticism. The problem is that fear drives us into fight or flight, which undermines our capacity to think clearly and rationally. Feeling devalued also diminishes our passion, commitment, and ultimately our performance. Leaders who rely on negative emotions may get the short-term results they're seeking, but the costs accrue over time. A harsh leader begets not just fear but also resentment, and those feelings are likely to influence people's performance and their loyalty in the long run.

In 2005, Jeff Blake, who heads marketing for Sony Pictures Entertainment in Los Angeles, had a heart attack and nearly died. Recognizing that he had to make some significant changes, he started a regular exercise program, but still found he spent a lot of time at work feeling frustrated, impatient, and angry. "It was huge for me to realize that when I am in a high-negative state, I have to step back," he told us. "The worst time to decide what to eat is when you're famished, and I came to understand that the worst time to make a decision is when you're feeling stressed and overwhelmed.

"That's the time to walk away, and that's what I learned to do—to take a walk around the studio lot. I use the first ten minutes of a walk to relax and get grounded and the last ten minutes to strategize about the next steps to deal with whatever challenge I was facing before the walk. That's been a real game changer for me. Folks like to know that the guy in charge is in control, and they don't hear me yelling anymore or slamming a door. I monitor my mood, and I intentionally manage my emotional state by incorporating breaks throughout the day, especially if I find myself in high negative."

Matthew Lang was a rising young leader at Sony Europe when we began working with the senior Sony Europe team several years ago. Aggressive, impatient, and driven, Lang was valued for his sharp mind and his ability to get things done. In January 2005, he was assigned to take over the Nordic countries—Sweden, Denmark, and Norway. His charge was to reverse a long, slow sales decline in that region. Appalled by what he saw as "a culture resigned to mediocrity," he set out to shake up the organization. At the time we met him, early in his new role, Lang was feeling frustrated and unhappy with his progress. He was also skeptical that anything we had to offer was going to help him in his business.

"I always thought it was okay that my behaviors were dictated by the mood I was in," Lang acknowledged. "It didn't occur to me that I had control over what I was feeling or that my mood affected the way others felt. When I started, I was very aggressive, like a bull in a china shop. I was easily triggered, and I was often grumpy and pissed off. The emotional quadrants helped me understand the impact of my being in the Survival Zone. The first place I made changes was physically. I started going to the gym in the mornings. Instead of working with my head down all day, I began taking regular breaks, and the result was that I felt better afterwards. When I stopped feeling like a victim, I was able to lead in a different way."

Next, Lang took his own executive team through our program. "I think it woke people up to the fact that we're each in control of our lives," he says. "The same way I had, our leaders started saying to their people, " 'It doesn't matter if we have difficult market conditions. You can do a good job no matter what's going on. We believe in you, and we're invested in you.' We were able to turn our region from bust to boom. We didn't do it with a new strategy or better products or different processes. It was about valuing our people. We succeeded because people began to feel different at work."

Like a number of the senior executives at Sony who most embraced our work, Lang decided to become a trainer himself, and he began delivering our curriculum throughout his organization. In 2007, based on his success in the Nordic countries, he was assigned to take over Sony South Africa, a critical region for the company not just because it had very high potential for growth but also because the multibillion-dollar World Cup soccer tournament will be held there in 2010.

Once again, Lang took his leadership team through the program and then began cascading it down through his organization. "It's had the same effect on business performance," he says, "a dramatic improvement in sales and profitability." Revenues increased 58 percent in Lang's first full year. Roy White, the HR leader for Sony Europe, is convinced there is a direct relationship between Lang's emotional shift and his division's performance. "Matthew's transformation as a leader has contributed tens of millions of dollars to the bottom line at Sony," says White.

More than 3,000 leaders and line employees at Sony Europe have gone through our program. One of the key benefits, says White, is the introduction of a common language for talking about emotions. "In our senior management population, we've reduced the time leaders spend in the Survival Zone by at least fifty percent. A big part of the reason is that we now have a simple way of holding each other accountable. It's become common for people to say to each other, 'What zone are you in?' and 'What story are you telling?' We've had a shift in our senior team's level of awareness. It's like we've all grown up a bit and taken more responsibility for the effect that our feelings have on others. That's allowed our organization to be able to challenge itself around unhelpful emotions. It's also made us far more resilient in the face of the huge stresses in the business."

MANAGING THE ROLLER COASTER

Awareness by itself is essential for leaders at all levels, not just because their emotions influence those they lead but also because events in their own lives can so quickly and dramatically change the way they're feeling. In one fascinating study, researchers asked a group of subjects to watch a range of people on a video and estimate how much each of them weighed. Afterwards, they were shown one of three short movies. The first was meant to prompt feelings of gratitude, the second anger, and the third no emotion at all. Finally, they returned to the first task and were offered help in making more accurate estimates of people's weight.

The subjects who watched the gratitude movie were the most likely to accept help; those who watched the anger-inducing movie were least receptive. Unless we're observing our own emotions—and intentionally taking control of them—we're often the product of our most recent experiences. Think about a leader who arrives at work after just a few hours of sleep, an argument with a spouse, or having been delayed by a traffic accident. What impact would the negative emotions she might be feeling have on any given decision she faced? How receptive would she be to new ideas? How much more likely would she be to take out her frustration on someone at work?

Awareness also helps leaders be more alert to their own triggers. "The key for me," explains Sarah Henbrey, a Sony leader who also now teaches our work to other employees, "was understanding the connection between my triggers and to my own sense of value. Instead of reacting when I felt triggered, I learned how to step back and take a deep breath. I stopped making it so much about me. Even in the most challenging times, I find I can now be less focused on myself and more focused on building the value of others. It's when I'm feeling positive emotions that I have the best impact. In the survival zone, you actually squander energy and destroy value."

Sony has changed the way it evaluates its leaders in Europe to encourage more attention to the effect they have on those they lead. "In the past we accommodated leaders who were technically skilled and hit the numbers," explains Roy White. "Now they also have to be able to harness the energy of their people. We want people to be led positively, because we know that translates into productivity. We've redone our compensation structure for leaders to take into account the satisfaction levels of people working for them. If leaders have a lot of unhappy people, they get paid less, and if they don't improve, we eventually let them go."

Thinking about performance through the lens of positive and negative energy has broad organizational implications. David Patton, the CEO of Grey Advertising in London, saw this play out vividly after taking his executive team through our work. "The agency business is a roller coaster of emotions," he explains. "You go from the joy of winning new business to the exhaustion and despair of being rejected after laying your value on the line to make a pitch for new business. We used the framework of the quadrants to help channel people's emotions in a more intentionally positive way and generate a different way of thinking. We recognized that we needed to pause to celebrate our successes along the way, or else people get burned out and feel taken for granted. We also needed to reflect on what we can learn when we aren't successful. That's also an opportunity to grow, and looking at it that way helps keep you away from negative emotions that drag you down."

One of the most extraordinary shifts in emotional climate we've observed has been at Ford, in the period since Alan Mulally came from Boeing and took over as CEO in 2006. The change is a measure of how profoundly the emotions of the top leader can influence those below him. As much as any leader we've met, Mulally recognizes the power of emotion. His positive energy is hard to resist.

"How people feel might be the most important thing for personal and team success," Mulally says. "People have to know you care, so you regularly express appreciation. You say 'Thank you' a lot. You look for things to celebrate. You treat people with respect. My view is that we're here to appreciate each other and to enjoy the journey, regardless of the outcome. For some people, when I got here, this was new information. But pretty soon you realize it works and it's a better way to operate."

Mulally's insight is supported by the research. In Baumeister's review of the literature on "belongingness," he found that many of the strongest emotions we feel, both positive and negative, are influenced by the degree to which we feel connected to others. "People seem to need frequent positive interactions with the same individual," he writes, "and they need these interactions to occur in a framework of long term, stable caring and concern." We hunger for close relationships not just in our personal lives but also at work, and we especially need to feel valued by those who manage and evaluate us.

Even in the military, the most appreciative leaders seem to be the most effective. In one study in the U.S. Navy, after annual awards were given to the most efficient, safest, and most highly prepared squadrons, researchers decided to look the leaders of these most highly rated squadrons. They turned out to be more positive and outgoing, more emotionally expressive and dramatic, warmer and more sociable (including smiling more), friendlier and more demonstrative, more appreciative and gentler than the leaders of average squadrons. The average leaders tended to fit the stereotype many of us have of the military. They were more "legalistic, negative, harsh, disapproving, and egocentric" as well as "more authoritarian and controlling, more domineering and tough-minded, more aloof and self-centered. They also needed to show they were right more often."

FIRST, DO NO HARM

Because gestures of appreciation are so rare in most organizations, a little goes a long way. In one study, researchers found that giving a small gift of candy to medical residents improved the speed and accuracy of their diagnoses. Another study found that a 10 percent increase in something called "motivating language" from leaders boosted worker satisfaction by 10 percent and performance by 2 percent. The neuroanatomist Jill Bolte Taylor came to believe that positive encouragement lay at the heart of her recovery from a stroke that nearly killed her. "I needed those around me to be encouraging," she wrote. "I needed to know that I still had value. I needed to have dreams to work toward. I needed people to celebrate the triumphs I made every day because my successes, no matter how small, inspired me." Every leader would do well to heed Taylor's prescription.

As simple as it seems, writing notes of appreciation is one of the basic behaviors we encourage in senior leaders. Doug Conant, the CEO of Campbell Soup Company, is said to write up to twenty handwritten messages a day to employees. He believes, as we do, that a note written by hand and sent through the mail is more personal and powerful for the recipient. At Wachovia, Ben Jenkins, now retired as president, created a ritual of taking one executive a week out to lunch. The only sit-downs he'd previously had with his direct reports were to hear monthly reports on their numbers or to give them yearly performance reviews. Instead, over meals, he made it a priority to recognize their accomplishments and to talk with them about their lives and their aspirations rather than their immediate work responsibilities.

As a young reporter at *The New York Times,* I was at my desk talking on the phone one morning when Joe Lelyveld, then a fast-rising editor at the paper, walked by. I barely knew him, but Lelyveld, who would one day become the paper's managing editor, picked up a blank pad on my desk and wrote, "Yours is the best story in the paper today." That incident occurred thirty years ago, and I still vividly remember its inspirational impact. I also recall clearly the sense of fear and dread that A. M. Rosenthal, the paper's managing editor at the time, prompted among reporters whenever he walked through the newsroom. Rosenthal had an explosive temper, and his criticisms could be searing.

The Hippocratic Oath applies to physicians, but it's just as relevant to leaders: First, do no harm. Because the impact of bad is stronger than good, the first rule for an effective leader is simply to avoid devaluing emotions: anger, intimidation, disparagement, and shame. In one of his most famous findings, John Gottman, a leading researcher in the field of marriage, discovered that in the most successful marriages, the number of positive interactions exceeds the negative ones by five to one. Put another way, it takes five positive comments to offset the impact of a single negative one. A workplace culture characterized by appreciation and high regard for employees undeniably drives higher engagement and loyalty. At the same time, the harm caused by a negative, disparaging culture may be even more potent.

Many companies we've worked in simply avoid the expression of emotions altogether. Instead, bland politeness and superficial pleasantness prevail, and conflict and disagreement go underground. Aggression morphs into passive aggression. The result can be corrosive backbiting and distrust, which makes people feel even more unsafe than they do when they're criticized more openly. The latter at least leaves them knowing where they stand.

Conflict avoidance was the culture we encountered when we began working with the senior team at Sony Pictures Entertainment. The atmosphere at meetings was superficially collegial and cordial. It was rare for people to disagree openly but also rare for them to work together effectively. Led by Co-Chairman Amy Pascal, the team decided to confront the issue directly. Among the rituals they designed together to create a more authentic level of dialogue was one they named "Code." Anytime another colleague said something that left you feeling you weren't getting the full story, you had the right to say, "Code." This single word served as shorthand for "I really want to know what you're feeling, so be straight with me." It was a way of surfacing the unspoken without resorting to attack or disparagement. The ritual created both a permission to tell the truth, even about difficult issues, and a shared expectation that team members would do so. Pascal, for example, found it particularly helpful in her relationship with her co-chairman, Michael Lynton.

She gave us this example: Say that she'd asked Lynton to attend a marketing meeting she was running, and at the last minute he canceled because something urgent came up. Since both of them were eager to accommodate the other, he might say to her, "Just go ahead without me," and she might say, "Okay fine." Subsequently, though, Pascal would find herself wondering if he really was okay with it and Lynton might wonder if Pascal really was fine with his *not* attending. Because both of them disliked conflict, neither would mention their concerns. "Code" gave them a simple, shorthand way to address the issue directly.

"If I realize it's *not* okay with me," explains Pascal, "then I have the responsibility to say to Michael, 'Well, actually it's a pain for you not to be there. We've got some big issues to decide, and I could really use your help.' If Michael says 'Code,' that forces me to stop and think about whether it's really okay with me that he isn't coming. If it is, I can just say, 'No, really, it's not a big deal, I can totally do it myself.' Or if it's not okay with me, I say that. Either way, I put all my cards on the table. Neither of us wastes energy later feeling resentful. It's a way of cutting through the typical disingenuous Hollywoodspeak—the 'I loved your movie, you look so wonderful' nonsense that everyone says to each other but rarely means. It's about telling the truth, even when it's hard. That's how you build a culture of trust."

TRUST AND TRANSPARENCY

The safer and more valued people feel, the more resilient they are in the face of high demand and uncertainty. Not even the best-run organizations can avoid challenges, conflict, and stress, especially in tough economic times. But leaders at all levels can profoundly influence the way an organization responds under pressure and the stories it tells about its challenges. When we first began working at Ford, prior to Alan Mulally's arrival, the company was in a severe downward spiral, hemorrhaging money. Fiefdoms and silos dominated. Fear ran high, as did distrust. It was hard to imagine an organization more mired in survival mode.

That's not the way Mulally saw it. To him, Ford remained one of the world's great brands, and he viewed turning it around as one of the world's great challenges. One of the first actions he took was to institute a weekly Business Plan Review at 8 A.M. on Thursday mornings, which includes the leaders in charge of Ford's four main profit centers and its twelve functional units, ranging from manufacturing to marketing to product development to government relations. Mulally was determined to make sure that everyone spoke to everyone else, and openly. Each executive was asked to report each week on how his or her area was doing, color-coding their reports green for "good," yellow for "caution," red for "problems." The first week a sea of green folders appeared. Mulally would have none of it. "Guys, this company lost a few billion dollars last year," he said. "Isn't there something that's not going well?"

A few executives began to acknowledge the issues they were facing.

Mulally didn't flinch, even when the news was terrible. Instead, he made it a point to thank the executive for being clear and transparent. Mulally treated bad news as a form of good news as long as it was delivered promptly and directly. "It's one thing for someone to stand up in victim mode and say, 'Life is hopeless and I don't know any way out of this mess,' " he explains. "It's another to deal with reality as it is, ask for help if you need it, and then move forward to solve the problem. It's all about how you respond. If someone calls you a son of a bitch, take it as a chance to learn. You say, 'Thank you very much for telling me, and I'd like to know more about why you think that.' It's incredibly liberating when people can feel safe saying the truth, no matter what it is. We have a clear plan going forward, but sometimes we have to modify our plan to meet the current reality."

Mulally set out to create a culture grounded in realistic optimism. That requires facing the facts, no matter how brutal they may be, and then having the faith and the focus to find the best possible solution—the same approach James Stockdale adopted as a prisoner of war. The reward is that minimal energy is spent in blame, second-guessing, and interdivisional politics, leaving more energy to devote to the business itself. Transparency and openness are fundamental, and that includes dealing with the outside world. That's why Mulally invites a broad range of outside guests to attend and observe his team's weekly business plan meeting.

Zappos, the hugely successful online clothing and shoe company founded in 1999 and purchased by Amazon for more than $900 million in 2009, defines positive energy as a core value and key driver of strategy. With no particular product to set itself apart from competitors, CEO Tony Hsieh built the brand around providing great customer service—but he began by building a great work environment for Zappos' employees. The vast majority, as we noted earlier, are customer service representatives earning between $12 and $18 an hour. One way the company makes its employees feel valued is by offering them perks such as free lunches, access to a life coach for any workplace issues they might have, a budget for every team to decorate its main meeting room in any way it chooses, and all kinds of social events, from happy hours to ice cream socials.

Any Zappos employee who sees a colleague doing something special—a "Wow," in company parlance—has the right to give that person a $50 bonus (with a limit of one per month). Hsieh and his top executives sit at side-by-side desks in a large room, along with everyone else in the company, giving all employees easy access to their bosses. In the vast majority of company call centers, workers operate from a bland, unchanging script. A key metric used to judge their efficiency is the average time they spend on a call—the less the better. At Zappos, customer service representatives are encouraged to express their personalities, connect with customers, and stay on the line as long as it takes, on the assumption that customers will be more likely to return if they feel well treated. It's a simple principle that companies overlook when they ask their employees to operate like machines. Treat employees well, make them feel more valued, and they will treat their customers well. Energy, after all, is contagious.

CHAPTER THIRTEEN ACTION STEPS

- Think of a time when you were most inspired by a leader or a direct supervisor. What adjectives would you use to describe that person? How do you seek to inspire others? Are you intentional about doing so?
- Write a note of appreciation to someone with whom you work. Tell the person specifically what you appreciate about him or her. Write at least one note of appreciation to someone in your life once a week. We're far quicker to notice what's wrong than to celebrate what's right in others. Remember that people are energized and inspired by feeling recognized and appreciated. The next time you are in a meeting, find a way to end it on a positive note so that people leave feeling better than they did when they arrived.
- Identify a difficult situation you have failed to address. Avoiding conflict typically creates more harm than communicating directly and honestly about it. The key is not to assume you're right but rather to enter any conversation with openness and curiosity. Try this: "Here's the story I'm telling myself about what happened here. Have I got that right?"

PART IV

SELF-EXPRESSION/MENTAL

CHAPTER FOURTEEN

A Poverty of Attention

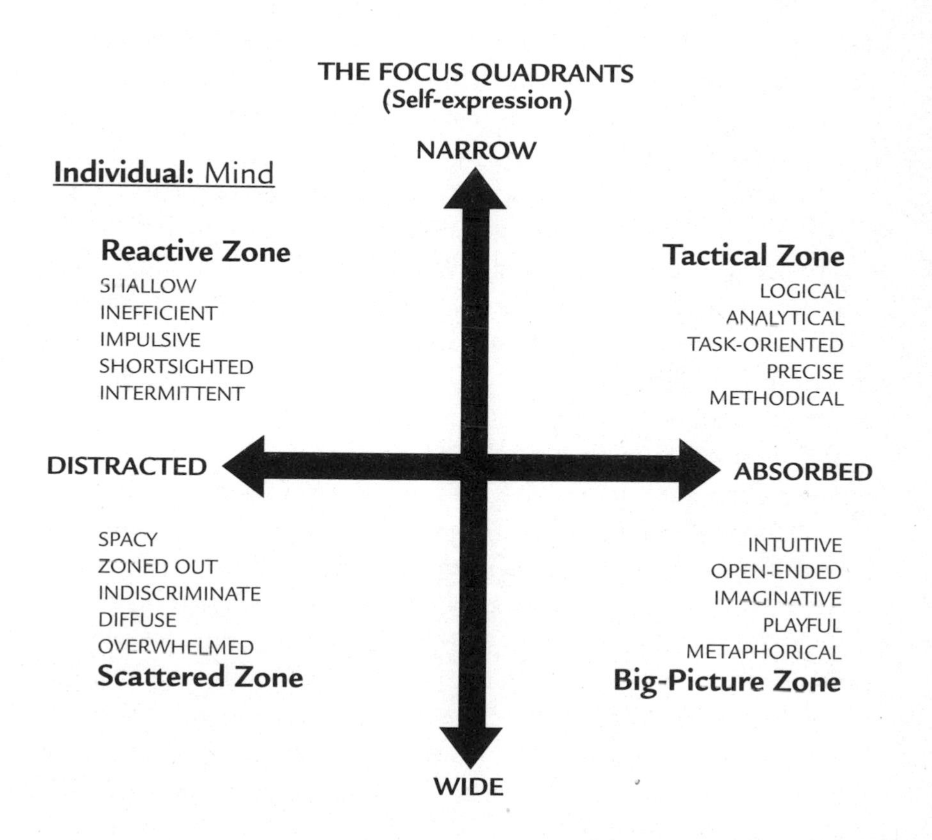

When was the last time you heard your e-mail ping? How quickly did you respond? How many windows are open on your computer right now? Have you searched for something on Google during the past hour or two? Checked your account on Twitter, Facebook, or LinkedIn? Watched a YouTube video? Bought anything online? Checked stock prices? Skimmed the news headlines? When was the last time you sent a text while walking from one meeting to another?

What's the longest you've gone without checking e-mail at all during the past month? How long do you stay focused on any one thing you're doing? When was the last time you took an hour out of your day just to think creatively or long term, without interruptions? How often do you sit back for a few moments, take a deep breath, and quiet your mind? Can you remember an occasion recently when you truly felt on top of things?

"Every one knows what attention is," William James wrote back in 1890. "It is the taking possession of the mind, in clear and vivid form, of one out of what seem several simultaneously possible objects or trains of thought. . . . It implies a withdrawal from some things in order to deal effectively with others."

Is there any doubt that our attention is under siege? More than two billion e-mails are sent every day. There were an estimated 75 million bloggers in 2009, and some 50 million Web sites. More than 500,000 new books are published each year, along with some 400,000 scholarly journals and 18,000 magazines. In 2005, when Google decided to stop updating the number of Web pages it regularly searches, the number had reached 8,168,684,336.

"It sometimes feels like I'm the ball inside a pinball machine," one senior executive at a large bank told us. "I'm always bouncing from one thing to another. I come in every morning, and the first thing I see on my desk is my computer screen staring at me, with all the messages that came in overnight. I start answering them, and then my phone starts ringing, and people start streaming into my office with questions and requests. I'm paying half attention to them because I've got two other screens in front of me telling me what's going on in the markets and in the world. If I look out on the trading floor, what I see are hundreds of traders, one next to the other, doing pretty much the same thing I'm doing: staring at their screens, typing on their keyboards, and talking into their phones. This goes on all day long—one demand after another, split up only by meetings in which everyone spends half their time answering e-mails on their BlackBerrys. The funny thing—the sad thing, really—is that there are a lot of nights when I walk out of the office at seven or eight P.M., after twelve hours, and I literally can't remember what I did all day."

Knowledge is power, as Sir Francis Bacon put it back in 1597, but there may well be an inverse relationship between the volume of information available to us and our ability to make sense of it. Herbert Simon, a polymath who wrote more than a thousand scientific papers and won the Nobel Prize in Economics, saw our current attentional crisis coming forty years ago. "What information consumes is rather obvious," he wrote in 1971. "It consumes the attention of its recipients. Hence a wealth of information creates a poverty of attention."

Which would you prefer: a day in which you made small progress on a range of tasks or one in which you made substantial progress on one important project? The vast majority of people tell us that they prefer depth to breadth and quality to quantity. But that's scarcely the way we live our lives.

Anyone who has children knows that they rarely do one thing at a time. Among those ages fourteen to twenty-one, more than one-third juggle somewhere between five and eight different media while doing their homework—listening to music, checking Facebook, texting, Twittering, and bouncing among Web sites. The rest of us aren't much different. In a much-cited study, Gloria Mark, a researcher at the University of California, Irvine, studied workers at two high-tech firms and found that on average they spent eleven minutes on any given project. Even those eleven minutes were split into tasks no longer than three minutes each. At Microsoft, the researcher Mary Czerwinski found that its programmers juggled eight computer windows at any given time and spent an average of twenty seconds in front of one window before moving to another. Czerwinski herself has said she considers twenty minutes of uninterrupted work a major victory.

The consequence is that our lives have been divided into smaller and smaller increments of focus. We do more things than ever, but we've lost control of our attention. More than 50 percent of American workers say they're interrupted so often that they find it difficult to get their work done. We're too busy trying to keep up even to focus on the fact that the way we're working isn't working.

THE FOCUS QUADRANTS

Just as we move between four different emotional states depending on what's going on in our lives, so we each experience four attentional states. They're depicted in the focus quadrants at the start of this chapter, page 177. The horizontal axis refers to the *quality* of our attention, from distracted to absorbed. The vertical axis refers to the *span* of our attention, from narrow to wide.

Much as we perform best in the high-positive or upper-right emotional quadrant, so the upper-right focus quadrant is where we focus best when it comes to achieving specific goals. Just think about any great performer in action. You need only watch the eyes of an athlete such as Roger Federer, Michael Phelps, or Derek Jeter to see just how locked in and singularly focused they are. It's no different for a heart surgeon, a fighter pilot, a ballet dancer, or an attorney delivering closing arguments in a courtroom. All of their attention—their cognitive energy—is concentrated on the task at hand. It's the capacity to keep other distractions at bay, even under fierce pressure, that helps set them apart from less skilled practitioners.

The psychologist Mihaly Csikszentmihalyi named this kind of absorbed focus "flow" and defined it simply as "the state in which people are so involved in an activity that nothing else seems to matter." The ability to control our attention, he argues, is fundamental to optimal performance and also to the highest levels of satisfaction. Others share his view. "The skillful management of attention," writes Winifred Gallagher in *Rapt: Attention and the Focused Life,* "is the sine qua non of the good life and the key to improving virtually every aspect of your experience, from mood to productivity to relationships."

The external obstacles to absorbed focus are greater than ever and the demands on our attention continue to increase inexorably. "The way we live is eroding our capacity for deep, sustained perceptive attention," Maggie Jackson writes in *Distracted: The Erosion of Attention and the Coming Dark Age.* "As we cultivate lives of distraction, we are losing our capacity to create and preserve wisdom . . . and slipping towards a line of ignorance that is paradoxically born of an abundance of information and connectivity."

Given the way our brains are designed, we actually learn less well when we're presented with a great deal of information all at once. We do far better when it's delivered intermittently, in spaced cycles, because that gives us time to deeply absorb it and commit it to long-term memory. When we try to take in too much at once, we can easily be overloaded. Two Harvard University researchers, Anthony Wagner

and Daniel Schacter, leading experts in memory, undertook
in which they asked students to memorize a list of words. T
group was shown the words all at once, repeatedly. The second g
was shown the words intermittently, over a longer period of ti
When it came time to remember the words, the second group dramatically outperformed the first.

"Learning occurs best when new information is incorporated gradually into the memory store rather than when it is jammed in all at once," writes John Medina, director of the Brain Center for Applied Learning Research at Seattle Pacific University and the author of *Brain Rules.* "Repeated exposure to information in specific time intervals provides the most powerful way to fix memory into the brain." Instead, faced with vastly more information and more ways to share it, our response is akin to that of kids set free in a candy store. We try to have it all. We've normalized a short attention span to such a degree that many of us wear it almost as a badge of honor. It serves as evidence of our busyness, efficiency, and dexterous ability to juggle numerous balls at the same time.

More often than not, we're not even aware that we're failing to make conscious and intentional choices about where to put our attention. We simply shift focus reactively and reflexively whenever something new draws our interest. This is the hallmark of the upper-left quadrant, which we call the Reactive Zone. Think for a moment of your Pavlovian response to the ping of an incoming e-mail. Are you responding because it's critical to do so or by rote? It's as if someone is throwing balls at us all day long and we assume that our primary job is to keep them all in the air. We accord more value to the number of activities we're juggling than we do to contextualizing, synthesizing, and prioritizing—the real routes to creating value that lasts.

Rather than setting and sticking to an agenda of our own, we cede our attention to the most urgent request or demand of the moment. How many of you, we ask our clients, believe that you're pretty skilled at multitasking? A few hands rise, tentatively at first, and then more invariably follow, as if the first responders have given everyone else permission to acknowledge a primary coping strategy they nearly all employ. How many of you, we ask next, believe that multitasking is a necessary skill given the demands you're facing? At this point, nearly every hand goes up. Multitasking, conventional wisdom holds, is the only way to deal with the competing demands we face over the course of a day.

Once again, we've assumed that human beings operate in the same way that machines do. Multitasking is a phrase that grew out of computing. In the early 1960s, programmers discovered they could increase their efficiency by enlisting microprocessors to run multiple applications simultaneously. Human beings lack a comparable capacity. Unlike computers, we're hardwired to undertake tasks sequentially. Our brains are incapable of paying attention to two separate things at the same time. In order to move from one task to another, we must effectively tell ourselves, "I want to do this now instead of that." This process is known as "goal shifting" or "task shifting." It creates something called "switching time," which is the increment of time it takes us to move from one source of focus to another.

THE MYTH OF MULTITASKING

At considerable cost, we've convinced ourselves that we're capable of doing more than one thing at the same time. Nowhere are the consequences of this false belief more vivid than when it comes to driving. How difficult can it be, we ask ourselves, to drive and talk on the phone at the same time? Why not use those long commuting hours to catch up on calls so we can continue to be productive? The answer is sobering.

Talking on a cell phone makes us four times as likely to have an accident—the same as a driver who has a blood alcohol content of .08 percent, which qualifies as intoxicated in most states. The risk is equal for drivers holding their phones to their ears and for those speaking through a wireless device. In both cases, researchers suggest, the drivers generate mental images of the unseen person at the other end of the line, which conflicts with their capacity for spatial processing. "It's not that your hands aren't on the wheel," says David Strayer, the director of the Applied Cognition Laboratory at the University of Utah, "it's that your mind is not on the road."

Switching time, and its attendant costs, rise with the complexity of the task. The more attention required for a given task, the less that's available for another and the longer it takes to shift from one focus of attention to another. When it comes to driving, for example, texting is far more dangerous than talking on the phone. Researchers at the Virginia Tech Transportation Institute found this out by putting video cameras in the cabs of a hundred long-haul truck drivers over an eighteen-month period.

The truck drivers were an astonishing *twenty-three times* more likely to have a collision when they were texting than when they weren't. On average, they spent five seconds focused on the texting, which was enough to travel 100 yards as if they were effectively blindfolded. "Texting is in its own universe of risk," says Rich Hanowski, who oversaw the study. Subsequent research has confirmed that even drivers in smaller, far more maneuverable vehicles are at nearly equal risk to truck drivers when they text.

Perhaps the most primal reason we multitask is out of a hunger to feel more connected. Technology is an extraordinary enabler. Acceptance, belonging, and feeling in the loop are especially urgent needs for adolescents, which helps explain a recent finding by the Nielsen Company. Teenagers sent and received an average of nearly 2,300 text messages a month in 2008—twice the average of just a year earlier. Perhaps ironically, the relentless growth of texting may also reflect the fact that brief messages aren't very satisfying. Much as we do with any source of pleasure that begins to provide diminishing returns, our first instinct is to increase the dose. In the case of texting, the collateral damage is that the more messages we send and receive, the more frequently we interrupt whatever else it is we're doing.

Linda Stone, a former Apple and Microsoft researcher, has coined the term "continuous partial attention" to describe this phenomenon. "We've stretched our attention bandwidth to upper limits," Stone has written. "With continuous partial attention we keep the top level item in focus and scan the periphery in case something more important emerges. . . . To be busy and to be connected is to feel alive. But the consequence is we're over stimulated, over-wound and unfulfilled."

Consider how this paradox plays out in the workplace. Think for a moment about the last time you were in the midst of a conversation with someone at your office and found yourself peeking out of the corner of your eye to read an incoming e-mail. Or an occasion during which you were talking on the phone to someone but also reading your e-mails or even quietly tapping out some replies. Partly, the motivation is to get more done, to keep up. In all likelihood, it's also a reflection of our insatiable thirst for novelty—the hunger we all feel for the next new thing.

Ironically, multitasking often leaves us feeling emptier and more disconnected. Partly, that's because divided attention makes each interaction more superficial. Also, if you are switching between multiple tasks, it stands to reason that the same is true for the people with whom you're interacting. When was the last time, for example, that you were on the phone and heard a gentle "clack, clack, clack" on a keyboard in the background? How did it make you feel? "Devalued" and "unimportant" are the most common answers we hear, and it could scarcely be otherwise. Multitasking sends an unmistakable message: "You're not worth 100 percent of my attention."

Split attention also ensures that you won't absorb everything the other person is saying. "That's okay," one client told us, "because I get the *gist.*" What she really means is the headlines. When we settle for the gist, we sacrifice the essence—complexity, subtlety, and depth.

When we split our attention, we also remember and retain less. If we're singularly focused, the brain's hippocampus, the key to building enduring memories, is in charge. When our attention is more distracted, the striatum, a subcortical part of the brain associated with rote activities, takes over. The consequence is that our memories are likely to be more vague and disjointed. Researchers at UCLA also found that when subjects were put through a multitasking exercise, they were significantly less capable of applying their learning contextually. They retained the facts, but they sacrificed the capacity to apply them more broadly—to generalize and create a broader principle from them.

The other reason we struggle with retention when we multitask is that we have a very limited store of something called "working memory." That's the short-term memory we use to navigate in any given moment, drawing on the most immediate information we need. As an example of the limits of working memory, Maggie Jackson cites research demonstrating that people remember significantly fewer facts related to a television news story when there is a crawl running continuously underneath. Our working memory isn't big enough to retain both the story and the crawl, and we end up losing parts of both. Jackson also notes that when we focus on more than one thing, "simultaneous data streams flatten content, making prioritization all the harder." Trying to do multiple activities at the same time effectively desensitizes us to differences and distinctions between them. It's all just data. Think of Raymond, the autistic savant played by Dustin Hoffman, spewing facts to no particular end in the movie *Rain Man.*

Nor are we likely to get better at multitasking. There is no experimental evidence to suggest, for example, that young people in their teens and twenties, who've grown up with technology, are any more capable of effectively multitasking than the rest of us. At Oxford University, researchers tested a group of eighteen- to twenty-nine-year-olds against thirty-five- to thirty-nine-year-olds on a task that involved translating images into numbers. When they interrupted the two groups along the way, the negative impact on their speed and accuracy was the same. The one real generational difference may be that younger people actually seem to prefer multitasking to doing one thing at a time. "It's almost as if they prefer to just constantly scan the environment and grab new information rather than ponder what they have," says Stanford University researcher Cliff Nass. "We don't know whether there are advantages to that, but so far we haven't found any."

David Meyer, widely viewed as the leading researcher in the field and the head of the Brain, Cognition, and Action Laboratory at the University of Michigan, is convinced that we won't ever find any advantages. "Training can help overcome some of the inefficiencies by giving you more optimal strategies for multitasking," he says. "Except in rare circumstances, you can train until you're blue in the face and you'd never be as good as if you just focused on one thing at a time. Period. That's the bottom line."

OUT OF SIGHT, OUT OF MIND

The most surprising drawback of multitasking is the growing evidence that it isn't even efficient. In a study Meyer and his colleagues conducted in 2001, they found that when subjects switched back and forth between two separate problems, it took them 25 percent longer to complete them than to do the tasks sequentially, one at a time. The difference was the cumulative switching time required during multitasking. In a parallel finding, the UC Irvine researcher Gloria Mark found that each time the computer programmers she studied switched from one task to another, it took them an average of twenty-five minutes to return to the original task, if they returned at all.

Once we're distracted by something new, we often forget about the original task. Given the limits of our working memory, out of sight often literally means out of mind. Ironically, one of the most common ways the programmers Mark studied kept track of their competing tasks was technologically primitive. They wrote them down on Post-it notes and plastered the notes around the edges of their computer screens. This jerry-rigged approach seemed to help them avoid forgetting unfinished tasks as they switched between them. The cost was that it kept the tasks right in front of them as potential sources of further distraction.

The ultimate consequence of juggling many tasks is not superficiality but rather overload. That's depicted in the lower-left zone in the Focus Quadrants at the beginning of this chapter. We call this "scattered attention," and it reflects of the difference between a short attention span and the inability to focus at all. "I just can't think straight" is a feeling we've all had at times, in response to hunger, fear, or simply having too much on our minds. When difficulty paying attention becomes more severe and chronic, it's sometimes be diagnosed as attention deficit hyperactivity disorder (ADHD) and treated with drugs such as Ritalin and Adderall. But in the world we live in, there's an increasingly thin line between what's viewed as necessary and even optimal when it comes to paying attention and what is literally pathological.

Consider these primary symptoms of attention deficit hyperactivity disorder as defined in the *DSM-IV Diagnostic and Statistical Manual of Mental Disorders of the American Psychiatric Association:*

- Often has difficulty in sustaining attention in tasks
- Often does not seem to listen when spoken to directly
- Often has difficulty organizing tasks and activities

- Often avoids, dislikes, or is reluctant to engage in tasks that require sustained mental effort.
- Is often easily distracted by extraneous stimuli

Do you know anyone who manifests most or all of those traits? More to the point, do you know anyone who doesn't? Edward Hallowell, a psychiatrist who specializes in treating ADHD, puts it this way: "Once applicable only to a relative few, the symptoms of ADD now seem to describe just about everybody." At nearly every organization in which we've worked, the work culture is characterized by the ADHD symptoms above, in large part because a short attention span and fractured focus are now so widely accepted as the norm. We've failed to recognize that attention is a capacity that must be both intentionally trained and regularly renewed.

When we default reactively or lazily to distraction—the province of the left-hand quadrants—we diminish our cognitive capacity, the richness of our experience, and ultimately our effectiveness. As Maggie Jackson puts it, "We are allowing ourselves to be ever-more entranced by the unsifted trivia of life. To value a split-focus life . . . is above all to squeeze out potential time and space for reflection, which is the real sword in the stone needed to thrive in a complex, ever-shifting new world. In the name of efficiency, we are diluting some of the essential qualities that make us human."

Given more information to digest and more ways to communicate with each other, we're more challenged than ever to build our capacity for absorbed attention. "Paying rapt attention," explains Winifred Gallagher, "whether to a trout stream or a novel, a do-it-yourself project or a prayer, increases your capacity for concentration, expands your inner boundaries, and lifts your spirits, but more important, it simply makes you feel that life is worth living."

How best, then, to seize back control of our attention?

CHAPTER FOURTEEN ACTION STEPS

- Resist trying to do two things at the same time. You'll inevitably give short shrift to both. If you're talking to someone on the phone, don't simultaneously check and answer e-mail. The person you're talking to will inevitably feel devalued if you do—and rightfully so. In effect, you're saying. "You're not worth 100 percent of my attention."
- Try turning off your e-mail completely for at least one hour a day, in order to devote all of your attention to a significant challenge you're facing. Your chances of success will increase if you choose the same time every day, so it eventually becomes something you do automatically.
- Ask a colleague whether the five characteristics of ADHD listed on pages 186–187 characterize you. What action could you take immediately to improve the quality of your focus and attention?

CHAPTER FIFTEEN

One Thing at a Time

The renowned psychologist David Lykken defined mental energy as "the ability to persist for long periods thinking productively about a problem, to shut out distractions [and] to persist in search of a solution."

On the one hand, many researchers now believe that regardless of your inborn talent, you can achieve excellence in almost any domain through single-minded focus and practice. On the other hand, mobilizing sustained, single-minded focus is difficult, energy-draining, often uncomfortable and doesn't come to us naturally. We're hardwired to be alert, vigilant, and quickly attentive to every new potential danger and threat. We also face more distractions in our lives than ever before. Though few of them are truly threatening and most are relatively trivial, they're often very seductive and compelling.

Unfortunately, there are no shortcuts to excellence, including the advantage of inborn talent. Think back to Anders Ericsson's study of the young violinists at the Berlin Academy of Music. The most significant difference between the best violinists and the others was the total number of hours they'd invested in their craft. "The goal of deliberate practice is not doing more of the same," says Ericsson. "It involves engaging with full concentration in a special activity to improve one's performance." The top two groups both practiced approximately twenty-four hours a week. But the future soloists had logged a total of 7,410 hours by the time of the study. The future orchestra members had invested 5,301. The least accomplished—the future music teachers—had practiced 3,420 hours, or less than half as much as the best violinists. Several researchers have found that achieving true expertise requires at least 10,000 hours of deliberate practice over at least ten years. The most crucial ingredient, after motivation itself, is sustained absorbed attention—whether that consists of practicing to improve or actually performing. Small wonder that excellence is the exception rather than the rule.

The first step in taking more control of our attention is recognizing what happens when we don't. First, we're less effective at whatever we're doing. Beyond that, the more we allow ourselves to be distracted, the more diminished our capacity for absorbed attention becomes over time. Much like an unused muscle, our attention grows weaker and shorter with disuse.

There are two kinds of distractions that fracture our attention. One is internal—the endless chatter of our own minds—and the other is external—what's going on around us. We struggle with both, but we arguably have less ability to influence the latter. Given the varied demands at work, many of our clients tell us that external distractions are simply a fact of life and not something they're in a position to control.

The most common and relentless source of interruption in most workplaces is e-mail. The numbers alone make this case. In 2009, worldwide e-mail traffic averaged 147 billion messages each day. By 2013, that figure is expected to more than double to 500 billion a day. The average U.S. office worker receives between 50 and 100 e-mails a day. Over eight hours, that's an interruption approximately every five to ten minutes. When e-mail pours into our inboxes, we must contend with an undifferentiated sea of important messages, alongside pitches, promotions, material copied to broad distribution lists and all kinds of spam. Just deciding what to delete is time-consuming. At least a third of all workers say they check their e-mail constantly throughout the day. According to a study by the American Management Association, U.S. workers spend an average of an hour and forty-seven minutes a day on e-mail alone.

Why exactly does e-mail exert such a magnetic pull on our attention? There are two primary reasons our clients tell us they feel compelled to check it as frequently as they do. The first is that they need to stay current in order to do their jobs effectively. The second is the expectation, both within their organizations and among their clients, that they will be highly responsive to requests.

At least equally powerful, we believe, is the mostly unconscious and Pavlovian impulse we have to respond to a sound which signals that someone wants our attention. Resisting that ping is akin to ignoring a ringing phone, a fresh chocolate chip cookie, or a crying baby. Since resisting is counterintuitive, it requires our will, the reservoir of which is diminished each time it's exercised. When something enters our field of attention, simply responding to it is the path of least resistance.

There are at least four other primary benefits our clients tell us they derive from responding quickly to e-mail. First, it's a way to keep their inboxes from getting even fuller. Second, it's a means by which to feel at least briefly efficient and productive, usually without significant effort or discomfort. Third, answering e-mail often provides a source of relief—a defensible reason to distract ourselves from more difficult and challenging tasks at hand.

Finally, while most e-mails ultimately prove to be inconsequential, each new ping also carries, at least briefly, the promise of a potential reward. As long as the pings keep on coming, there's always a chance that the next one you check will prove to be an interesting opportunity, a note of thanks or praise, an invitation to an event, or a friend checking in and making a connection. The only thing more horrifying to most of us than an inbox with two hundred new e-mails is one that doesn't contain any. We want to be wanted.

Our responsiveness to distractions is powerfully and often unconsciously influenced by our desire for pleasure—and our instinct to avoid pain. If there's an external expectation that we'll answer quickly, we don't want to take a chance of being chastised for not responding. In reality, we have considerable power to set people's expectations about how quickly we'll answer e-mails. Often, our compulsion to answer e-mail is just a reflection of our need to stay connected in order to feel productive in the short term with minimal effort. Answering e-mail is also a way to avoid the pain of mobilizing the sustained focus that more challenging tasks require. Gaining more control of our attention, it turns out, is intimately linked to our capacity to delay gratification.

We need only watch a toddler's attention skittering from one bright and shiny object to another to recognize that absorbed focus is not our genetic birthright. Toddlers are fueled largely by primitive emotions and lack the benefit of a fully developed prefrontal cortex.

They want what they want right now. But, if that pattern continues for very long into their lives, it doesn't bode well. Early attentional control turns out to be at the heart of later success and satisfaction.

DELAYING GRATIFICATION

The psychologist Walter Mischel first demonstrated this phenomenon in his deceptively simple and now famous "marshmallow" test. Mischel conducted his research in the late 1960s at the private Palo Alto, California, nursery school that each of his three daughters attended. He and other researchers have continued to explore the implications of his findings to this day.

Interested in understanding what made delayed gratification possible for some children and not for others, Mischel devised a challenge that he eventually posed to a succession of 650 four-year-olds over a period of several years. Each child was offered the chance to eat one marshmallow immediately, or two if the child was willing to wait while the researcher stepped out of the room for an unspecified number of minutes. Children who decided they couldn't wait were invited to ring a bell, at which point the researcher would return. The majority of the children gave up in less than three minutes, rang the bell, and settled for a single marshmallow. Thirty percent, however, held out for a full fifteen minutes, until Mischel or one of his researchers returned.

The primary distinction between those who waited and those who didn't became clear over time. It had to do with attention. The children who succumbed to temptation couldn't keep their eyes off the marshmallow and often stared directly at it. As a consequence, they very quickly burned down their limited reservoirs of will and discipline. The children who were able to wait somehow figured out that consciously resisting temptation wasn't going to work. Instead, they found a variety of ways to shift their focus away from the marshmallow, by turning their chairs around, covering their eyes, or distracting themselves by singing or playing a game.

The successful children managed to push the marshmallow, and therefore the temptation to eat it, out of their awareness. Mischel came to call this skill "strategic allocation of attention." "If you're thinking about the marshmallow and how delicious it is," Mischel told a journalist years later, "then you're going to eat it. The key is to avoid thinking about it in the first place."

This is where attention and emotions become intermingled. For most of the children, the marshmallow prompted an emotional response—intense desire—that overrode their capacity to think, much the way that intense fear prompts the fight-or-flight reaction. This is what Mischel calls "a hot stimulus." The hotter the stimulus—and fear and desire are among the hottest—the more difficult it is to control our attention and ultimately our behavior. "Young kids are pure id," says Mischel. "They start off unable to wait for anything—whatever they want, they need."

In 1981, more than a decade after his initial experiment concluded, Mischel decided to send a questionnaire to parents and teachers of all his original subjects, asking a series of questions about how the children had fared. It turned out that the ones who had been able to delay gratification at the age of four grew up to be more confident, self-reliant, trusting, dependable, and persevering. They also developed more lasting friendships, responded more resiliently to stress, and eventually scored an astonishing average of 210 points higher than the low delayers did on their SATs. The low delayers also turned out to be more stubborn, indecisive, self-critical, resentful and likely to have behavioral problems in school. They were also more likely to be overweight, to abuse drugs, and to be less resilient in the face of stress. In short, they continued to struggle with controlling their impulses. As a consequence they had less control of their attention.

Why do some kids—and adults—learn to take charge of their attention more successfully than others? Mischel and his colleagues ultimately discovered a fascinating correlation between the way toddlers dealt with separating from their mothers at the age of nineteen months and how they performed on the marshmallow test at the age of five. The toddlers who cried the most when their mothers left were also more likely to have trouble resisting the marshmallows when they got older. In both instances, we might hypothesize, the children were reacting to a desire for something they felt they urgently needed and felt they couldn't do without. Marshmallows replaced mothers.

In John Bowlby's research, the more secure children feel, the more emboldened they are to separate from their mothers and explore the world. Lacking what the developmental psychologist Erik Erikson termed "basic trust," the insecure nineteen-month-old cries when her mother leaves, out of fear that the mother will never return. The insecure five-year-old opts for the single marshmallow out of a similarly urgent desire for something sweet and soothing. It promises to make her feel better right now, and in her world, that's all that matters. The more secure five-year-old, less dominated by fear-driven impulses, has the capacity to move her attention away from the marshmallow in exchange for a bigger reward later. The prefrontal cortex overrides the amygdala.

Mihaly Csikszentmihalyi captures this brilliantly in *Flow:* "Preoccupation with the self consumes psychic energy because in everyday life we often feel threatened. Whenever we are threatened we need to bring the image of ourselves back into awareness, so we can find out whether or not the threat is serious, and how we should meet it." Conversely, the safer and more secure we feel, the more attention we can allocate to our long-term goals. "Self-consciousness, which is the most common source of distraction, is not a problem for such a person," Csikszentmihalyi goes on to explain. "Instead of worrying about how he is doing, how he looks from the outside, he is wholeheartedly committed to his goals." A growing body of research suggests that we may have a genetic predisposition to different levels of intrinsic anxiety, but it's also clear that our security is profoundly influenced by our experiences with attachment.

This is a profound lesson for parents and teachers, but also for leaders and managers. If you want those in your charge to be effective at delaying gratification and focusing their attention effectively, it goes a long way to make them feel cared for and secure. It can also help to specifically teach attentional skills, which are rarely an explicit part of any school curriculum, much less of the learning agenda in organizations. Mischel and his colleagues, for example, have experimented by teaching poor delayers among children simple mental tricks to help them redirect their attention away from a hot stimulus such as a marshmallow, in the same way that more successful delayers do instinctively. After relatively modest training, many of the kids who hadn't been able to hold off eating a marshmallow for more than a minute could now wait for a full fifteen minutes.

We rely on a similar principle in our own work to drive more enduring behavioral change. As we explained in chapter 3, we teach our clients to build "rituals," highly specific behaviors performed at specific times so they become automatic and no longer require conscious will or discipline. In effect, we're teaching them how to turn their attention away from other potential distractions. In the case of e-mail, for example, many of our clients build rituals around turning it off altogether for certain defined periods of time in order to focus in a more absorbed way on the most challenging task at hand.

Steve Wanner, the partner at Ernst & Young who was working twelve- to fourteen-hour days when we first met him, typically arrived home in the evening feeling exhausted. He found it difficult to fully engage with his wife and four children in the evenings. One of the primary drains on Wanner's energy was his habit of answering e-mails constantly, either on his BlackBerry or his computer, from the time he woke up until he went to bed at night. Much as most four-year-olds can't resist a marshmallow if they stare directly at it, most of us struggle to resist e-mail if we constantly watch or hear it enter our inbox. At our urging, Wanner created a ritual of answering his e-mail at only specific times of day and otherwise turning it off altogether.

Wanner's main concern was that clients or colleagues would see him as unresponsive or that he might miss an urgent message. To address that concern, he added an away message explaining that he answered only at designated times but that if anyone had a more urgent need to reach him, to simply call him on his cell phone. He also called each of his most important clients to explain what he was doing and why. Where previously he had been unable to keep up with all his messages, Wanner discovered that the new ritual made it possible to clear his inbox each time he opened it—the reward of fully focusing his attention on one task at a time, for designated periods of time. While he invited anyone who needed him to call his cell phone, almost no one did.

Dozens of our clients have adopted some form of Wanner's ritual. As he did, they find that the concern about missing something important almost invariably proves to be unfounded. E-mail, it turns out, creates its own sense of artificial urgency. When you're not checking it constantly and you tell key people in your life, "Feel free to call me if it's urgent," it forces them to ask, "Do I really need an instant response?" In most cases, the answer turns out to be no.

PRIORITIZING OUR ATTENTION

It's not simply e-mails that fracture our focus. We create plenty of distractions for ourselves by juggling tasks, making ourselves perpetually available to others, opening several windows on our computers, and focusing on whatever feels most urgent at the moment, without regard to whether what we're doing is really important. In our reactive rush to stay ahead of a wave we fear will drown us, we're forever racing to keep up with external demands. We're far less effective at setting our own agenda and sticking by it.

Assume for a moment that you can learn to resist distraction and to do one thing at a time. You're still left with a key challenge: having collected your attention, where ought you to put it? That's a question we ask each of our clients, in part because it's one they rarely pause to ask themselves. Often as not, the initial response to our question is an uncomfortable silence. Most of us just don't spend much time thinking long term. Do you? Where does it make most sense for you to be investing your attention? Given a few moments to reflect, most of our clients arrive at some variation on this simple answer: whenever possible, I ought to be putting my attention in the service of what's most important.

Obvious as that may seem, the act of prioritizing—focusing on what's likely to add the greatest value over the longest term—doesn't come to us naturally. It requires both awareness and intentionality. At a practical level, it means setting aside regular time to reflect on and define priorities, rather than simply plunging into the next task that comes into your mind or reacting to the next request that flashes up on your computer screen.

The single most effective mental ritual we've discovered is one we call "Doing the most important thing first." Clients design their own versions of the ritual, but the basic elements are always the same. The first step is to decide in advance the most important thing to do on any given day. Typically, that means reflecting on it the night before or, if it's a longer project, at the beginning of a week. Most clients find that this ritual works best when they schedule the task as the very first thing they do when they arrive at work each morning. Obviously, the number of potential distractions and interruptions tends to increase throughout the day. Moreover, most of us are freshest in the morning and progressively lose the energy necessary to tackle difficult challenges as the day wears on.

As with all rituals, we've found that specificity is a key to success. That means setting not only a clear starting time but also a clear stopping time, no more than ninety minutes later. The goal is to be fully engaged throughout whatever period time you choose to work. It's also helpful to allot *no less* than forty-five minutes to the task. It takes time to become mentally absorbed, especially in challenging work. It's also essential to eliminate potential distractions by turning off e-mail, not answering calls, and letting others know that you don't want to be interrupted unless something literally can't wait. Finally, when you've reached your designated stopping time, it's important to take a true renewal break. If you've really absorbed yourself in a difficult task, you should be sufficiently mentally depleted that you crave an opportunity to rest and refuel.

Many of our clients are surprised to discover how powerful this ritual can be. Above all, it's a way to ensure that you devote time each day to your most important and challenging work. But it's also energizing. By launching each day with a strong dose of focused productivity, you head into the rest of your day secure that no matter what else happens, you've already accomplished something significant.

QUIETING THE INTERNAL DIALOGUE

Powerful as it is to learn to shift attention away from external distractions, we must also contend with the relentless chatter in our own minds. On the face of it, we should have more control over what's going on inside ourselves than we do over what's going on outside. In fact, our minds seem to have minds of their own. Even as we're working on a project, our attention is often drawn to the past and the future: hopes and regrets, fears and fantasies, daydreams and disappointments, ambitions and insecurities. The capacity to stay fully present—to do one thing at a time—is a challenge contemplative traditions have been grappling with for thousands of years.

To get a quick sense of how your own mind operates, get a pen and a piece of blank paper and put it by your side. Now find a comfortable place to sit, if you don't already have one. Now I'm going to ask you to close your eyes and focus on your breath. Don't think about anything else. Just follow your breath as it goes in and out, and don't seek to influence it in any way. Do this for whatever feels like approximately two minutes. You can put this book down and begin now. When you're done, pick it back up.

Okay, you've now finished the first part of the exercise. Now pick up your pen and paper. Here's your assignment: write down everything you thought about during the time you were just following your breath and ostensibly not thinking about anything. Do your best to re-create the sequence of your thinking, even if the thoughts seem trivial. Put the book down one more time, and then pick it up again when you've finished writing.

If you're like 95 percent of our clients, you've compiled a reasonably robust list of what was on your mind. A couple of the items might have something to do with thinking about your breath, how you felt while you were doing the task, or whether you'd done it long enough. In all likelihood your mind also went off on several other tangents. Maybe you noticed noises in the room, or you remembered something you need to get done. Perhaps you felt anxious or uneasy or found yourself musing about what you're going to be doing later today. It's possible you noticed a pain in your back, your neck, or your knee or a growling in your stomach. Maybe something you thought of reminded you of someone you know, and you started thinking about that person and something you'd done together. Perhaps you scolded yourself for having so many stray thoughts, or wondered if others doing this exercise were having as hard a time focusing as you were.

The answer to that last question is yes. Not everyone remembers a string of thoughts, but it's rare that anyone claims to have stayed exclusively focused on the breath. William James once sagely observed that the human mind won't focus on any one object for more than a few seconds. More accurate, it won't do so without significant training.

We build the muscle of attention much the way we do a biceps or a triceps: by subjecting it to increments of intense stress—and then relaxing. The stress, when it comes to attention, is staying singly focused on one thing at a time. Many of us associate meditation with spiritual practice, but at a more practical level, it is simply attentional practice. The most basic form is often referred to as "concentration" meditation. There are many variations, but one simple one is to sit in a comfortable position and count your breaths. For most of us, that's easier than trying to follow the breath in and out. The more deeply we breathe, the more relaxed and less vigilant we become and the easier it is to focus attention on one thing, such as counting.

To experience the difference between counting and following your breath, you might try the exercise we did back in chapter 3. Close your eyes and breathe in through your nose to a count of three. Then slowly breathe out through your mouth to a count of six. Focus solely on the counting, and do it for thirty seconds or a half-dozen breaths. You can put the book down again and start now.

In all likelihood, you found it easier to stay focused this time than you did during the earlier breathing exercise following your breath. One reason is that counting gave you a clear object of attention. A second is that intentionally extending the outbreath prompted deeper relaxation. The third is that you did the exercise for just thirty seconds, rather than a minute or two. Most teachers of meditation recommend that students practice for at least twenty minutes at a time. We believe that's usually far too demanding when you're first starting out, and often counterproductive.

BETWEEN BOREDOM AND ANXIETY

Csikszentmihalyi has described "flow" as a state of absorption balanced delicately between boredom and anxiety. When we have too little challenge, our attention wanders because we're bored. When the challenge is too great, anxiety overwhelms our capacity for continuous attention. Trying to focus on one thing for twenty minutes at a time, we've found, leads most beginners to either boredom or to anxiety that their minds are wandering so much. It's more effective, we believe, to focus in a highly concentrated way for thirty or sixty seconds than to wander in and out of absorbed attention over longer periods of time. As the muscle of attention gets stronger, you can increase the length of your practice by increments, much as you might progressively increase the weight you lift in a strength-training program.

Like many other clients, Fujio Nishida, the president of Sony Europe, instituted the breathing ritual we mentioned earlier as a way to manage stress. He found that even a few minutes once or twice a day gave him a sense of calm that allowed him to think more clearly and effectively, especially in the wake of a challenging event or a difficult interaction.

"Mindfulness meditation" is a second form of attentional training that can be valuable. Rather than trying to quiet the mind of all thought, mindfulness emphasizes simple awareness. As thoughts, feelings, and sensations arise, the practice is simply to note each one and then let it pass without dwelling on it. Building this skill of self-observation, sometimes referred to as "witnessing," allows us to step back from the ongoing drama our mind constantly creates. Instead, we learn to view whatever arises with more equanimity, or what the Buddhists call "nonattachment." Here again, attention and emotions are deeply interconnected. On the one hand, decreased anxiety frees us to pay more focused attention to the task at hand. On the other hand, increased capacity for absorbed attention decreases our anxiety.

One of the symptoms of schizophrenia is an inability to focus intentionally. Schizophrenics typically perform poorly on tasks requiring vigilance, quickness of response, or sustained attention. Often, that's because they're preoccupied by emotions such as fear, paranoia, and depression. In a study conducted at Montefiore Medical Center, researchers administered attentional training to a group of twenty-seven inpatients diagnosed with chronic schizophrenia. After a baseline assessment, each patient received eighteen sessions of training conducted on a computer over a six-week period.

On average, the participants became more focused, less distractible, and quicker in response time compared to their baseline scores and to a control group of other schizophrenics. Perhaps more surprising, the experimental group experienced broad improvements in their psychological well-being, including fewer hallucinations, less emotional withdrawal, and less somatization, meaning the manifestation of psychological distress in physical symptoms. The more focus the subjects were able to mobilize on the external task, the less preoccupied they became with their own distress. If patients with a severe psychological disorder can improve their attention in a matter of weeks, what does that suggest about the average healthy person's potential for training attention?

Jon Kabat-Zinn and his colleagues at the University of Massachusetts Medical School have conducted a series of studies about the everyday value of mindfulness meditation. More than a decade ago, Kabat-Zinn developed an eight-week protocol that includes a two- to three-hour class each week followed by a one-day retreat—some fourteen hours of meditation in all. His early work was aimed at helping people suffering from various forms of chronic pain that had been resistant to traditional medical intervention, such as back and neck pain, headaches, and gastrointestinal disorders. In a series of studies, subjects who went through his protocol showed significant decreases in pain, less need for medication, and more physical mobility.

In a later study, Kabat-Zinn was able to demonstrate that patients suffering from anxiety or panic disorders experienced significant improvements after going through his program. Most recent, collaborating with the neuroscientist Richard Davidson at the University of Wisconsin, Kabat-Zinn took workers at a biotechnology company with no specific symptoms through his mindfulness protocol. The participants reported decreased levels of anxiety and increased positive emotions compared to a control group. In a study by another group of researchers, two sets of Chinese university students were trained for three months in concentrative and mindfulness techniques, and both significantly outperformed a control group of nonmeditators on tests of sustained attention. Interestingly, the mindfulness meditators, taught how to observe but not react to distractions, outperformed the concentrative meditators when both groups were subjected to an unexpected stimulus. One potential implication is that mindfulness is a more practical form of attentional training for people working in an open office environment where distractions and interruptions occur at random times throughout the day.

Relatively few of our clients have had any formal attentional training, but here's what one CEO, who declined to let us use his name out of a concern about what some of his conservative clients might think, had to say about his practice.

"I didn't start meditating because I was interested in higher states of consciousness. My goal was practical. My job involves dealing with all kinds of different people and activities, and it's hard to stay focused on any one. I'd always find myself ruminating about the last meeting or anticipating the next one. I took up meditation because I wanted to see if I could learn to slow down my mind. I began with breath counting, simple concentration. It's not like all my thoughts went away, but my mind definitely got quieter and I felt calmer. Beyond anything else, it helped me to stay more focused on whatever I was doing.

"After about a year I was introduced to mindfulness, and I was immediately drawn to it. Breath counting was fine, and it really helped me, but it wasn't very interesting. Mindfulness was much more intellectually engaging. It was fascinating to actually learn to observe my own mind the way I might watch a movie or a play. It was a revelation to discover that I could observe an emotion—anger or frustration or irritation or even sadness—without feeling like I had to react to it. No matter how intense the emotion, I got so I could name it—'anger, anger' or 'impatience, impatience'—and then just watch it pass by, which it almost invariably did. It wasn't as relaxing as breath counting, but ultimately I think it's had even more impact on my life at work. I'm much less reactive, more able to hold my fire and let things play out.

"What's really interesting is that it's *not* like learning to ride a bicycle. I have to keep practicing. If I let it go for a week or two, I start to see the difference in my focus, and also in how I feel. I don't need to meditate for very long—even a few minutes a day makes a big difference—but I need to do it regularly. I really believe now that focus is a skill every bit as foundational as reading or writing. Every school should build in meditation from the first grade. They could just call it attentional training. It ought to be part of companies too. I'm not yet fully comfortable saying that to our clients, but I talk about it all the time inside our company. Control your attention, and you control your life. I truly believe that."

CHAPTER FIFTEEN ACTION STEPS

- The most common source of external distraction at work is e-mail. Think about how you're currently managing it. Write down the costs and benefits of managing e-mail the way you do. Now list the ways you might retain those benefits while minimizing the costs.
- A second source of distraction is internal—the chatter in our brains. Meditation, or quieting our mind, is one way to gain more control of our attention. It takes practice. Start out by counting your breaths in and out up to ten. It shouldn't take you much longer than a minute. Can you stay focused on counting your breaths? Add more sets of ten as your concentration gets stronger.
- Once you're able to focus more effectively, the next challenge is where to focus. That means consciously defining your priorities. Schedule time at the end of the workday to identify the most important task you could address the following day. In the best of worlds, make that task the first thing you do the following morning, for at least sixty minutes, without interruptions.

CHAPTER SIXTEEN

Cultivating the Whole Brain

When we think of "paying attention," the first association many of us make is to sitting behind a desk in grade school. "Listen to what I'm saying," the teacher says. "Eyes on me. Don't let your mind wander."

The focus expected of us in school—and later in the workplace—is mostly the logical, deductive, analytic attention that characterizes the upper-right quadrant of the Focus Quadrants (see page 177). We call this narrow, absorbed attention "tactical," and it's the province of the left hemisphere of the brain. But there is a second kind of absorbed focus that paradoxically has more in common with daydreaming than it does with our traditional notions about paying attention. We call it "big-picture" focus, depicted in the lower-right quadrant, and it's associated with the right hemisphere of the brain.

In most schools and organizations and in the culture at large, the capacities of the left hemisphere are accorded far more value than those of the right. The consequence is that our right hemisphere is typically underdeveloped. Is there any doubt that Western culture has privileged the capacities of the left hemisphere—in the left-hand column below—over those in the right-hand column?

LEFT	RIGHT
Verbal	Visual
Rational	Intuitive
Quantitative	Qualitative
Analytic	Synthetic
Deductive	Inductive
Simplify	Enrich

Specialize	Integrate
Separate	Connect
Critical	Nonjudgmental
Goal-oriented	Big picture-oriented
Sequential	Simultaneous
Systematic	Empathic
Objective	Subjective
Literal	Metaphorical
Rule-bound	Unbounded
Outcome-driven	Process-driven

The dominance of our left hemisphere—especially inside most companies—is a testament to the enduring power we've accorded logical thinking and scientific method ever since the Enlightenment. That shouldn't be entirely surprising. The power of rigorous critical thinking has driven remarkable advances in science, medicine, technology, and the growth of economies and democracies around the world.

Because the left hemisphere is uniquely specialized for language, it effectively serves as our spokesperson. By contrast, our right hemisphere literally lacks a voice. It wasn't until the neuroanatomist Jill Bolte Taylor's left hemisphere stopped working after she suffered a stroke that she was able to appreciate, for the first time, the unique capacities of her right hemisphere. "Prior to this experience," she writes, "the cells in my left hemisphere had been capable of dominating the cells in my right hemisphere. The judging and analytical character of my left hemisphere dominated my personality."

This is precisely the conclusion that neurobiologist Roger Sperry came to during the split-brain research for which he eventually won the Nobel Prize in Medicine. Sperry set out in the late 1950s to study severe epileptics who had undergone an operation called a commisurotomy. This radical surgery is aimed at bringing epileptic seizures under better control by severing the corpus callosum, which connects the two sides of the brain. The consequence is that the two sides can no longer communicate the way they ordinarily do. Based on ingenious experiments with these patients, Sperry was able to demonstrate that each of our hemispheres is highly specialized: the left for logical, sequential tasks and the right for visual and more subjective ones, including seeing patterns and combining ideas in new ways, understanding metaphor, and recognizing emotions through body language, and tone of voice. As the psychologist Robert Ornstein has noted, the left hemisphere specializes in text and the right in context—*what* is said versus *how* it is said.

When the right hemisphere is more active, we're able to step back from the urgent demands of whatever we're doing and take a wider view, often incorporating a longer-term perspective. Rather than working step-by-step toward a conclusion, we literally become more "insightful"—open and receptive to seeing things in different ways and making new connections. Hemispheric specialization, Sperry concluded, is not an "all-or-none" phenomenon. The two hemispheres are always communicating, especially during the most complex tasks. But it is the left hemisphere that is systematically trained. As Sperry put it, "[T]here appear to be two modes of thinking, verbal and nonverbal . . . respectively, and . . . our educational system, as well as science in general, tends to neglect the nonverbal form of intellect."

QUIETING THE LEFT HEMISPHERE

There are several ways to access and evoke the experience of right-hemisphere focus, but perhaps none so reliable and powerful as an exercise devised by Betty Edwards, a former art professor who is the author of the book *Drawing on the Right Side of the Brain.* At one level, the book is a primer in how to draw. More profound, it is about how to train the right hemisphere, specifically by learning how to see in a different way than we ordinarily do. Edward's first exercise, which became the basis for her PhD thesis, is a very simple one. No words can approximate the experience you will have by actually doing it.

The exercise has two parts. Before you begin, you'll need to get two pieces of blank paper at least the size of the pages of this book, as well as a pencil with an eraser (not a pen). You'll need a quiet place to work in which you're not likely to be interrupted. On the first piece of paper, the assignment is to draw a self-portrait. Unless you draw regularly—and very few of our clients do—this might seem like a daunting challenge. All we ask is that you do the best you can on the first sheet of paper. If you'd like to take a quick look in the mirror first, to remind yourself of what you look like, do so now. But then draw yourself from memory.

When you're finished, take the second sheet of paper, and turn to the next page in this book. There you'll see a sketch, which we've obviously turned upside down. Resist looking at it right-side up. Instead, begin by drawing a rectangular frame on your paper exactly the same size as the one that surrounds the drawing on the next page. Once you've done that, copy the drawing itself, as closely as you can, on your own piece of paper, and not by tracing it. Start from the bottom, and work your way up. Don't try to name anything you're drawing or to make it look like anything specific. Just draw from line to line and space to space. You can use your thumb or finger to estimate distances between lines, if that helps. Be as meticulous about re-creating what you see as possible.

Typically, this drawing takes about twenty to thirty minutes, but don't check your watch, and don't be bound by any specific time limit. Instead, allow yourself to become immersed in the process and simply draw until you've finished. It's best not to read any further before doing this exercise.

Assuming you've finished, you can now turn your drawing right-side up so you can see how you did. You were copying Pablo Picasso's sketch of Igor Stravinsky. But now let's set aside both drawings for a few moments and focus first on your self-portrait. What was your experience of drawing it, and what's your assessment of how well you did?

In all likelihood, it looks only vaguely like you and lacks much richness, detail, or three-dimensionality. There's a good chance you've represented your hair with a bunch of straight or squiggly lines, your nose with a scrawl, and your mouth with two curved lines and a straight line in between. If that's so, your explanation may well be that you're not an artist and you can't really draw. This self-critical

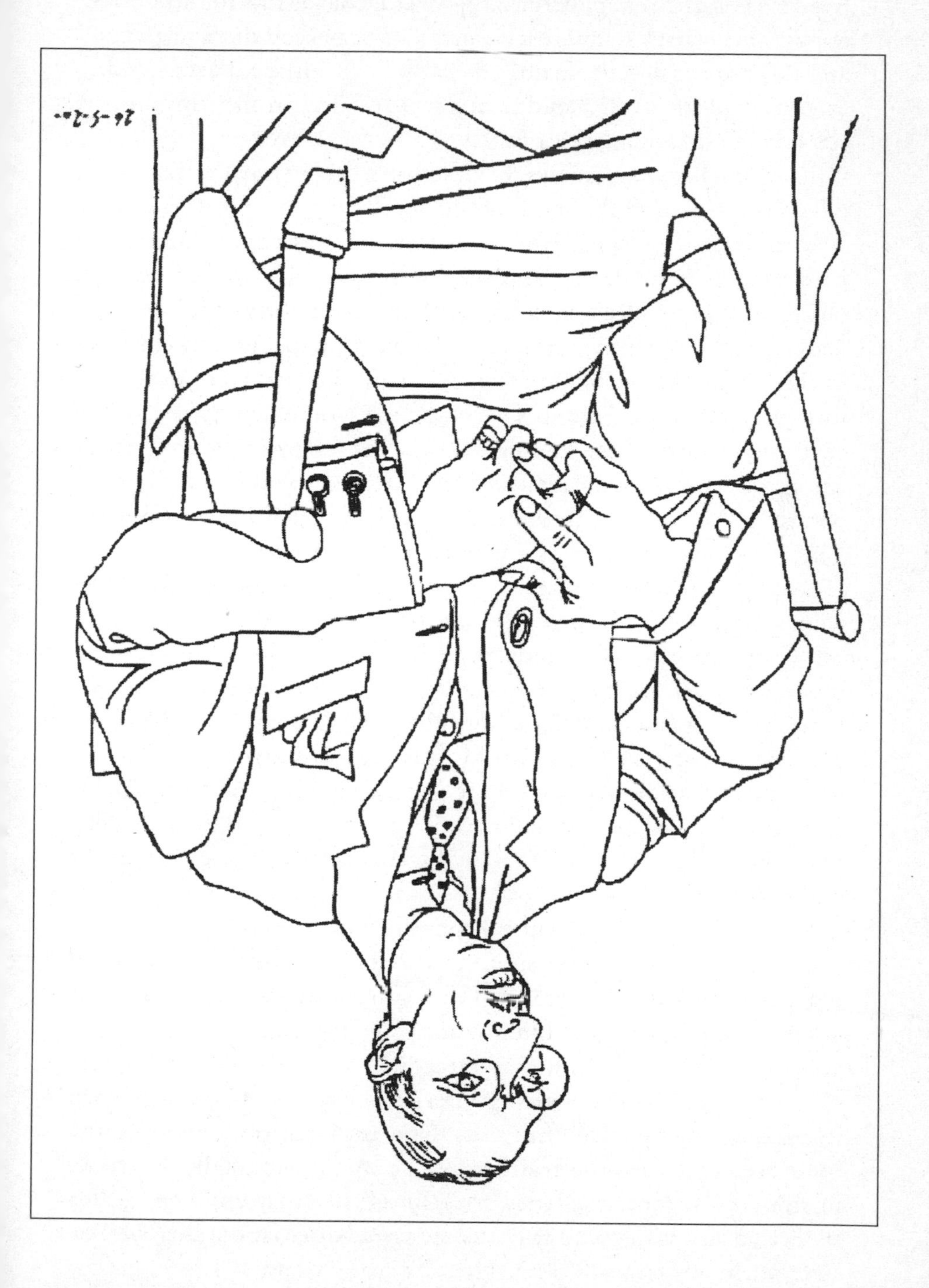

voice is the left hemisphere talking, and Edwards has made a career out of talking back to it. I had no previous drawing experience when I met Edwards and went through her five-day training. Based on that experience, I can attest that drawing realistically is something anyone can learn to do remarkably quickly.

In all likelihood, you overrelied on your left hemisphere, or what Edwards refers to simply as "L-mode," to draw your self-portrait. The left hemisphere is specialized to simplify, reduce, generalize, and name things. If we draw in L-mode, we're not interested in seeing a nose in all its complexity. Rather, the left hemisphere is goal-oriented and impatient to reach conclusions. It gives names to objects in order to classify them, so one nose is just like another. Asked to draw one, we tend to retrieve the symbol we have for it from memory, reproduce that, and move on. Edward's simple but profound insight was that by turning the drawing upside down, it becomes impossible for the left hemisphere to name what it sees. Confronted with a bunch of lines and shapes, the left hemisphere loses interest in the task.

The right hemisphere, by contrast, lacking the capacity to name things, is happy to immerse itself in the details of what it sees. Without language, it's also unburdened by time considerations. In "R-mode," we're in no rush to get anywhere or to arrive at a specific destination. If you took on the upside-down drawing task, it's likely that you experienced your mind quieting down, your self-critical voice giving way, the loss of a sense of time passing, and the palpable cognitive shift as you became absorbed in the task for its own sake. For many people, this is also a meditative experience, both relaxing and restorative.

Are you surprised by how well your drawing turned out? Is it better than you expected? For most of our clients, the answer is a resounding "yes." The explanation is not that you somehow unlocked latent artistic talent. Rather, it's that, by accessing R-mode, you were simply able to draw what you saw. "You already know how to draw," says Edwards, "but old habits of seeing interfere with that ability and block it." As the artist Don Dame puts it, "Drawing is the time-bound activity of seeing. It stills the brain's noise. . . . Art is a specialist's activity in this culture, and it is just a *symptom* of the process of seeing." It's not that drawing is necessarily an expression of artistic ability—it may or may not be—but rather that *learning* to draw is a means by which to train a unique way of seeing.

As for creativity, Edwards believes it can be trained like any other skill. The practical value of drawing is that it's a way to exercise and strengthen the capacities of the right hemisphere. They're valuable in everything from problem solving to innovation to strategizing to stepping back and seeing the big picture. In a left-hemisphere dominated world, these right-hemisphere capacities are dramatically underdeveloped.

The Internet, filled with search engines, wikis, and thousands of Web sites on every imaginable topic, makes vast amounts of information instantly available to anyone. The consequence is that left-hemisphere capacities, such as breadth of knowledge, memory for details, and even gathering, sorting, and organizing information, create less of an advantage in the workplace than they once did. But there is still no computer that can match the key capacities of the right hemisphere: creative and big-picture thinking; curiosity and openness to learning; and even empathy. Think of each of these as muscles that most of us have undertrained. In a fiercely competitive and rapidly changing marketplace, they're a largely untapped source of potential competitive advantage, both for individuals and for organizations.

RICHER, DEEPER, LONGER TERM

Seeing more deeply is the metacapacity we build when we actively train right-hemisphere focus. Above all, R-mode requires slowing down—and quieting down. "If ever there was a silent process," the psychologist Jerome Bruner has written, "it is the creative one." More, bigger, faster is the province of the left hemisphere. Richer, deeper, slower is the opposing but complementary strength of the right hemisphere. We can't march relentlessly toward a near-term goal and adopt a reflective, big-picture perspective at the same time. Far too often, we choose to focus on the former at the expense of the latter. Both are crucial to the highest levels of performance.

In absorbed L-mode, we move analytically, logically, and sequentially toward a goal by focusing narrowly on the task at hand. Consider an accountant doing a series of computations, a lawyer writing a brief, or a surgeon making a series of cuts. In R-mode, we can be just as deeply absorbed in a task, but we pay attention in a different way, seeing both the whole and the parts, noticing patterns, embracing paradox, ambiguity, and complexity. For example, we often dismiss intuition as magical thinking that charlatan psychics claim to have. But intuition is defined in the dictionary simply as "the power or faculty of attaining direct knowledge or cognition without rational thought and interference." In short, it's a nonverbal route to knowledge that arises not from rational deduction but from seeing and sensing more deeply.

NURTURING CREATIVITY

Where are *you* when you get your best ideas? In the shower? Working out? Driving? Walking in nature? In your dreams? Here's where you're likely not: at your desk, in front of your computer. We rarely get our best ideas when we're actively *trying* to get them, using our logic and our will. More common, they come to us when we're not consciously seeking them. This is the right hemisphere at work. The best ideas occur to us, paradoxically, when we let go of conscious control, which is something our left hemisphere is reluctant to do. The left hemisphere not only chafes at threats to its power but also sees itself as in charge of our safety. Letting go makes it, and therefore us, feel vulnerable. The right hemisphere, by contrast, has no self-consciousness and, as a result, no sense of self to protect.

The more we understand the value of letting go, the more comfortable we become selectively setting aside L-mode to think more freely, imaginatively, and visually in R-mode. As Edwards points out, the words we use to describe creative breakthroughs are almost always associated with seeing: insight, foresight, hindsight, seeing the light, coming into focus, getting the picture, or even something as simple as "I see it."

Researchers have now begun to map more precisely what happens inside the brain in these creative moments. In a series of studies, the researchers John Kounios and Mark Jung-Beeman used brain scanners and EEG sensors to study neural activity as subjects struggled to solve word puzzles. When the subjects reported that their solutions seemed to arise suddenly and spontaneously, rather than by deductive analysis, the EEG recordings revealed a flash of gamma waves in the brain's right hemisphere. The flash manifested just before the solution popped into the subject's awareness.

"Solving a problem with insight," Kounios says, "is fundamentally different from solving a problem analytically." The researchers also detected an increase in alpha brain-wave intensity in the visual cortex, which is associated with an inward focus of attention. "You want to quiet the noise in your head to solidify that fragile germ of an idea," says Jung-Beeman. The broader implication is that intentionally setting aside time to quiet the mind and activate the right hemisphere—through meditation or drawing, for example—is a powerful way to induce creative breakthroughs.

Artists understand intuitively how to move into this state, but the rest of us must learn it. Hannah Minghella, who heads production at Sony Pictures Animation, came from a highly artistic family, but in the aftermath of our work together, she's become more conscious about setting the conditions that fuel her creativity. "When I first got into my job, I tried to involve myself in everything," she told us. "As time progressed, I realized that wasn't sustainable and I needed to delegate more tasks so that I could have more downtime, both to restore myself and so I could think creatively.

"I've learned that I definitely don't do my most creative thinking at the office. I need to be completely on my own, in a quiet place, undistracted. If I need to figure something out in a script that isn't working, my ritual now is to make a cup of tea at home and sit down all by myself with a notepad, roll up my sleeves, and just write free form. That's when I usually have my best ideas. I've realized that my responsibility in this job is not to worry about the minutiae of administration or to be involved in every detail of our process, but to look for places where something has gone off creatively and to help get us back on track. I can only make that happen when I give myself the time and space I need."

Many of our clients, ranging from Sony's Matthew Lang to Mark Fields, Ford's president for the Americas, have discovered that taking a midafternoon break and going for a walk serves a dual purpose. It provides a source of renewal, but it's also a time during which solutions to problems they've been struggling with often arise spontaneously. During the writing of this book, my midmorning break was to take a run. If I'd been unable to solve some writing problem while sitting in front of my computer, a solution would almost invariably occur to me during my runs. I found it impossible to think intentionally and sequentially about a problem while I ran, but I often had spontaneous insights or saw new connections between ideas. Much the way it is with a dream, these ideas tended to slip away very quickly. It was essential, I learned, to write down my insights the moment I finished a run. On occasion, knowing I had a specific problem to solve, I even resorted to taking a small, voice-activated tape recorder along on my runs.

LEARNING, LISTENING, AND RECEPTIVITY

If R-mode serves creativity, it also facilitates learning. Our left hemisphere is filled with thoughts, ideas, beliefs, and memories of past experiences that profoundly influence the new information it takes in. On the one hand, this instinct drives discernment and critical thinking. On the other hand, as Edwards puts it, "Preconceptions, whether they are visual or verbal, can blind one to innovative discoveries."

To a considerable extent, the ego-driven left hemisphere believes it already knows everything it needs to know. It's often more eager to confirm its existing beliefs than to explore new ideas. It's also wired to reach conclusions as quickly as possible. As Bolte Taylor put it following her stroke, "Our left mind's language center is specifically designed to make sense of the world outside of us, based upon minimal amounts of information. . . . Our left brain is brilliant in its ability to make stuff up and fill in the blanks when there are gaps in its factual data. . . . I need to remember, however, that there are enormous gaps between what I know and what I think I know." Finally, the voice of self-judgment resides in the left hemisphere and often speaks loudest when we're struggling to learn something new.

The right hemisphere, lacking language, has no way of knowing what it knows and no self-critical voice ringing in its ear. It delights in new learning. Visualize a toddler playing, laughing, and exploring, full of curiosity and innocent wonder. With their limited language skills, toddlers are largely free of a self-critical voice. They're hungry to learn and unconcerned with outcomes. It's an ideal way to grow and develop, both for children and for adults. It's also a state that can be cultivated through meditation.

When Zen Buddhists talk about "beginner's mind," they're referring to an openness to every experience, unfettered by preconceptions, agendas, or expectations. The same stance facilitates absorbed listening, a capacity notably absent in many leaders we meet. This not only limits their learning but takes a toll on those they lead. Feeling truly heard and understood is deeply nourishing for all of us. The more skilled we get at accessing R-mode, the more receptive to others we're capable of being.

Empathy—the capacity to be sensitive, sympathetic, and responsive to what others are feeling—is the third primary strength of the right hemisphere. "Our right brain perceives the longer wavelengths of light," Bolte Taylor writes in *My Stroke of Insight.* "As a result, the visual perception of our right mind is somewhat blended or softened. This lack of edge perception enables it to focus on the bigger picture of how things relate to one another. . . . In contrast, our left brain perceives the shorter wavelengths of light, increasing its ability to clearly delineate sharp boundaries."

In short, when the right hemisphere is dominant, our sense of separateness diminishes. This may provide a neurological explanation for the sense of oneness—what both Hindus and Buddhists call "*samadhi*"—that highly practiced meditators sometimes experience when they are most deeply concentrated. In effect, boundaries disappear. In the days after her stroke, Taylor found that she was not capable of experiencing separation or individuality. "In the absence of my left hemisphere's analytical judgment, I was completely entranced by the feelings of tranquility," she writes. "Freed from all perception of boundaries, my right mind proclaims, 'I am a part of it all.' "

At the most practical level, intentionally quieting the left hemisphere is a way to relax the instinct to judge and rush to premature conclusions, which facilitates greater empathy. Numerous studies show that the most inspiring leaders are consistently those who tune in to what others are feeling and listen to them with genuine interest and respect. Along with a handful of leaders we've worked with over the years, Amy Pascal, the co-chairman at Sony Pictures Entertainment, has an instinctive ability to make you feel as if you're the most fascinating person in the world when you're in her presence. At Sony, it's referred to, sometimes ruefully, as "being in the light." That's because as warm a place as it is to bask, many people are vying for Pascal's attention and, not surprising, no one feels they get enough of it.

There is intense controversy about whether observed differences in male and female brains are learned or genetic. Simon Baron-Cohen, a British psychologist, is the leading proponent of the latter view. "The female brain is predominantly hard-wired for empathy," he argues in *The Essential Difference.* "The male brain is predominantly hard-wired for understanding and building systems. . . . To systematize you need detachment. . . . To empathize you need some degree of attachment in order to recognize that you are interacting with a person, not an object." By contrast, in *Pink Brain, Blue Brain* the neuroscientist Lise Eliot argues with persuasive evidence that "when it comes to differences between boys and girls . . . the fact is that the gaps are much smaller than commonly believed and far from understood at the level of the brain or neurochemistry."

Ultimately, the issue is less about gender than about the limitations of any brain that operates at the extremes. Asperger's syndrome and high-functioning autism, for example, are typically characterized by rigid, narrowly focused attention, as well as severely impaired capacity for empathy. People suffering from these disorders typically live highly ordered, controlled lives. They focus narrowly on small details and stick obsessively to routines and systems. At a less pathological level, we've observed many analytically gifted, left-hemisphere-driven leaders who lack the capacity to connect emotionally with those they lead. At the opposite end, extreme empathy may lead to an inability to create boundaries with others, while high creativity may be accompanied by a spacy inability to follow through and translate ideas into actions.

THE STAGES OF CREATIVITY

Neither hemisphere of the brain provides the full range of qualities we need to operate at our best in a complex, multilayered world. Our first imperative, then, is to stop choosing sides between them and instead find better ways to tap the strengths of each so the whole is greater than the parts. Creativity is a good example. Because it can't be understood purely in logical terms, many of us have tended to view it as mysterious, ineffable, and even magical. In fact, thinking creatively turns out to be a classic whole-brain activity that requires both hemispheres, and more of one than the other, depending on which stage we're at in the creative process. The better we understand these stages, the more systematically we can train and enhance creativity in ourselves and others.

A surprising degree of consensus has emerged during the past hundred years about the basic stages of creative thinking. In the late nineteenth century, Hermann von Helmholtz, a physicist and physiologist, became the first scientist to suggest that creative ideas emerge in three predictable stages. The first, he said, is saturation, which is essentially the gathering of facts. The second is incubation, which is the mulling over of the information, often unconsciously. The third is illumination, when some new combination of the data leads to a breakthrough or an "Ah-ha!"

In 1908, the French mathematician Henri Poincaré suggested a fourth stage, which he named "verification," to describe the point at which a creative insight is rigorously tested for accuracy. More recent, several researchers have suggested an additional stage that precedes the other four. The psychologist George Kneller named this "first insight," which he characterized as the point at which creative challenge is defined. The five-step process therefore looks like this:

FIRST INSIGHT ▶ SATURATION ▶ INCUBATION ▶ ILLUMINATION ▶ VERIFICATION

In *Drawing on the Artist Within*, Betty Edwards makes a convincing case that each step in the creative process draws more specifically on one hemisphere of the brain or the other. In our terms, that suggests a movement between the upper- and lower-right Focus Quadrants. *First insight* is an R-mode activity. The very notion of setting a creative challenge requires stepping out of the box of what we already know. It's the inspiration a scientist has for a new experiment, the outlines of a plot for a novel that suddenly occurs to a writer, or an entrepreneur's idea for a new business. "The formulation of a problem," wrote

Albert Einstein, "is often more essential than its solution, which may be merely a matter of mathematical or experimental skill."

Saturation, the gathering of information, involves immersing one's self in the known, which is foremost a left-hemisphere activity. This second stage in the creative process involves not just gathering the information but also reading through it, sorting, evaluating, organizing, outlining, and prioritizing. This tends to be laborious, methodical work, and it is sometimes shortchanged, but always at a cost. As George Kneller puts it: "One of the paradoxes of creativity [is] that in order to think originally, we must familiarize ourselves with the ideas of others." Information, in short, represents the raw material from which original thinking emerges—and the more knowledge one has, the better the base. In Anders Ericsson's terms, saturation represents a critical component of deliberate practice, building the base of knowledge that lies at the heart of true expertise.

In any extended creative endeavor, we're likely to hit roadblocks at certain points along the way. Imagine the feeling of being stuck on a problem. Your mind seems to be going in circles or you find yourself spacing out. The harder we try at those times, the more confused and frustrated we often become. That's when the R-mode *incubation* phase begins. In many cases, this occurs unintentionally after we throw up our hands and walk away from the problem, at least temporarily. When we understand incubation as a critical stage in the creative process, it can be something we move to intentionally after recognizing we've exhausted our logical, left-hemisphere capacity to solve a given problem. This is one of the reasons we urge our clients to break up their days—and especially their periods of intense focus—with a walk or by meditating or exercising.

It's also in R-mode, after we've stopped trying to solve a problem logically and sequentially, that the fourth stage of creativity, *illumination,* occurs. This is the moment of breakthrough, when the solution comes to us unbidden, a gift that seems to arise spontaneously. For the chemist Friedrich August Kekulé, the breakthrough he'd been wrestling with occurred one afternoon in 1857, when he fell into a reverie while working on a textbook. He had a half-waking dream about a snake seizing its own tail. That image, he later explained, led directly to his hypothesis that the carbon atoms in benzene formed a closed ring. Solving the structure of benzene became the key to understanding the basis of many organic compounds. While working on *The Last Supper,* Leonardo da Vinci regularly took off from painting for several hours at a time and seemed to be daydreaming aimlessly. Urged by his patron, the prior of Santa Maria delle Grazie, to work more continuously, Leonardo is reported to have replied, immodestly but accurately, "The greatest geniuses sometimes accomplish more when they work less."

The final stage of the creative process is *verification.* Often this requires the application of rigorous scientific method, which represents the best of left-hemisphere thinking. Even the most creative insights aren't worth much if they can't be translated into a form in which they can be understood and used by others. This L-mode stage may require long hours in a laboratory, meticulously testing a finding, or hunched over a computer, translating an understanding into words. Verification is the difference between a clever hypothesis or intuition and a solution that reliably and enduringly changes lives. It's through the capacities of the left hemisphere that we translate insights and ideas into laws, generalizable principles, and practical applications.

Understanding the difference between the capacities of the two hemispheres of our brain allows us to intentionally foster the conditions that best serve each one. Absorption is the core capacity we need to use either hemisphere optimally. The capacity to move flexibly between L-mode and R-mode—drawing on either one or both, according to the task—is the essence of the whole brain operating at its best. "Using the two modes together," says Edwards, "you can learn to think more productively, whatever your creative goals may be." To thrive—individually and organizationally—we need nothing less.

CHAPTER SIXTEEN ACTION STEPS

- Seeing more deeply and creatively is the capacity we build by training the right hemisphere of the brain. The first step is learning to slow down and quiet our minds of internal chatter. Schedule at least one half-hour period this week in which to brainstorm around some issue at work. You can help to access your right hemisphere by doodling, daydreaming, going for a long walk, or undertaking any activity that frees you from having to think consciously.
- The most inspiring leaders are those who consistently tune in to what others are feeling and listen to them with interest and respect. The next time you have a meeting or conversation with someone, practice listening closely without interrupting. Give that person your undivided attention, and see what it feels like. What did you learn or discover that you wouldn't have otherwise?
- Begin any creative project by immersing yourself in what's already known. This is the step known as "saturation," and, contrary to the assumption many of us make, the best ideas tend to emerge by extending, deepening, rethinking, and reframing what's already known.

CHAPTER SEVENTEEN

Autonomy for Accountability

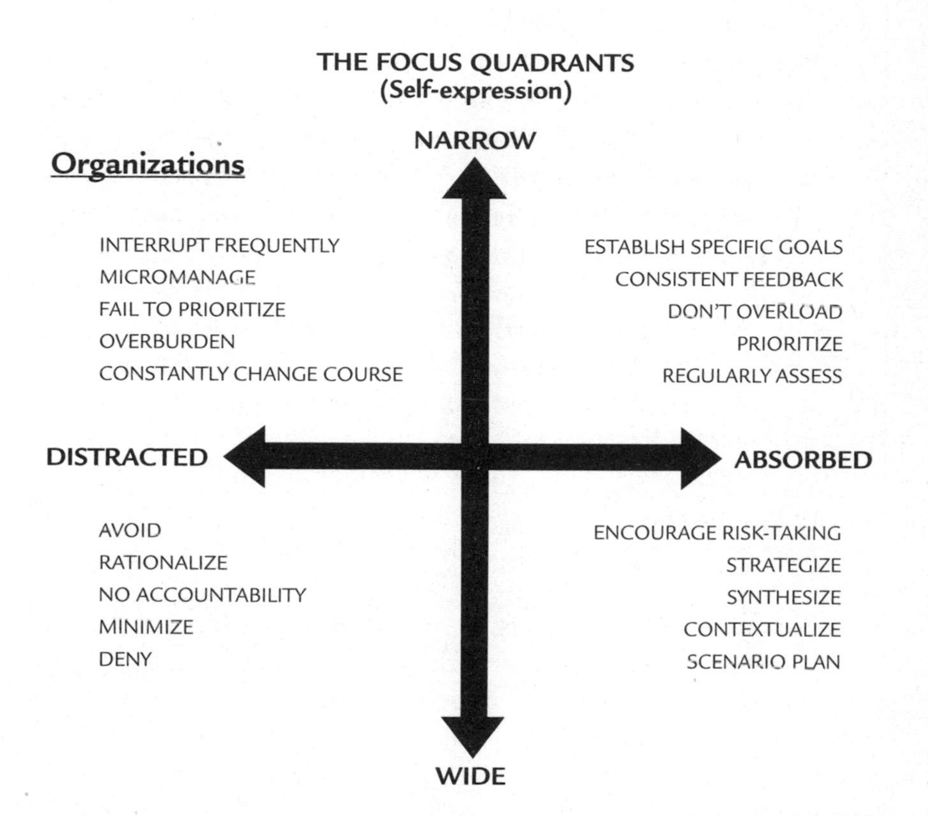

The best way for organizations to encourage higher productivity and more innovation is by promoting more absorbed focus. To a remarkable degree, however, leaders unwittingly collaborate with their employees to fracture their focus and distract their attention. In most organizations, the expectation of instantaneous responsiveness pushes everyone into reactive mode, making it difficult to stick to any agenda. In the race to do more, bigger, faster, what gets sacrificed are boundaries, stopping points, and finish lines. We rarely have the opportunity to become fully absorbed in a task. Organizations settle for our continuous partial attention—to their detriment and to ours.

Given the powerful cultural currents driving distraction, it's essential for organizations to adopt countervailing policies and practices that encourage more absorbed focus. One of the first opportunities is helping employees manage information overload more effectively. That requires not just creating very explicit organizational policies regarding e-mail, but also leaders willing to model new behaviors. At Sony Pictures, for example, the senior executive team wrestled with alternatives before deciding to set an 8-A.M.-to-8-P.M. limit on the times during which they would be expected to respond to internal e-mail. Outside those hours, they are free not to respond. If there is an urgent reason to reach a colleague, the agreement is that you pick up the phone and call the person. Not every executive has followed the policy, but a significant number have adopted it with good success.

"The expectations have really changed," says David Hendler, SPE's CFO. "There is less activity around e-mail after hours and more understanding if you don't respond immediately. I slip every now and then, but mostly I have stuck to the eight-to-eight rule. I'm no longer on my BlackBerry when I'm with my wife and kids, and they really appreciate it. That drives more energy while I'm working. I'm not drained or distracted by thinking 'Oh, I should be spending time with my family.' "

We've worked with a number of companies to institute an organizational ritual banning e-mailing altogether during meetings. It was common at Dannon, as it is at many companies in which we've worked, for executives to bring their laptops to meetings and use the time to catch up on e-mail. The rationale was always some variation on, "We can manage more than one thing at the same time and in that way we're more efficient." But the result bordered on the bizarre: no one truly listened to what anyone else was saying. "When we banned e-mail, it totally changed the character of the meetings," explains Juan Carlos Dalto, who was Dannon's CEO at the time. "Suddenly the focus of our meetings was on the real important discussions and people really concentrated on straight talk and productive debates. For the first time, it became a forum in which we had real strategic discussions with broad participation, and we were able to make important decisions based on everyone's input."

In many companies, meetings themselves are a source of distraction from higher-value work that people feel they could otherwise be doing. "Two principal types of mental activity dominate here," says Sony Europe's HR vice president, Roy White. "There's e-mail mode, where you sit at your desk for long hours bashing away at the keyboard, and there's meeting mode, where you typically sit long past your attention span. Neither mode optimizes people's ability to be productive or creative." Much as with e-mail, the ease with which meetings can be arranged online has prompted their proliferation. It's not uncommon for people to be scheduled in meetings back-to-back all day long, with no real time in between any of them. Many of our clients say they spend more time in meetings than anywhere else. Few companies have ritualized meeting practices and the consequence is that they often lack a rigorous agenda or a clearly defined goal. It's no wonder that people in meetings often find themselves itching to return to the e-mails piling up in their inboxes.

A number of our clients have begun scheduling meetings not on the half hour or the hour but on the quarter hour, for fifteen minutes or forty-five minutes. Odd as that sounds, it's one way to send a signal that meetings will start and end on time. It's also a way to shift people's thinking about how long a meeting ought to be. Our ultimate goal is to get leaders to intentionally question whether any given meeting is truly necessary and then to ask how long it really needs to be.

As an experiment, David Pope, now a senior leader at Wells Fargo, decided to cut every meeting to half of its previous length. Sure enough, he discovered that just as much was accomplished, and he suddenly had an extra hour or two a day freed up for other activities. More often than not, we've found that the shorter the meeting and the clearer the goal is, the more focused the level of attention and the better the outcome. The other value of short meetings, especially ones that don't end on the hour, is that they often leave participants time to reflect on and metabolize what they've just discussed and to get some renewal before the next obligation. Conversely, when meetings are scheduled to run longer than ninety minutes, it's important to schedule true recovery breaks, or people's attention will almost certainly wander.

FOCUSING IN A ROOM FULL OF PEOPLE

Our immediate work environment plainly influences our capacity to focus. Frank Lloyd Wright was one of the early advocates of open-plan design, not just for private homes but also for corporate offices. Wright's aim was to liberate people from living and working in small boxy spaces. Henry Ford and the efficiency expert Frederick Winslow Taylor took up the idea for just the opposite reason: to save money by squeezing as many people as possible into a small space. In recent years, the move to democratizing the workplace has emboldened a new wave of advocates for open-plan design. The laudable goals include fostering better communication, more face-to-face interaction, more responsiveness to issues as they arise and less hierarchy. Senior executives at companies such as Gillette, ING Direct, and Zappos all sit in open-space environments. The costs, however, are considerable and often underappreciated. An open plan nearly guarantees a high level of distractibility and fractured focus. Nearly all of the research suggests that the costs of working in such offices far outweigh the benefits. In a comprehensive study conducted in 2009 and titled "Why Your Office Could Be Making You Sick," the researcher Vinesh Oommen found that the consequences of open-plan offices include higher levels of stress, higher blood pressure, and more susceptibility to illness, as well as more interpersonal conflict, higher turnover, lower satisfaction and diminished productivity. The key contributing factors are the higher level of noise, the increased frequency of interruptions, and the costs to privacy in open-space environments. It's simply much harder to focus in an absorbed way when the people around you are typing, shuffling papers, and talking to one another and on the phone.

In a second study, conducted by the Center for the Built Environment at the University of California, Berkeley, more than 23,000 occupants in fourteen buildings were surveyed. Those in separate offices were dramatically more satisfied with noise levels and privacy than those in open spaces or in cubicles with partitions. Surprisingly, the

Berkeley study also found that those in cubicles had more complaints than those in fully open environments. Cubicles were introduced in the 1950s as an attempt to create more privacy and personal space in the wake of complaints by employees working in open space. It turns out that it's often more difficult to have a private conversation in a cubicle than in an open environment, where it's easy to check visually to see if anyone else is listening. People working in a fully open workplace also seem to have lower expectations about privacy and are more compelled to adapt. Conversely, they enjoy more of the social benefits that arise from being in an open space than do those confined to cubicles.

In practice, most of us crave both privacy and connection. Because they allow for neither, cubicles may represent the worst of all worlds. The best workplace, we believe, is one that provides a range of environments that serve people's varying needs. The quiet and privacy of a separate office plainly facilitates the most absorbed focus. For brainstorming in groups, a more comfortable, informal environment encourages relaxed, open-ended thinking. A fully open environment works better for those doing less intellectually demanding tasks and also for work in which ongoing collaboration is a high priority.

"Many of our people work in an environment which is virtually indistinguishable from a busy train station in terms of interruptions and distractions," says Andreas Ditter, former vice president, Sony Audio Europe, and now managing director, Sony Pictures Home Entertainment Germany. "One of my solutions is that I've started using walking meetings as a way to get out of the office, change channels and gain focus. It really works effectively, because it accomplishes two things at the same time: an opportunity to have an exchange of ideas and a chance to move and renew."

In the UK, Sarah Henbrey, Sony Europe's director of organizational development, began wearing headphones in the office after going through our training. "It's incredible what a difference such a small thing can make," she says. "In the past you'd either feel guilty about putting on headphones and shutting people out, or you'd worry they thought you were vegging out to music. Now people have a common language and understanding about distractions, so wearing earphones is just a way of saying you're focused on something." At the same time, we helped Sony create a space called "The Village Green" at its European headquarters in Basingstoke. Modeled on a traditional English village green, the space has been designed like a park—in this case with AstroTurf rather than grass—and it's become a meeting ground that helps get people out of their offices.

Among all of the companies at which we've worked, Google may have the best mix of spaces at its headquarters in Mountain View, California. The campus includes some two dozen buildings, and people travel between them by walking, but also by using bicycles that the company makes freely available. The buildings contain an assortment of private offices, cubicles, and open environments. Throughout the campus, there are also more than a dozen small cafés, in which coffee and snacks are available and where employees go to meet or hang out. Google's main restaurants have open bench seating, encouraging people to sit together and intermingle. There are also rooms explicitly set aside for brainstorming, often filled with gadgets, toys, and knickknacks that encourage people to play and explore, and to get out of their ordinary linear ways of thinking.

BREAKING OUT OF THE BOX

What does it take to ensure that organizations support the second kind of absorbed attention—R-mode lower-right-quadrant thinking—which serves innovation, strategy, and long-term planning? The simple answer is intentionality. Setting aside separate spaces for creative thinking, for example, makes a statement about the priority it has been accorded in the organization. The more visually appealing and the less linear the space, the more conducive it is to R-mode thinking. But unless leaders make an explicit commitment to setting aside regular time for such thinking, it's unlikely to occur with any regularity. One ritual we encourage leaders to adopt is scheduling time for reflection and for team brainstorming and strategy sessions. This is the sort of work the author Stephen Covey so aptly termed "important but not urgent."

The risk is that people experience such meetings as so irrelevant to urgent challenges and everyday business that they ultimately get abandoned. For Derry Newman, the CEO of Solarcentury, which builds and provides solar technology across Europe, the solution has been to intentionally balance right- and left-hemisphere thinking in his organization's initiatives.

"We have many people here who see immediately how to progress a piece of thinking or a new idea," Newman told us. "But then they see another idea and another, and very rapidly we fall into initiative fatigue. Before we did this work, we had become great at starting things, but not at seeing them through." Newman drew on our sprinter/marathon metaphor to balance longer-term innovative thinking with more immediately pressing work.

"We started to establish more boundaries," Newman explains. "For example, we've broken our longer-term project plans into shorter sprints. I've asked our managers to think in terms of three-week sprints. It's had a powerful effect. We can maintain high levels of mental focus for three weeks now, knowing we will have a chance to recover and renew before we take on the next three-week sprint. During the recovery periods, we have time to step back and look at where we are and where we're going. It feels less overwhelming, and it builds people's confidence. They can now get their arms around smaller chunks of high-challenge work without losing sight of the big picture. It's brought a significant degree of calmness and focus to the way we work. We've also brought in forty-five percent more business with the same number of people since we started working this way."

The other key to innovation is a culture that prizes learning and truly invests in it. There are now "chief learning officers" in many large companies, but time allotted to employees for their development typically remains scarce. Because most learning doesn't generate an immediate payoff, everything but technical training tends to be viewed as nonessential and low priority. The opposite may be true. Arie de Geus, a former head of planning at Royal Dutch Shell, conducted a study of companies that have lasted the longest. "The ability to learn faster than competitors," he argued, "may be the only sustainable competitive advantage."

The obvious bias in most organizational learning is to the left hemisphere—observable facts and information that can be understood and absorbed as quickly as possible. "Can you give us the basics in a half day?" we're often asked about our own work, as if providing a list of suggestions and a raft of data would be sufficient. It's difficult to convince most leaders that meaningful change is possible only if they're willing to give their people the time to reflect on, discuss, and metabolize new ideas and to experiment with new practices. The prospect of devoting several days to building new capacities, much less an entire week, is increasingly unthinkable to most senior leaders we've met. Some organizations do run three- and four-day executive retreats once a year, bringing together experts from various fields to give short presentations. We call these "big bang" experiences. They can be powerful in the moment, but they typically have a short half-life, and it's rare that employees are offered any sort of follow-up.

We've been most successful in organizations when we've had the opportunity to work with people over an extended period of time, regularly refreshing, revisiting, extending, and deepening the principles and practices we teach. That shouldn't be any surprise. After all, we're asking people to change behaviors they've practiced, reinforced, and habitualized over many years.

"We are what we repeatedly do," Aristotle observed more than two thousand years ago. Anders Ericsson and others have demonstrated that people can systematically improve their skills, but only through deliberate practice: focused repetition at regular intervals over extended periods, accompanied by regular feedback. Coaching, for example, can be effective in organizations for the same reason it is in sports. It supports people's learning, holds them accountable to their commitments, and provides them with specific, ongoing feedback in the areas in which they're trying to improve. Any organization that fails to build a robust learning program for its employees—not just to increase their skills but also to develop them as human beings—ought to expect that its people won't get better at their jobs over time and may well get worse.

WE ARE NOT YOUR CHILDREN

The last key to helping people focus their attention better may be the most counterintuitive. It involves giving them more autonomy in the way they work—and then holding them more accountable for the value they deliver. Instead, the all-too-common dynamic in today's workplace is parent-child. Most employers tell employees when to come to work, when to leave, and how they're expected to work when they're at the office. Treated like children, many employees unconsciously adopt the role to which they've been consigned. Feeling disempowered and vulnerable, they lose the will and confidence to take real initiative or to think independently. Doing what they're expected to do often becomes more important than doing what makes most sense, what's most efficient, or even what might create the highest value. The real measure of people's effectiveness in an organization ought to be based on the value they create, not the number of hours they work. That requires a relationship between consenting adults, grounded in trust, fueled by mutual responsibility, and regulated by periodic accountability.

Most leaders and managers we work with set clear expectations about the hours they expect their employees to work. Very few organizations take responsibility for defining in clear and specific terms what success looks like for any given job outside sales. The result is that employees are often uncertain what exactly is expected of them. Too often, they default to working long hours on numerous tasks, trying to cover all the bases without necessarily doing anything that truly adds value.

Creating clear goals and deliverables is what makes it possible to truly hold people accountable. That's not easy for complex jobs that include responsibility for managing people and processes, or doing creative and strategic thinking. But it can be done, we've found, even in the least measurable of jobs. At Sony Pictures, for example, we worked with two senior movie executives to help them define precisely what they expected from each of their employees who had a role in finding and developing scripts and overseeing production. Subjective and unpredictable as that process is, the leaders we worked with were able to calculate with reasonable specificity how many pitches and submissions it typically requires to find one script worth buying and how many scripts must be developed on average to get one worth producing. With that information in mind, it was possible to say to their executives, with far more precision, "This is what we expect you to deliver in your role."

Once you've arrived at the metrics for a given job, the number of hours people work, or how they choose to do their job should become secondary. As Hew Evans, Sony UK's HR director, puts it, "If your manager knows what you're doing all the time, you're not doing your job and neither is he." To put this thinking into wider practice, we've introduced a simple exercise at a number of companies. First, we work with managers to help them define the deliverables for each of their direct reports. Then, in a single two- to three-hour session, we take employees—everyone from senior executives to administrative assistants—through a process of defining their ideal work schedule. What, we ask them, would allow them to be most productive and most satisfied, on and off the job?

Would a given person prefer, for example, to start earlier in the day and end earlier, or perhaps to work in the morning, take time off at midafternoon to be with children returning from school, and then resume working in the evening? Would another person be more efficient by working at home several days a week and avoiding a two- or three-hour round-trip commute? Might still another employee prefer to work longer days, in two- or three-hour stretches, taking time off between them to work out, have lunch with a friend, run an errand, or take a midafternoon nap, in order to be able to work more effectively in the early evening?

At IBM, for example, a thousand software developers working in different time zones have been given the flexibility to decide when they work. Many of the developers have also chosen to split their workdays into smaller chunks, taking time off intermittently through their days to deal with other aspects of their lives. The time it takes to update a given product's software has been reduced from eighteen to twenty-four months five years ago to four to six months today. As Patty Dudek, an IBM vice president, puts it, "If we want top talent to work on something and we give them all the flexibility they need to balance their lives, they're then more than willing to step up to the challenge when we need them to drop everything."

The ideal work schedule looks different for each of us, given the vast differences in people's temperaments and life circumstances. Obviously, there may be times, in a team environment, when collaboration and even sacrifice are necessary to achive a shared goal. With that in mind, the second step in our process is for managers to meet individually with each of their direct reports to discuss their proposed schedules. When managers come to these discussions with a feeling of trust, our experience is that most individual preferences can be accommodated.

At Chubb Insurance, for example, a group of employees was given the opportunity to choose the work hours that best suited them. Some 400 have participated so far, and in the Chicago office nearly 75 percent of the employees—120 out of 163—work nonstandard schedules they've created. The productivity gains have been striking: an increase from 82 percent to 91 percent in customers contacted within twenty-four hours and from 90 percent to 100 percent in timely benefit payments to claimants. "It's making people more responsible and accountable for what they do," says John Finnegan, Chubb's CEO. "The test is that they can do it better than they've done it before."

We've taken autonomy a step further in our own small company. We don't ask anyone to answer e-mail after hours or on the weekends. If there is an urgent need to reach someone, we'll call, but that is rare. Except for the handful of employees whose presence is required to keep our offices open and running, we set no specific hours. Even for the employees who do work fixed hours, we leave them free to find ways to cover for one another, so they can take time off during the day if they choose to do so. We have no sick days or vacation policy. Instead, we assumed that our people are committed to getting their work done and that they'll take a vacation when they need it. We invest almost no time or energy in monitoring how our employees get their work done—and they do.

Best Buy is the only large company we're aware of that has instituted a broad-based program which gives employees the level of autonomy we've been describing. Results Oriented Work Environment (ROWE) was launched at Best Buy's headquarters in 2001 and is now offered to all of the approximately 3,000 corporate employees at its Minneapolis headquarters. The program's creators, Cali Ressler and Jody Thompson, share many of our assumptions. "The employer's job is to create very clear goals and expectations for what needs to get done on a daily, weekly, monthly, and yearly basis," they explain. "The simplest definition of a Results Only Work Environment [is that] each person is free to do whatever they want, whenever they want, as long as the work gets done. Everything else—when they come in, how much time they spend in their cube, how long their lunch lasts—is no longer [the employer's] concern. The point here is to always redirect focus back to the work."

Two outside researchers studied the impact of the ROWE program on approximately 325 employees at Best Buy and compared them to an equal number of employees who remained in a traditional work environment. After six months, significant numbers of those in the ROWE group reported that they had more time to take care of all aspects of their life, experienced fewer work interruptions, and were getting more sleep than they had previously. Interestingly, the most dramatic changes occurred in turnover. Among three separate ROWE groups totaling 377 employees, the number who left the company decreased by 90 percent, 52 percent, and 75 percent, respectively, between 2005 and 2007. Because Best Buy estimates the average cost of turnover per employee at $102,000, Ressler and Thompson estimate the total cost savings to the company to be approximately $6.7 million. They've now instituted a second pilot among 137 employees at a division of Gap and experienced similar results.

Ultimately, of course, the issue that matters most is not how many employees leave but how well those who stay perform. Perhaps no factor influences productivity more directly than people's capacity for absorbed attention. In a world rife with potential distractions, it's in the self-interest of organizations and their leaders to help their people stay focused on the priorities that have the potential to create the greatest value. When employees are given the opportunity to design workdays that better suit their needs, common sense tells us—and a growing body of evidence demonstrates—that they perform at significantly higher levels.

CHAPTER SEVENTEEN ACTION STEPS

- The ability to focus on one thing at a time increases productivity and promotes innovation. What one new policy or modification of an existing one would support those you lead in focusing better on one task at a time? For example, consider creating one e-mail-free day a week, or even a half day, during which people are encouraged to focus on projects that require high concentration.
- Our immediate work environment directly influences our capacity to focus. Identify one change you could make to the physical environment that would improve other people's capacity for absorbed attention—or your own. If people share an open space, could they wear earphones when they're working on a challenging project? Could you let colleagues know when you don't want to be interrupted? If you're a leader, could you create a quiet room for anyone's use—akin to a quiet car in a train?
- In the absence of intentionality, the urgent will nearly always overwhelm the important but nonurgent. Create a separate, relaxing, informal space at work that is exclusively devoted to creative thinking and brainstorming. Then schedule a regular time—once a week or once every two weeks—in which you bring together colleagues to brainstorm new ideas, discuss longer-term projects or set strategy.

PART V

SIGNIFICANCE/SPIRITUAL

CHAPTER EIGHTEEN

Who Are You, and What Do You Really Want?

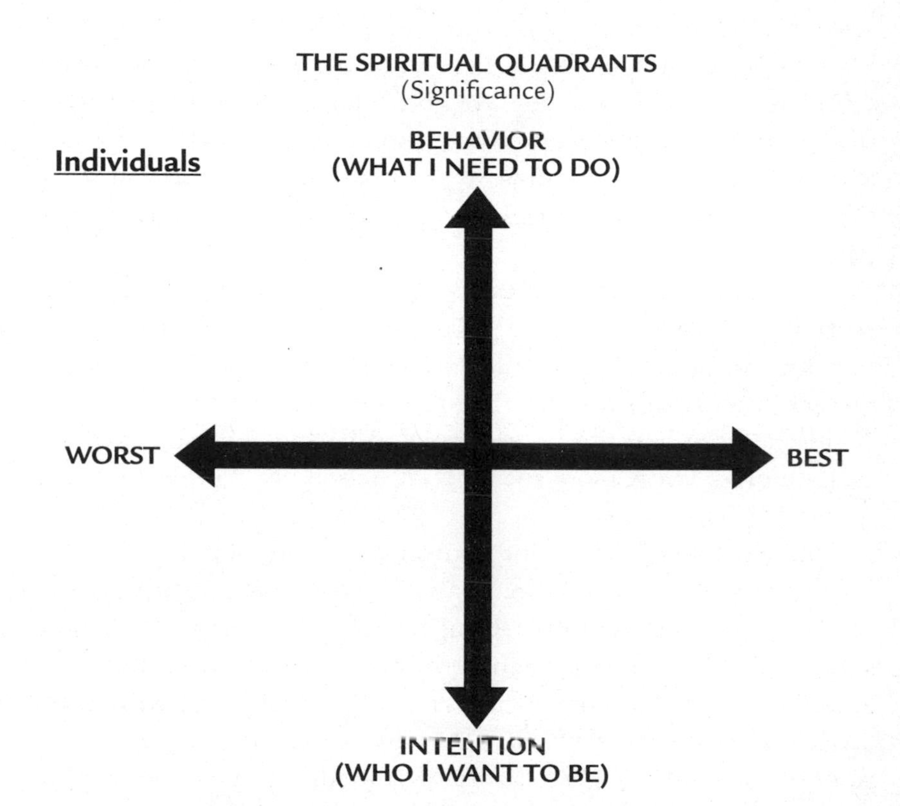

What if you returned a telephone call from someone you didn't know, and you reached an answering machine and got this message:

"Who are you, and what do you really want? Leave a message at the beep." That's quite a challenge. How would *you* answer? After all, they're arguably life's biggest questions.

Who are you? As in: "What do you stand for most deeply?"

And what do you really want? As in: "What's your purpose in life?"

Spiritual energy is the uniquely powerful source of energy we derive from deeply held values and a clear sense of purpose beyond our self-interest that we embody in our everyday behaviors.

Deeply held values define the person you aspire to be. They're what we're rooted in and what we stand for. They provide an internal compass that helps us navigate the storms we all inevitably face and make the right choices even on the occasions when we're tempted to take a more expedient route. Values are a source of identity, clarity and strength. Virtually anything in our lives can be taken from us—a job, a home, loved ones, or our health. But no one can take away your values, and knowing who you are goes a long way. A broad range of studies has shown that people whose motivation comes from within—variously referred to as intrinsic, self-authored, or authentic—are more energized, more engaged, more persistent, and ultimately higher performing.

A clearly defined sense of purpose ties our values to concrete intentions and gives us external direction—a reason to get up in the morning and a fuel to stay the course in the face of the inevitable setbacks that arise along the way. "He who has a why to live for," said Nietzsche, "can bear almost any how." When something really matters, we bring vastly more energy to it: more focus, conviction, passion, and perseverance.

Our spiritual self transcends our physical, emotional, and mental selves but also includes them. It's our highest level of development. Physical energy is our foundation, and if we neglect it, the impact shows up in our ability to manage our emotions. If we're run by our emotions, we find it more difficult to focus our attention and think creatively. At our best, we use all of our capacities—physical, emotional, and mental—in the service of embodying our deepest values and highest purpose.

As in the other three dimensions, we cultivate spiritual energy most effectively when we move between spending it and refueling it. Here the movement is between the reflective work of defining and regularly renewing our intentions and aspirations, in the lower-right quadrant of the figure on page 237, and the outer work of embodying those intentions in our behaviors, in the upper-right quadrant. Unlike each of the three previous sets of quadrants, you'll notice that the spirit quadrants contain no descriptive adjectives. Science can help us understand objectively what fuels our physical, mental, and emotional energy and what depletes it. In the spiritual dimension, the values, purpose, and behaviors that fuel us are more subjective, nuanced, and personal.

There are two distinct ways to nurture spiritual energy. The first, in the lower-right quadrant, is internal, and it depends on defining what you stand for—the person you want to be and the purpose you want to serve. The second, in the upper right, is external, and it's fueled by our behavior in the world.

Cultivating spiritual energy requires effort and reflection. There is no shortcut and no steps we can skip. Spiritual practice is challenging but ultimately energizing. It's up to each of us to find ways to invest our lives with meaning. Only then can we reap the rewards. Purpose and significance are not our birthrights.

"It did not really matter what we expected from life, but rather what life expected from us," Viktor Frankl wrote about his experience surviving in a Nazi concentration camp. "We needed to stop asking about the meaning of life, and instead to think of ourselves as those who were being questioned by life—hourly and daily. . . . Life ultimately means taking the responsibility to find the right answer to its problems and to fulfill the tasks which it constantly sets for each individual."

In practical terms, tapping into spiritual energy—the right side of the quadrants—means tapping into the energy of your best self. One way to define the person you want to be is to think for a moment about your most *admirable* qualities—the ones that make you feel best about yourself and nourish others. To undertake this exercise, get a pen and a piece of paper and draw your own set of quadrants like the ones at the beginning of this chapter.

Start by recalling at least two recent occasions in your life when you were acting in a way that made you feel deeply good about yourself. You can write down those behaviors in the upper-right quadrant. What were the values you were serving? Those belong in the lower-right quadrant. Next, try to remember occasions on which you behaved in ways that *didn't* make you feel good about yourself. Those belong in the upper-left quadrant.

Now, ask yourself how you would have behaved in that circumstance at your best. Add those examples to the upper-right quadrant. What values do those behavors reflect? Add those to the lower-right quadrant.

Okay, now, what are the opposite of those values? Put those in the lower-left quadrant. For example, if you have "generosity" in the lower right, then you'd put "selfishness" or "stinginess" in the lower left. If you have "considerate" in the lower right, the opposite might be "greedy" in the lower left. The opposite of "forgiving" might be "judgmental."

This is a challenging undertaking. It is difficult to see our own shortcomings, but it is also hard to give ourselves credit. It may be helpful to ask a person close to you—someone who knows you very well and whose opinions you trust—to help you on this exercise.

Once you've filled in the quadrants, you'll have two pictures of yourself. The unbecoming qualities and actions likely describe a person you'd want to avoid. The admirable qualities and behaviors you've listed are a reflection of what you value most in yourself. So which is the real you? The truth, of course, is that we're both of these selves, and we move along a spectrum between them, depending on the circumstances.

NARROW, SHALLOW, AND SHORT TERM

It's difficult to envision a more vivid example of the default to primitive instincts than the one that characterizes those at the center of the recent fall of the banking system. "There's plenty to criticize about American financial life," author Michael Lewis has written, "but the problems are less with rule-breaking than with the game itself. Even in the most fastidious of times it is boorishly single-minded. It elevates the desire to make money over other, nobler desires. It's more than a little nuts for a man who has a billion dollars to devote his life to making another billion, but that's what some of our most exalted citizens do, over and over again." Here is how the head of human resources at one of the large financial firms that ultimately fell put it to me in the midst of the boom: "I often wish our senior executives would tie the accomplishment of their goals to a higher purpose than just being the most profitable. Unfortunately, that's all most of our leaders know."

Money is the sugar in the spiritual diet. It tastes good, it's a source of pleasure, and it's not harmful in small doses. But anything that provides a powerful hit of pleasure, or a reliable way to avoid discomfort, has the potential to become addictive. The problem is that more money, like more sugar or more of any other drug, provides diminishing returns over time. In any addiction, the typical pattern is to chase the high, progressively upping the ante in a futile effort to recapture the initial pleasure it provided.

Soon after he quit but before the company fell, a former managing director at Lehman Brothers told us this story: "I was sitting in my office one afternoon and complaining to no one in particular about having to go on the road yet again. The guy at the desk next to me said, 'Yeah, I've got to fly across the country myself, and I'm gonna miss my daughter's first birthday.' Now, this guy had been at the firm for twenty years, and he was worth at least fifty million dollars. So I said to him, 'Why do you still do it?' He looked at me like I was some kind of idiot for even asking the question. 'Well, for the money, of course,' he said. But of course, it wasn't the money anymore. You keep doing this because it's who you think you are. It becomes your whole identity. You disconnect from everything else. I know that's true, because I experienced my own identity crisis when I finally quit. It felt like detoxing from a drug."

When the immediate material rewards are sufficiently seductive, the more primitive centers of the brain—"I want what I want now"—override the more reflective capacity of the prefrontal cortex. It's noteworthy, for example, that not a single CEO or senior executive at a large bank ever stood up and blew the whistle on the practices that led to the worldwide financial meltdown in 2008. Nor has virtually any one of them ever explicitly acknowledged any personal responsibility for what happened.

Several years ago, in the midst of the boom, I gave a talk to managing partners at a large investment bank known for its supreme self-confidence. The topic was how to sustain high performance in an era of relentlessly rising demand. I spoke about the role of the four different sources of energy and how intermittent renewal is a critical component of sustainable performance. When I finished, a partner in his late thirties or early forties—no one in the room was much older than that—raised his hand.

"You're making an assumption that we're concerned about sustainability," the partner said without a trace of irony. "The reality is that there are hundreds of talented people knocking on our door every year, dying to come and work here. If one person burns out or decides to leave, there are ten more prepared to step in, and every one of them is prepared to work 24/7. Why should we be worrying about something like renewal?"

Why, he was asking, should any of us worry about anything but earning as much money as we can as fast as we can? Three years later, the economy collapsed, the stock market crashed, and the firm nearly went out of business.

The partner's view was hardly a new one. Here's what Socrates had to say back in 400 B.C.: "I honor and love you, but why do you who are citizens of this great and mighty nation care so much about laying up the greatest amount of money and honor and reputation and so little about wisdom and truth and the greatest improvement of the soul? . . . I tell you that virtue is not given by money, but from virtue comes money and every other good of man."

THE VALUE OF REFLECTION

Clarifying and deepening our values through regular reflection is the antidote to a narrow, shallow, short-term perspective. Reflection requires quiet, uninterrupted time, the scarcest of commodities in the world most of us inhabit. We rarely step back to think about why we're doing what we're doing, where we're headed, or what the consequences are likely to be. Instead, most of us spend our days feeling compelled to act, react, and transact. We're unwilling to stop moving at least partly out of fear of what we might see—or see is missing. It's easier, oddly, to stay busy.

Perhaps surprisingly, our first spiritual challenge is accepting that our highest and lowest selves coexist inside us and forever compete for our favor. "To know ourselves, we have to know our own animal nature first," the psychiatrist Ian McCallum writes in *Ecological Intelli-*

gence. The genetic difference between humans and chimpanzees is no more than 2 percent, he points out, while the elephant, the lion, and even the spotted hyena all share more than 90 percent of our genetic makeup. McCallum evocatively captures the implications of these facts:

> It is important to remember that the game we are playing is a shared one. It's called survival. "I want it all and I want it now" is the brainstem speaking. The psychological instincts of the predator, the parasite and the scavenger are in our history and in our blood. They will not go away, which means there is no point in turning a blind eye to them. . . . We all have something of the hag and the hyena in us. We are all, in our own subtle ways, manipulators, con men and we all own a little bit of the beggar, too. We, too, are territorially and materially acquisitive. We are pathetic, but we are also wonderful. And when we know this, when we recognize our inflation or the scavenger, the conman and the road rage creature within us, then we can learn how to say yes or no to them.

The advantage human beings have over every other species is a modern brain, a prefrontal cortex that allows us to reflect and make intentional choices based not just on our logic, but also on our deepest values—who we want to be and how we want to behave as a consequence. This requires not just cultivating our highest values but also having the courage to recognize our basest instincts. "There is no sun without shadow," said Albert Camus. Or, as Carl Jung wrote, "I must have a dark side if I am to be whole; and inasmuch as I become conscious of my shadow, I also remember that I am a human being like any other."

Reflecting on our most deeply held values helps us distinguish between our survival-based motivations and our higher ones. In situations of conflict or disappointment, and especially when we feel threatened or triggered, one of the most powerful reflective practices is to ask ourselves a simple question: How would I behave here at my best? Plainly, it's easier to assign blame outside ourselves, to rationalize our reactive behaviors, or to find ways to avoid thinking about anything that makes us feel we're falling short. But seeing our shadow—asking ourselves "In what ways is this my responsibility, and how could I behave better?"—is a powerful spiritual practice. Seeing where we've fallen short gives us more clarity about who we want to be and how we want to behave.

Mindfulness is the highest level of awareness most of us can develop in our everyday lives. We introduced it in chapter 14 as a way to train attention, but it also has great value in the spiritual dimension. Mindfulness, you'll remember, is the practice of witnessing the arising and passing of our thoughts, feelings, and sensations without becoming identified with them. This level of awareness allows us to observe our thoughts and emotions but not to be defined by or feel captive to them. It's from the perspective of the witness that we can say, "Yes, I am that, but I'm more than that."

From the mindful perspective, the ordinary boundaries we create with our minds dissolve, and so, in turn, does the sense of separateness and alienation that so often characterizes our daily lives. We're truly able to see the big picture, the good and the bad in ourselves and others, with compassion rather than judgment. Higher consciousness, by this view, isn't some mystical aspiration. It simply means becoming conscious of more.

Avoiding our dark side is what we do in the lower-left quadrant of the Spiritual Quadrants—most often by shutting down our awareness. We each have an infinite capacity for self-deception, and we use it to protect ourselves. When we fall short or come under criticism, we find ways to deny, deflect, rationalize, minimize, and assign blame to others. We feel better in the short term, but the costs in the long term are considerable. "Every time we laugh at someone else's misfortune," writes Lyall Watson, "it is our shadow showing. Every time we take pleasure in the pain of a rival, it is a genetic pleasure."

Recognizing our own worst instincts requires not just openness but also humility. False humility is manipulation covertly aimed at winning praise. Genuine humility frees us of the need to protect an image of ourselves or stand above others. It gives us permission instead to accept, embrace, and learn from our limitations. In one recent study of leaders, those with the highest opinions of themselves turned out to be the least receptive to criticism or negative feedback. In another study, those with the highest levels of "self-esteem" were more likely to "irritate, interrupt and show hostility to others."

Carl Sandburg brilliantly captured our dual nature—our basest instincts and our need to take responsibility for our behaviors—in his poem "Wilderness," written in 1918:

> O, I got a zoo, I got a menagerie, inside my ribs, under my bony head, under my red-valve heart . . . For I am the keeper of the zoo: I say yes and no: I sing and I kill and I work: I am a pal of the world: I come from the wilderness.

The willingness to recognize our shortcomings also saves us from squandering energy on denial, rationalization and blame when we fall short. It frees us from the need to defend ourselves, and instead allows us to embrace all of ourselves. As McCallum puts it, "It does not matter who or where we are, our lives at all times will involve subtle and sometimes obvious combinations of these survival strategies. Whether we are lions, hyenas, or humans, we engage in these activities for the same reasons—for food, turf or territory, security, approval, sexual partners, rank, status, attachment, and belonging. . . . [W]e employ these strategies not only to establish ourselves, but also to promote and to protect ourselves."

The irony is that our efforts at self-preservation and self-protection so often cause precisely what we're seeking to hold at bay. We keep people at a distance to avoid feeling vulnerable and risking rejection. We get angry and hostile when we don't feel we've been treated fairly. We're selfish and self-serving when we fear we aren't getting enough of whatever we think we need. In each instance, what we seek, above all, is to feel safe, secure, and valued. We want to belong and to be connected to others, but our survival behaviors succeed only in pushing others away. In the process, we confirm our worst fears.

Strengthening our spiritual selves requires a leap of faith. When we reach out, we can be spurned. When we're generous, others may take advantage of us. When we own our shortcomings, we can be subjected to blame and scapegoating. When we put the interests of others above our own, we worry that no one will take care of us. It takes courage and commitment to live our deepest values and cultivate our best selves. But, as T. S. Eliot put it, "Only those who will risk going too far can possibly find out how far they can go."

Fear also blinds us to how much we receive in return when we extend ourselves. Take a look again at the qualities you chose to describe yourself at your best. How many of these values and intentions are connected to the way you treat others? Risky as it sometimes feels, we typically feel better about ourselves when we're serving something beyond our self-interest. The fact that we're rewarded when we give without precondition is just a bonus, but it makes evolutionary sense. Reciprocity, like generosity, ultimately serves our survival better than selfishness. It builds trust, deepens relationships, and reinforces values that serve the greater good.

Defining and regularly revisiting our values is just the first step. Applying our values to a specific purpose is the next step. Embodying those values and living that purpose in our everyday behavior is the ultimate move. How, in the face of all the pulls to survival behaviors, do we make that happen?

CHAPTER EIGHTEEN ACTION STEPS

- At the end of the workday or before you go to sleep, take a few minutes to ponder this question: "When did my more primitive, survival instincts guide my actions today?" Next, ask yourself, "How would I have behaved at my best?"
- Practice mindfulness. Once in the morning and once in the afternoon, stop and take a few moments, as you breathe in and out, to simply be aware of what's arising and then let it pass. You may notice physical sensations, emotions, or thoughts. Learning to observe yourself is a way to free yourself from the compulsion to act on every feeling that arises.

CHAPTER NINETEEN

We're All in This Together

It is through reflection that we define what really matters in our lives. It's defining a specific purpose that fuels our actions. As the character Princeton sums it up in the musical *Avenue Q:* "Purpose. It's that little flame that lights a fire under your ass. Purpose. It keeps you going strong , like a car with a full tank of gas."

The need for purpose is unique to human beings. We're the only species capable of reflecting on why we're here. "Your time is limited, so don't waste it living someone else's life," Apple CEO Steven Jobs told Stanford's graduating class in 2005, just a year after he was diagnosed with pancreatic cancer at the age of forty-nine. "Don't be trapped by dogma—which is living with the results of other people's thinking. Don't let the noise of others' opinions drown out your own inner voice. And most important, have the courage to follow your heart and intuition. They somehow already know what you truly want to become."

We can find purpose and motivation in many pursuits, from making a living, to doing our work with excellence, to expressing ourselves creatively, to building wealth and power. The energy of spiritual purpose is unique because it's typically derived from serving something larger than our self-interest. The hunger for purpose is universal and transcends any specific religion or set of beliefs. Adding value to others, and to the common good, gives us a powerful source of energy in the form of meaning and significance. The more we contribute, the more valuable we feel. So how exactly can we cultivate the behaviors that characterize us at our best—the energy of the upper-right spirit quadrant—and also take care of our more basic needs?

Teleologists believe there is an inherent and ultimate purpose in nature and therefore in our lives. Others, like Viktor Frankl, believe the reverse: that it's our responsibility in life to create a meaningful purpose. Either way, purpose represents a specific intention, a course of action, an aim we are either pointed toward or toward which we point ourselves. We're trained through our education to accumulate knowledge, build skills, and seek a career. We're rarely taught how, practically and intentionally, to develop a sense of purpose.

We saw this vividly in the fall of 2008, when we began working with ninth-graders at the Riverdale Country School, an independent high school in the Bronx, on a project we called "The One Big Thing." Our goal was to give these fourteen- and fifteen-year-olds the opportunity to pursue a project they felt passionate about in a school day otherwise filled with classes they were required to take.

To our initial surprise, many of the kids found it challenging to identify something they really wanted to do. Few of them had ever been given the opportunity and the encouragement to pursue an interest purely for its own sake. Over the months, a high percentage of the kids embraced the challenge and brought great enthusiasm to projects that ranged from building a skateboard to composing a rock opera to creating a fantasy baseball league to building a dollhouse to writing and performing a rap. (You can watch a video about "The One Big Thing" at www.theenergyproject.com.)

The pilot was so successful that nearly all of the participants signed up to do it again as tenth-graders. We've also launched it with a new group of ninth-graders, and twice as many of them signed up the second year. The most common response we get from adults who watch the video is "Wow, I'd really like to do that myself." What would you choose to do if your organization allowed you to devote 10 or 20 percent of your time to a project you felt passionate about doing? What would happen if you suggested to your supervisor that you devote some percentage of your time to such a project? Simply thinking systematically about what interests you most deeply can be highly motivating and inspiring.

DO WHAT YOU LOVE

Purpose is grounded in a feeling. "What do I most love doing?" is the natural starting point. We all bring more energy to the activities we enjoy, and pleasure itself sustains our energy. Think about a time when you felt most alive or when your enjoyment of doing something was so great that you completely lost track of time. Were you doing it by yourself or in collaboration with others? What exactly made it so engaging? In my own case, for example, it's figuring out why people do what they do and understanding how the disparate aspects of our lives fit together and influence one another. I love doing this on my own, and equally so in collaboration with others.

It was during the final days of a long economic boom that Drew Gilpin Faust gave her first baccalaureate ceremony address, as Harvard University's new president, to the graduating class of 2008. Her talk was prompted by conversations she'd had with dozens of undergraduates who were struggling with career choices. "Is it necessary," she asked the students, "to decide between remunerative work and meaningful work? . . . Finance, Wall Street, 'recruiting' have become the symbol of this dilemma, representing a set of issues that is much broader and deeper than just one career path. . . . You are worried because you want to have both a meaningful life and a successful one. If you don't try to do what you love—whether it is painting or biology or finance; if you don't pursue what you think will be most meaningful, you will regret it. Life is long. There is always time for Plan B. But don't begin with it. . . . Find work you love. It is hard to be happy if you spend more than half your waking hours doing something you don't."

From an energy perspective, it's also more efficient to nurture the skills that come most easily to us. These emerge through some immeasurable blend of genetics, the encouragement of others, the investment we make in disciplined practice, and the rewards we get for our efforts along the way, especially early in our lives. Ultimately, though, passion can almost always trump genetics. As Anders Ericsson and others have shown so convincingly, we're all capable of developing expertise at virtually anything if we're willing to work at it deliberately enough. The limitations we set are mostly our own. Passion is an extraordinary fuel for persevering through frustration as we move along the learning curve. It also helps keep us committed to growth once we've achieved excellence. If you don't truly love what you do, simply being good at it will never be deeply energizing or satisfying.

WALKING THE TALK

There are multiple dimensions of a satisfying, well-lived life, and it helps to begin the search for purpose by clarifying our priorities. What follows is a simple version of an alignment exercise we do with clients. You can do it here or re-create it on a separate piece of paper. In column 1 below, rate how important each of these dimensions is in your life on a scale of 1 to 10, with 1 low and 10 high. This isn't a forced ranking, so you can give each category as high or low a number as you'd like:

In column 2, estimate how much energy you invest in this dimen-

	1	2	3
WORK/CAREER			
FINANCIAL SUCCESS			
SPOUSE/PARTNER			
CHILDREN			
FAMILY			
FRIENDS			
FITNESS			
CREATIVITY/ SELF-EXPRESSION			
ENJOYMENT/ HAPPINESS			
LEARNING/ GROWTH			
SERVICE TO OTHERS/ CONTRIBUTION			

sion of your life, using the same scale. Finally, for column 3, subtract the numbers in column 2 from those in column 1, and write down your answers. It's possible that you'll get a negative number in one or two categories, and that's fine. If you're not sure about an answer, try to imagine what someone who knows you well would say—or simply ask that person.

Column 1 is a reflection of what you value—what you aspire to in that dimension of your life. Column 2 is a reflection of how you actually live. Column 3 is a measure of the gap between the two. Obviously, the ideal number for every category in column 3 is zero, which would mean that in every facet of your life you invest your time and energy directly in proportion to how important you feel it is to you. That level of alignment is exceedingly rare. In all likelihood, you'll have several categories for which there is a notable gap between column 1 and column 2. In our experience, a gap of 2 is worth exploring, and a gap of 3 or more is highly significant.

Typically, people assign a high value to most of the categories in column 1, but have lower numbers for several of them in column 2. Occasionally people discover they're investing more time and energy in a dimension than they feel it deserves. That's most common, we find, in their jobs, where people feel compelled to work hard but aren't especially engaged by what they're doing.

In most cases, however, those we've worked with find their intentions in column 1 run out ahead of the time and energy they invest in column 2. There are many reasons this is so, but it's when we feel under threat and most overwhelmed that we tend to behave in contradiction to our deepest values. Such behaviors show up in the upper-left spirit quadrant. What do your own worst behaviors look like, especially in the areas of your life where you've revealed the greatest gaps?

Often the gap is simply about neglect—doing nothing at all or less than you believe you should in a given area of your life. If that's the case, what's the story you've been telling yourself that has made the gap acceptable until now? What's the cost to you and to others in your life? Are you okay with the trade-offs you're making, consciously or unconsciously? It's in the crucible of high demand that we're challenged to translate our best intentions into our best behaviors. If you say your children, or your spouse, or your health, is a 10 in importance in column 1, but you give them only a 5 or a 6 in terms of time and energy, what do you need to do to close that gap? What ritual could you build that would create a better alignment between what you say you value and how you actually live?

CLOSING THE ALIGNMENT GAP

For Simon Ashby, vice president of operations at Sony Europe, the disconnect he found most distressing was in his relationship with his daughter. "When I first began doing this exercise," he told us, "I thought to myself, 'I'm pretty well sorted out across these things.' On closer reflection, I realized that the time I spent with my daughter probably wasn't the highest quality. She's from my first marriage, so I only have a certain amount of days with her. The story I was telling myself was 'I'm a forty-five-year-old man and she's an eleven-year-old girl, and what have we in common?' We'd just sit around when we were together, and I wasn't really that involved with her. I decided to make a ritual that I would always plan ahead what to do with her when we were together. We began to take all kinds of excursions, but what it really did was to make me truly be with my daughter when we were together. Four years later, she's fifteen—always a difficult time for kids—and we have a terrific relationship. My daughter is so important in my life, and I don't know how good I would have been if I hadn't been intentional about my time with her over the last few years."

For Adam Williams, the head of strategy for Sony UK, struggling with the gap between what he valued and how he actually lived resulted in an unexpected insight. "Being able to reflect deeply on these questions led to a breakthrough," he told us. "I'd always thought I needed to emulate my father and uncle and set up my own business. At the back of my mind, throughout my career in the corporate world, I'd be thinking, 'What is the business I need to set up?' But when we did the spirit work, I began to ask myself, 'If I was really motivated to be an entrepreneur, then why haven't I done it? Why I am still doing this work?' I realized it had been about the expectations set by my father's achievements. In reality, the scope of work at Sony—the intellectual challenge, teamwork, and freedom to be an innovator—

was something I'd be very unlikely to achieve in setting up my own business.

"Seeing that really reenergized me. It put me back in charge of the choices I was making, and it made me feel as if I had renewed my contract with the company. If I worked a long evening, I felt clearer about why I was doing it. If I took time off in the afternoon to attend my children's sports day, I didn't feel guilty, because I was giving my all at work. It just seemed that these things were now joined up. I think I'm a better father and husband as a result. I don't carry my work home anymore, and I'm able to switch between work and family more effectively. The lightbulb moment for me was the realization that no one was making me do what I was doing. I'd made a choice, and I'd made it for a reason. I love what I do."

MAKING WORK MATTER

The second key to fueling purpose is putting what you love to do and do best into the service of something beyond your immediate self-interest. "The big insight I got doing this work," explains Matthew Lang, the managing director of Sony South Africa, "is that I don't get my value from capabilities like marketing or sales. I get it from empowering people and bringing out the best of their skills. Having that clear definition of purpose means it now takes precedence over everything else. And because I'm clear about what I want and who I want to work with, I've gotten much more focused. It's also made my job easier and much more satisfying."

Pedro Jesus is a twenty-nine-year-old sales manager in the consumer division of Sony Portugal who has won numerous awards for his leadership. His job is in sales, but that isn't how he finds his purpose. "I feel most aligned with myself when I help others to find their inspiration and creativity," he says. "Occasionally this brings me into conflict with the more pragmatic concerns of the people who work for me. Their job is to make sales, and they can get frustrated with me because I want them to bring vision and creativity to everything they do. But I also know that on balance, they would rather I challenge them to seek creative breakthroughs than simply let them settle for the status quo.

"In doing this work on my spirit, I realized that it's all connected. Not taking better care of myself physically, because I was working so hard, was actually undermining my passion and my purpose. I've gotten much more honest with myself now, and the result is I've given up smoking, reduced my alcohol intake, and made sleep more important. I've built boundaries between work and home that make me feel more satisfied and more in control. I've become the guardian of my spirit rather than just its beneficiary."

UBUNTU

Purpose extends our sphere of influence not through the accumulation and exercise of power, but by giving us a clear route to adding value to others. As Ian McCallum puts it, "We are obliged to nurture an intelligence capable of making the shift from short-term survival thinking—me versus you—to one that consciously grasps the long-term significance of I and Thou." Practically, we must operate less from our primitive instincts and more from the wiser, more embracing perspective of our best selves.

In modern Africa, the word *ubuntu* is used to describe the way in which generosity of spirit connects us to the energy and affirmation of a larger community. "A person with *ubuntu*," explains Archbishop Desmond Tutu, "is open and available to others, affirming of others, does not feel threatened that others are able and good, for he or she has a proper self-assurance that comes from knowing that he or she belongs in a greater whole and is diminished when others are humiliated or diminished."

No career automatically provides a purpose, but no job precludes our finding a purpose in it, either. It isn't the role we fill that prompts a sense of purpose but how we choose to approach whatever work we do. As Marian Wright Edelman puts it, "We must not, in trying to think about how we can make a big difference, ignore the small daily differences we can make which, over time, add up to the big differences that we often cannot foresee."

Some years ago, I took my oldest daughter to get her license at the local motor vehicle bureau. It was a typical day in a government office, marked by long lines, disgruntled customers, and stone-faced clerks.

I sat down with Kate to wait our turn, and after several minutes I noticed a single clerk who was smiling and laughing with each client who came to her window. "I guarantee you," I said to Kate, "there's some good reason that woman is so different than every other employee here."

As it happened, we eventually ended up being called to this woman's counter. "I have one question I want to ask you," I said, to Kate's mortification. "All the people you're working with look as if they can't wait for the day to end. You've got a big smile on your face, and you seem like you're in a great mood. Why is that?"

"I'll tell you exactly why that is," the woman said, reaching out for a photograph in front of her. She turned it around. It was a young boy, perhaps six years old. "That's my son," she said. "This job is what's making it possible for me to take care of him and send him to a good school, so he can get the education I never did and get the kind of job I never could. Anytime I start feeling a little frustrated, I just look at that picture, and I feel good again. That's why you see me smiling."

This woman knew exactly why she was coming to work every day. Whatever limitations and frustrations her fellow clerks felt doing their jobs, she felt energized by her deeper purpose all day long. One happy consequence was that she shared her positive energy with every person who had the good fortune to show up at her counter. She made *them* feel better, which made her feel better about herself. Without any conscious intent, she created a virtuous circle that got wider with every connection she made. Much as Kate and I did, the people she encountered walked out the door of the Department of Motor Vehicles feeling a little better about life, instead of a little bit worse.

WHEN MEANING IS THE PRIMARY FUEL

Purpose and the community it creates can be a source of positive energy even when our more basic needs go largely unmet. When we spent time with intensive care unit nurses at the Cleveland Clinic, we discovered they felt severely overburdened by their jobs in a range of ways. Chronic staffing shortages forced them to stick closely by the bedsides of their critically ill patients. They rarely had time for meals, much less breaks, and they often worked twelve- to fourteen-hour shifts without eating anything and sometimes without even sitting down. And as hard as they worked, they felt painfully devalued by the doctors whose patients they looked after.

What kept these nurses so passionately committed to their work, even though they had no time to take care of themselves and received little or no appreciation from their superiors? Above all, they told us, it was the deep sense of satisfaction they derived from caring for their patients. In short, they survived almost entirely on spiritual energy, the feeling that what they were doing truly mattered and made a difference.

Even the opportunity to save people's lives is not, it turns out, a guaranteed source of purpose and significance. The Cleveland Clinic surgeons we met worked under conditions nearly as demoralizing as those the nurses described. They put in long hours, were expected to meet high quotas for the number of surgeries they performed, and felt undervalued by the hospital's administrators. They were much better compensated than the nurses, and they enjoyed far more prestige. But many of the surgeons, we found, brought less passion to their work than the nurses did.

The biggest difference, we eventually concluded, was that the surgeons felt much less emotionally connected to their patients. "Yes, I save lives every day," one surgeon told us. "But I sometimes feel like I'm working in a factory. I barely have time to see my patients, except during surgery, when they're knocked out. My favorite experience is when I can find the time to call patients after they've left the hospital, just to see how they're doing. I can't tell you how surprised and thrilled they are to get those calls and how much satisfaction I get from making them. But the truth is, I don't have time to call my patients nearly often enough."

THE TRAGEDY OF THE COMMONS

Having a purpose larger than our immediate self-interest serves others and makes us feel better about ourselves, but it's also increasingly crucial to our survival. That's because we live in a world of increasing population and accelerating demand for the earth's finite resources and critical threats to the planet's sustainability.

In 1968, an ecologist named Garrett Hardin foresaw our current predicament and wrote an article about it for the journal *Science* entitled "The Tragedy of the Commons." Hardin began by pointing out that despite extraordinary advances in fields such as science, medicine, and engineering, there remains a class of problems that can't be solved by technical means but instead require a fundamental shift in our values and in our resulting behavior.

To illustrate his point, Hardin painted a hypothetical scenario: "Picture a pasture open to all. It is to be expected that each herdsmen will try to keep as many cattle as possible on the commons." This approach works fine for all of the herdsmen, Hardin explained, as long as the capacity of the land exceeds the number of cattle that make use of it. At some point, however, the ratio reverses. The land is no longer sufficient to support all of the cattle and a day of reckoning arrives. This is the tragedy of the commons. "Each man," wrote Hardin, "is locked into a system that compels him to increase his herd without limit—in a world that is limited. Ruin is the destination toward which all men rush, each pursuing his own best interest in a society that believes in the freedom of the commons."

Much as we might seek to deny it or avoid it, this is the tragedy that we, too, increasingly face. We're all herdsmen, living in a system that encourages us to increase our herd without limit. But the ethic of self-interest is sustainable only in a world of unlimited resources. Consider just population statistics. In the early 1800s, the world's population hit 1 billion people. As the environmental writer Douglas Chadwick points out, it took *a million years* to reach that first billion. It took just 130 more to reach 2 billion, and only 30 more to get to 3 billion, in 1960. By 2000, that number had doubled to 6 billion. A decade later, as I write these words, there are 7 billion people on Earth. At the current rates of increase, we'll reach 10 billion by midcentury.

For better or for worse, we're all in this together. Much as rising demands in our own lives are overtaxing our personal energy reserves, so it's depleting the external reserves we depend on: food, water, clean air, and fossil fuels. To survive, we must find ways to renew the resources we use up, both internal and external. Our challenge is to add value to the commons, not deplete it. When we focus too narrowly on our short-term satisfaction, we're contributing to our long-term demise.

CHAPTER NINETEEN ACTION STEPS

- We bring more energy to the activities we most enjoy. What do you love doing? Think about a time when you were doing something that made you feel more fully alive or that you found so absorbing you lost track of time. Write down in as much detail as possible each aspect of this experience. Were you doing it alone or in collaboration with others? Where were you, and did the environment make a difference? What precisely did you find most exhilarating? What lessons from this experience can you apply to your everyday work?
- It's one thing to say something is important to you, another to live in alignment with that belief. Go back to page 252 and complete the "Walking the Talk" exercise, if you haven't already. Which gap between column 1 and column 2 do you find most unacceptable? What is one behavior you could add into your life to close that gap?
- Having a purpose that transcends our immediate self-interest extends our sphere of influence by providing a clear route to adding value to others. Our small, daily choices can add up over time and ultimately make a big difference. Choose one behavior you could add into your life every day that would add value to others.

CHAPTER TWENTY

Purpose for Passion

THE SPIRITUAL QUADRANTS

To fuel spiritual energy, an organization must define a set of shared values and a purpose beyond its continuing profitability. That begins with asking the same questions of itself that we pose to individuals: "Who are you?" (What do you stand for?) And "What do you really want?" (What is your purpose?) Most large organizations dutifully take on this task, but often without much enthusiasm or commitment. Not surprising, the results seldom have much impact. Can you name the values, the vision and the mission of your organization? Do they have any influence on your motivation or behavior?

Consider the example of a large company with characteristically lofty values: integrity, respect, excellence, and communication. Those were the stated values of Enron, the company whose massive accounting fraud led to its bankruptcy and the imprisonment of its top executives. Here was Enron's definition of integrity: "When we say we will do something, we will do it; when we say we cannot or will not do something, then we won't do it." Or respect: "We do not tolerate abusive or disrespectful treatment. Ruthlessness, callousness and arrogance don't belong here." Say what?

Or how about Reynolds American, the tobacco company whose cigarette brands include Camel, Salem, Winston, and Pall Mall? "We do the right thing," its values statement says. "We treat every person with respect, fairness and integrity." The right thing? Is that possible when your business is making and marketing cigarettes? The Reynolds America mission, meanwhile, is to be "the innovative tobacco company totally committed to building value through responsible growth." But what exactly *is* responsible growth for a tobacco company that acknowledges on its Web site that "Cigarette smoking is a leading cause of preventable deaths in the United States" and that "No tobacco product has been shown to be safe and without risks." Wouldn't it be more accurate for Reynolds to say its mission is to "convince people around the world to smoke as many cigarettes as possible, without being put out of business by the government or the courts?"

These may be extreme examples, but there is a deep disconnect between what many companies say they stand for and what they actually do. These disconnects take a toll on employee engagement and on their productivity. A review of more than 150 leadership studies found that integrity is the value employees care most about in their leaders. Honesty is second, and humility is third. The other qualities employees most value include care and appreciation, respect for others, fairness, listening responsively, and reflectiveness. "These leaders," the study concluded, "were more likely to motivate people, inspire trust, promote good relationships and achieve goals including increased productivity, lower rate of turnover and improved employee health."

The best evidence of an organization's values and mission is the behavior of its leaders. "Many leadership theories emphasize the need for the leader to articulate an inspiring vision," writes Laura Reave, the author of the review of leadership studies. "But what is important is not so much words but rather actions: the level of ethics demonstrated, the respect and compassion shown to others." Employees are seven times more likely to be loyal to leaders they believe have high integrity, for example, than to those they do not.

AN INSPIRING PLACE TO WORK

So what are the lived values and the purpose of *your* organization based on the way it treats people, the products it creates, the services it provides, and the way it deals with customers and clients? Do those values and that purpose make you proud to work there? To whatever extent they don't, what does your organization need to do—or stop doing—to become a more inspiring place in which to work?

If you lead or manage others, here are the sorts of questions you might ask yourself and request others to answer about you:

- Do you actively support people in taking care of themselves physically? Do you model these behaviors yourself?
- Do you truly value, regularly recognize, and express appreciation to those who work for you?
- Do you respect and trust your employees and treat them as adults capable of making their own decisions about how best to get their work done?
- Do you believe passionately in what you're doing, and do you give the people who work for you a compelling reason beyond a paycheck to come to work every day?

"Leaders who emphasize spiritual values," Reave concludes, "are often able to awaken a latent motivation in others that has been found to increase both their satisfaction and productivity at work. These leaders do not so much transform individuals as awaken existing motivation."

The most universally despised of all qualities among leaders is egocentricity—selfishness and self-absorption. People are more inspired by a compelling purpose, the research shows, than by a leader's personal charisma. In two-thirds of the companies that Jim Collins studied in *Good to Great,* for example, he found that the presence of a leader with a "gargantuan" ego eventually contributed to "the demise or continued mediocrity of the company." The best leaders, Collins concluded, "subjugate their own needs to the greater ambition of something larger and more lasting than themselves."

Two widely recognized schools of leadership draw explicitly on spiritual energy as a critical element. "Transformational leadership" is a term coined by the historian James MacGregor Burns in 1970 to describe great political leaders. The core principle is value-driven attentiveness to the needs of followers: supporting, coaching and mentoring them; celebrating their contributions; pushing them to take risks, learn, and grow; and inspiring in them a strong sense of purpose around meaningful goals. Transformational leaders set high standards and encourage those they lead to be less concerned with their personal agendas and more concerned with looking out for one another and for the organization as a whole. Transformational leaders also tend to be focused on "why"—the purpose of their actions. By contrast, conventional "transactional" leaders are more narrowly concerned with "how"—the tactics and steps required to reach any given goal.

Robert Greenleaf coined the term "servant leadership" in 1970, six years after his retirement from AT&T, where he spent forty years in charge of management development. Servant leadership starts, he has written, "with the natural feeling that one wants to serve. . . . Then conscious choice brings one to aspire to lead. That person is sharply different from one who is *leader* first, perhaps because of an unusual power drive or to acquire material possessions. . . . The difference manifests itself in the care taken by the servant-first to make sure that other people's highest priority needs are being served. The best test, and difficult to administer, is: Do those served grow as persons? Do they, *while being served,* become healthier, wiser, freer, more autonomous, more likely themselves to become servants?"

Alan Mulally is an example of a rare CEO who sees his job as a calling. "In my mind, my life's work is to serve," he explains. "I have one life, an integrated life that includes my work, my personal life, my spiritual life, and my family life. I manage all those pieces into my schedule, and I don't separate them out. I make sure everything I do serves one of those, and I commit my time and energy to those pieces in an integrated way. I build in exercise and tennis and hanging out with my wife. When my kids were growing up, I might go to a business meeting and then to a soccer game or a school recital. It's all part of the whole.

"The more each of us know what we're really contributing to, the more motivated and excited and inspired we are. The higher the order, the more energy it generates. So if you ask me if I'm here to make a living, or to be the best CEO in the history of mankind, or to make safe and efficient transportation that enables people to have a better life, I'd say it's the latter. I have one life, and I want to commit myself to something important. I want to go for the highest calling I can, and I do everything I can to help everyone I work with do the same thing."

DOING THE RIGHT THING

By coincidence, we've worked extensively at two very different divisions of Sony: Sony Pictures Entertainment, which is based in Los Angeles and makes movies and television, and Sony Europe, which is based in Surrey and markets and sells the company's consumer electronics across Europe. In their own ways, both companies set out to redefine and reenergize themselves by reconsidering their values and purpose, beginning with the way they invested in their employees.

For Michael Lynton and Amy Pascal, the co-chairmen of Sony Pictures, the changes they've overseen grew out of an explicit desire to better meet employee needs. The company was already successful, but Pascal, in particular, was determined to change the culture for the better. We began our work with the senior leadership team, focusing on them first as individuals. When leaders see an impact in their own lives, they're far more motivated to extend their experiences into the organization. Many Sony leaders made initial changes at the physical level, but over time they also created rituals around living their deepest values more fully in their everyday behaviors.

Pascal, for example, recognized that she instinctively avoids conflict and decided it was important to build a ritual that would help her to be more direct. She began by asking herself a simple question—"What is the right thing to do here?"—when she found herself in a situation that felt uncomfortable. She defined "the right thing" as doing what would serve Sony Pictures best in the long term, even if it made her personally uncomfortable in the short term. Often, that meant saying no to someone she liked or respected and didn't want to offend. Over time, the senior team created a variation on this theme for themselves, in the form of the "Code" ritual we described in chapter 13. "Saying the word 'Code' forces the other person to tell you what they're really feeling or what they really need when it's easier not to say anything," Pascal explains. "Ultimately, it's just one more reminder to people about being real."

Lynton, who is more introverted and less instinctively social than Pascal, built a ritual around being more intentionally appreciative of others. He made it a practice, for example, to regularly write notes and call people in the company as a way of recognizing their accomplishments. Other executives built rituals that not only helped them to be more efficient but also to better embody their values. Gary Martin, who heads studio operations, made it a practice to turn off his e-mail entirely at certain points during the day and to take time in the afternoon to walk around and talk to his people about something other than business. David Bishop, who runs Home Entertainment, built a ritual around multitasking. "I'd often be on the phone with someone and reading my e-mails at the same time," he explains. "I realized that I wasn't truly listening to people, which is important to me, and I also wasn't really giving the right attention to what I was reading. Now I do one or the other but not both. I'm a better leader, and I'm more efficient in my job."

Keith LeGoy, the head of distribution for Sony Pictures Television International, focused his ritual on triggers—both as a practical tool but also as a way to treat people with more generosity of spirit. "The first step is awareness," he explains. "The quadrants helped give a name to triggers and why they happen. It sort of normalized them as something that everybody experiences. Now when I feel triggered, the first thing I do is stop, take ten seconds, and breathe deeply. That helps me to avoid getting emotionally pulled in. Then I can begin to think and reengage my more rational side. I'll ask myself, 'How can I collaboratively approach this person in order to accomplish what I want?' I don't negate them. I try to hold their value and understand their point of view even if I don't agree with it. When you demonstrate to people that you truly value their perspective, they're disarmed and appreciative. It also gives me a more balanced view, so it's a win-win."

Pascal and Lynton shared their vision with all employees at a town hall meeting in the fall of 2008. It was grounded in a commitment to very specific values. "We've done well as a company," Lynton began, "but Amy and I have been wrestling lately with this question: What comes next? Where do we go from here? We decided that we needed to change the fundamental culture of Sony Pictures. And that's not about putting words on paper, it's about creating a feeling in your gut. Our culture has to make people excited and energetic about coming to work each day. Amy and I believe that creating a culture which can help us deal with chaos, work more closely together, and be more excited about our work depends on creating a community that's based on trust and transparency."

The core value they highlighted was an extension of Pascal's own commitment to "doing the right thing." "There are lots of behaviors that get in the way of winning by making people feel devalued," Pascal told the gathered employees. "When people feel devalued, they become unfocused, and when you're not focused, you can't win." She offered some examples: "You're trying to talk to somebody, and they're checking their BlackBerry. You walk into someone's office to have a conversation, and they make three phone calls while you're standing there. You're on your way to a meeting, only to find it's been canceled again or is starting twenty minutes later. These behaviors generate bad feelings. We want to provide you with as many resources and tools as possible to help everyone break these habits. It isn't just about being number one. That alone can't sustain us over time. It's about focusing on 'doing the right thing.'

"Everybody knows what it means to do the right thing. It means serving the greatest good even when it doesn't seem to be in your immediate self-interest. It means you don't make choices out of fear of failure or just because they seem expedient. You don't make choices that are quicker or easier or because it's what everyone else is doing.

I'm convinced that if we institute a culture of doing the right thing, we will be number one . . . and much more."

The second aspect of the vision had to do with the kind of culture they wanted to create for employees. "We're already known as talent-friendly," Pascal went on. "These talent relationships are not going to be any less important, but our relationships with each other are simply going to be more important. We want to be an *employee*-friendly studio. That's what is going to make our company not only successful but also great. And the way we are going to make Sony Pictures the best place to work for all of you is by investing in you. We want you to feel excited when you come to work in the morning but still energized when you go home at night. We want to create a culture where you feel valued and there is a spirit of reciprocity and mutual respect."

Three years after we launched our work with the senior executives, nearly every one of the 6,000 employees at Sony Pictures had gone through some version of our training, including those in Europe and Asia. Lynton and Pascal stuck with their commitment despite the difficult economy. More than 90 percent of those we've trained say it has helped them bring more energy to work every day. Eighty-eight percent say that the experience has made them more focused and productive. Eighty-four percent say they feel better able to manage demands and more engaged in their jobs.

At the organizational level, Sony Pictures has created a series of support structures for employees. It has built an intranet site devoted to the work we did and issues a regular newsletter describing people's experiences and insights. The company now subsidizes a healthy meal and a salad bar at a newly built employee cafeteria. It has also stocked vending machines with healthier foods and hired a dietician who is available for consultations with employees. The company has built a new, fully equipped gym on the lot that offers exercise classes, as well as yoga, nutrition, and wellness classes. It has created a large grassy commons area where people can relax and hang out. Sony also offers its employees paid time off each month to volunteer their services to nonprofit organizations.

"This has been about believing that the culture of the company is as important as the product," Pascal explains. "We're not fully there yet, but we now have a common language and shared principles, and this experience has been enormously bonding. The culture we're creating is the adhesive. It's what holds the company together and makes you nimble and flexible enough that you're able to respond to whatever is happening in the marketplace."

PERHAPS WE CAN CHANGE MORE THAN WE THINK

At Sony Europe, the process evolved in a very different way. We began our work there in the wake of several years during which the consumer electronics division had struggled with rising competition from South Korea and China. Ultimately, the company was forced to close several factories and initiate significant layoffs, putting more demand on those who remained and driving down morale. In 2005, the division got a new president, Fujio Nishida, who had worked previously for Sony in Japan, Canada, Australia, and the United States. It was Roy White, the head of human resources under Nishida, who brought us in with a mandate to help reenergize employees who were feeling discouraged and burned out. White himself was feeling the same way.

"For two years," White explains, "I was barely holding on—struggling with budgets, reducing head count, managing the unions, and doing all the things in HR I don't like doing. Things that drained my spirit." White recognized that people were working longer and harder than ever and that it wasn't sustainable. He was committed to reenergizing the workforce, but he was also passionate about creating a truly great place to work—one in which people came to their jobs with a sense of purpose and pride.

Much as Lynton and Pascal did at Sony Pictures Entertainment, Nishida agreed to pilot our work with his team of executives from all around Europe. "We were definitely taking a risk that these very senior, hardened executives would see this as a complete waste of time," White explains. "As it turned out, the feedback was incredible. The first response we got was 'It's such a relief that I'm not the only one who feels overwhelmed.' The second thing was that our leaders began to make significant changes in their lives. The third thing was that they began to see bigger possibilities for the company. We clearly tapped into something deep."

Our work began with taking four groups of senior executives—

seventy in all—through a four-day version of our curriculum. At that point, Nishida and White made the decision to roll it out to 2,000 leaders and managers across the organization. Several leaders chose to make the work available to employees at every level. In some cases, they led the sessions themselves after training with us. "The work we did gave us permission to discuss basic needs such as eating, sleep, and exercise and make the link with business performance," explains Nishida. "It also helped many senior managers make really significant changes in their lives without the organization having changed first. That got many of us thinking, 'Perhaps we can change more than we thought we could.' It helped us build the confidence and the trust to take on the most fundamental assumption in our business—that if the parent company didn't change, then neither could we. We began to see each other in a new light, outside the limitations of the existing culture, so the true talents of our people could shine. We found a new voice and sense of purpose."

Steve Dowdle, the managing director of Sony UK, took the lead in implementing changes that ultimately spread throughout Europe. "This has not been a tinkering exercise," he said. "It's a radical transformation from product-centric to customer-centered and from being told what we're supposed to do to defining for ourselves who we are. We began by giving people the tools to build their own capacity, but then we needed to build the capacity of the organization as well. The work we did on ourselves—especially the spiritual work—helped us focus on the need to create a stronger purpose for the business. I had to take our new business model to Japan five times to get approval. I'm tenacious, but without knowing why you really want something to change, the forces of corporate pragmatism set in and you settle for less. The clarity of our new purpose—to serve the customer better than anyone else—helped us move from being a product-focused arm of Japan to a much more dynamic, locally focused business. That's been incredibly energizing and inspiring."

Roy Dickens was the executive charged with bringing the new customer-focused strategy to life in the United Kingdom. "What I came to understand," he says, "is that I love change. Not for its own sake but because it brings out the best in me as a leader—creating, motivating, and inspiring a team with the passion to change the status quo. When you lead a team through change, you create a sense of family and community, which is good for everyone. As we implemented the new strategy, it quickly became apparent that my job would be one of the first to go. What amazed me was that I didn't fall into survival mode, even when I realized I was designing myself out of a job. I let go of the fear, and it was liberating. The reason that was possible is that I was doing something I believed in." As it turned out, Dickens was rewarded for his efforts with a new job as head of Sony's retail operations.

"I've seen the value at every level of the work we did," says Matthew Lang, Sony South Africa's managing director. "For me, the physical benefits have been huge, because I know now that I won't burn out. At the emotional level, I've learned a set of tools about how to manage myself and others that will serve me for the rest of my life. At the mental level, it was liberating, coming from a background as an engineer, to pay more attention to my gut instincts and to realize that I could actually learn to be creative. Maybe most important of all is the spirit level. I feel like I now have a map for my life, and I know I'm not alone in that. The best people in our organization have a renewed sense of purpose, which gives us more energy to face the challenges ahead. Without the culture shift, which has been profound, I think we would have lost many of our best people. We're a much better company to work for because so much more trust is being placed in people."

In Roy White's view the key to the transformation was tapping the energy of a purpose that came from within employees themselves. "We eventually created a tipping point," he explains, "a critical mass of people prepared to be brave enough to work on what they cared about and what they believed was right. I think that's what really came out of this work. It's always there in people, isn't it? It's just giving them the permission to allow that side of themselves to grow."

In December 2008, Fujio Nishida recorded a holiday video message for all Sony employees across Europe. He sent it out in the midst of a recession that had battered Sony's electronics division, but he chose not to dwell on the immediate problems. "What is the future of this company?" he exhorted employees to ask themselves. "Is it something I can be proud of? That I would be happy that my children or grandchildren joined? Purpose and creativity are essential. Just focusing on business and financial objectives, you never think of that. But we can change Sony's destiny from here and that's a big idea. I want all nine thousand people thinking about that."

IT ALL FITS TOGETHER

An organization truly is a living organism—a human community that can realize its highest potential only when each individual is fully valued and feels fully vested in a shared purpose. The better people's needs are met, the better they feel and the better the organism functions as a whole. An organization that invests in its people across all dimensions of their lives and rallies them around an inspiring purpose is actually investing in itself. As individuals grow and increase their capacity, the organism as a whole gets stronger.

Think about this in your own experience. When you deeply believe in something and feel passionate about it, you bring far more energy to it. You have more reason to take care of yourself physically. You're more motivated to build better relationships and exercise control over your emotions. You have more motivation to resist distractions that keep you from focusing on what really matters most. It's all connected.

The best leaders are those with the most spacious, embracing vision of their roles. The wider, deeper, and longer range our awareness is, the bigger our world becomes. "I was never an overly reflective or philosophical person," Eugene O'Kelly, the former CEO of the accounting firm KPMG, wrote in the last months of his life, before he succumbed to brain cancer at the age of fifty-three. "Before my illness, I had considered commitment king among virtues. After I was diagnosed, I came to consider consciousness king among virtues. I began to feel that everyone's first responsibility was to be as conscious as possible all the time. . . . Looking at how some of the people around me had managed their lives, I lamented that they had not been blessed with this jolt to life. They had no real motivation or clear timeline to stop what they were so busy at, to step back, to ask what exactly they were doing with their life. Many of them had money; many of them had more money than they needed. Why was it so scary to ask themselves one simple question: Why am I doing what I'm doing?"

Regularly asking yourself what you stand for and how you want to behave as a result—resisting the default into denial and self-deception—is the key to growing, learning, and evolving. As individuals and as leaders that requires a willingness to embrace ourselves in all our contradictions, complexities, and imperfections. It's contingent on having the strength to resist choosing sides too quickly in the fruitless pursuit of certainty.

It depends on acknowledging the power of our self-serving survival instincts but also having the courage to make conscious choices to behave at our best, especially when we're tempted to default to our worst.

It means recognizing that as addicted as we can become to the speed and intensity of our lives, we're more creative and productive when we move intentionally between effort and renewal, action and reflection.

It's about balancing care for others with care for ourselves, the former because it gives life more meaning, the latter so we can realize our highest potential.

Above all, awareness requires recognizing that we're ultimately interdependent. Together we can enrich and renew the world we share rather than hasten its demise. That's true for each of us as individuals. It's even truer for those of us who are leaders and have the power to influence those we lead. And it is truest of all for organizations. It's in the workplace that we gather together every day and have the greatest collective opportunity to serve the highest good.

This is not just about a new way of working, it's also about a different way of life. It requires is an evolutionary shift in the center of gravity in our lives from "me" to "us." That's an enormous leap, and time is running short. "We have to wake up," writes Ian McCallum, "to the privilege of what it means to be human."

In a world of rising population and dwindling resources, the choice we face is stark. We can continue to be the continuing creatures of our undoing and the dinosaurs of the future, or we can serve as the "keepers of the zoo" and the true guardians of the extraordinary world we've been given.

The world is changing. Are you?

CHAPTER TWENTY ACTION STEPS

- What specific action can you take at work to serve a purpose beyond your immediate self-interest? Even if you can't change the organization you work for, can you behave every day in ways that are more in alignment with your own values and purpose? If you're a leader, can you articulate a purpose that is inspiring and compelling to those you lead?
- The most ineffective leaders are egocentric, selfish, and self-absorbed. How can you step beyond your own needs to better serve the needs of those you lead? If you're an individual contributor, how can you do so with your colleagues?
- The next time you find yourself in a difficult or challenging situation, ask yourself this question: "What is the right thing to do here?" Most of us know deep down the difference between doing the right thing and the wrong thing. Under pressure, we sometimes take the expedient route and then rationalize the choice we've made. Hold yourself to a higher standard.

The Big Ideas

CHAPTER ONE
More and More, Less and Less

The way we're working isn't working, in our own lives or for organizations. The relentless urgency that characterizes most corporate cultures undermines thoughtful deliberation, creativity, engagement, and sustainable high performance.

- The primary value exchange between most employers and employees is time for money. It's a thin, one-dimensional transaction that leaves both sides feeling unsatisfied.
- Rather than trying to get more out of people, organizations are better served by investing more in them and meeting their multidimensional needs in order to fuel greater engagement and more sustainable high performance.
- Human beings need four sources of energy to operate at their best: physical (sustainability), emotional (security), mental (self-expression), and spiritual (significance).
- It's not how much time we invest into our work that determines our productivity but rather the value we produce during the hours we work.
- We're not meant to operate in the same way machines do: at high speeds, for long periods of time, running multiple programs at the same time. Human beings are designed to pulse between the expenditure and the intermittent renewal of energy.

CHAPTER TWO
We Can't Change What We Don't Notice

Human beings have made extraordinary advances in science, medicine, and technology, but we've devoted remarkably little attention to understanding our inner world. We've accumulated vast knowledge but woefully little self-knowledge. Without a richer understanding of what motivates us—and what stands in our way—we will remain insufficiently equipped to take on the vastly more complex challenges ahead.

- Awareness is the key to recognizing the consequences of the choices we're making and their impact on others.
- We each have an infinite capacity for self-deception. We become skilled at denial because it helps us to avoid discomfort in the short term, but it exacts a toll in the long term.
- Learning to observe our feelings as they arise, rather than simply acting them out, allows us to make more reflective, intentional choices about how we want to show up in the world.
- We must learn to embrace opposites. By celebrating one set of qualities and undervaluing another—courage or prudence, confidence or humility, tenacity or flexibility—we lose access to essential dimensions of ourselves and others.
- Because all virtues are interconnected, any strength overused ultimately becomes a liability. Honesty without compassion, for example, is cruelty. We create the highest value not by focusing solely on our strengths or ignoring our weaknesses but by being attentive to both.

CHAPTER THREE
We're Creatures of Habit

Will and discipline are wildly overrated. Even when the need for change is obvious and our intentions are strong, we often fall short. Making changes that last requires building positive rituals—highly specific behaviors that become automatic over time and no longer require conscious intention.

- We are creatures of habit. Ninety-five percent of our behaviors occur automatically, unconsciously or in reaction to an external demand. Only 5 percent of our actions are consciously selected.
- Research suggests that we have one reservoir of will and discipline and it gets progressively depleted by each act of conscious will. Stress of any kind reduces our self-regulatory reserves.
- The more our behaviors are repeated and routinized, the more they occur without conscious effort and the less energy they require.
- The key to building successful rituals is to define the behaviors in a highly precise way and to do them at specific designated times.
- Resistance to making change is built into the process, and long-term success requires addressing the reasons we don't want to make any given change.

CHAPTER FOUR
Feeling the Pulse

Our most fundamental need is to spend and renew energy. Most of us spend more energy than we adequately renew. All systems in our body pulse rhythmically when we're healthy—heartbeat, brain waves, body temperature, blood pressure, and hormone levels.

- Even in sedentary jobs, physical energy is the foundation on which high performance rests. Failing to take care of ourselves physically ensures that we'll ultimately be suboptimal at whatever we do.
- Every activity in our lives has an energy consequence—eating, movement, sleep, work, and relationships.
- Maintenance and refueling are essential to sustainable high performance. The higher the demand we're facing, the greater and more frequent the need for renewal.
- We're most effective at work when we alternate between active forms of renewal, such as exercise and play, and more passive forms, such as meditation, napping, and sleep.

CHAPTER FIVE
Sleep or Die

If physical energy is the foundation of all dimensions of energy, sleep is the foundation of physical energy. No single behavior more fundamentally influences our effectiveness in waking life. Sleep deprivation takes a powerful toll on our health, our emotional well-being, and our cognitive functioning.

- Ninety-five percent of us require seven to eight hours of sleep a night to be fully rested. The average American sleeps between six and six and a half hours a night.
- Sleep is one of the first behaviors we're willing to sacrifice in the attempt to get more done. Numerous studies of great performers suggest that they sleep more, not less, than average.
- There is a powerful correlation between inadequate sleep and obesity. It's during sleep that we produce the hormone leptin, which signals satiety and helps us control how much we eat.
- The only truly viable solution to insufficient sleep is to go to bed earlier, in part by beginning to quiet down at least thirty to forty-five minutes before trying to sleep. Alcohol is a short-term sedative but may induce shallow sleep and less overall sleep time.

CHAPTER SIX

Making Waves

Intermittent renewal is critical to sustainable high performance. Over the course of a day, we oscillate every ninety minutes from a higher to lower level of arousal and alertness. These are called "ultradian" cycles. In effect, our bodies are asking for a break every ninety minutes. More often than not, we ignore these signals, especially in the face of high demand.

- The key to effective renewal is not how long we do it but how well we do it. As with any other capacity, we get better at effectively renewing by practicing it more systematically.
- Passive renewal—breathing deeply, meditating, listening to music, reading for pleasure—is about lowering physiological arousal. Active renewal is a different way of changing channels, by raising the heart rate through aerobic exercise, weight lifting, or more strenuous forms of yoga or Pilates.
- We are designed to sleep twice over the course of a twenty-four-hour period, the second time in the midafternoon. A short nap of twenty to thirty minutes can powerfully enhance performance over the subsequent two to three hours.
- Much as we perform better with multiple short cycles of rest during the day and an extended period of sleep every night, so research shows that we are healthier and more productive when we take regular vacations.

CHAPTER SEVEN
Use It or Lose It

Regular exercise, especially intense energy expenditure followed by deep recovery, dramatically increases our capacity not just physically but also mentally and emotionally. Too little movement, like too little sleep, weakens and diminishes us in all dimensions of our lives.

- Ideally, we should be doing some form of at least moderately intense physical activity six days a week for twenty to forty-five minutes a day. That time can be split between two or three sessions over the course of a day, so long as each one is at least ten minutes.
- Any movement is better than no movement, and even walking is effective in increasing our overall level of fitness.
- Steady-state aerobic training involves raising the heart rate for an extended period of time. Interval training—pushing the heart rate up to high levels for thirty to sixty seconds at a time and then recovering back to a resting rate—is an even more powerful way to build cardiovascular capacity.
- Strength training two to three times a week, is at least as important as endurance training. Building greater strength increases everything from metabolism to coordination to bone density to balance.

CHAPTER EIGHT
Less Is More

From an energy perspective, the key to nutrition is maintaining a stable, steady level of blood sugar. Food is our primary source of glucose, and it fuels not just our bodies but also our brains. Many of the foods that we choose to eat provide a quick hit of energy but serve us poorly in the long term.

- When our blood glucose levels spike too high or drop too low—when we eat too little for too long or too much at once—we function less efficiently at all levels.
- The simplest rule is to eat when you begin to feel hungry but never so much that you feel stuffed.
- Breakfast is especially crucial to regulating our blood sugar levels because it typically follows the longest number of hours we go without eating.
- Small, frequent meals serve us better than two or three large ones. To maintain a steady source of energy, it's best to eat something at least every three hours, or five to six times a day.
- Sugars and simple carbohydrates provide the least enduring sources of energy. Low-fat proteins and complex carbohydrates are the best source of energy.
- We cannot control our eating by resisting temptation, because we quickly burn down our reservoir of will. Instead, choose in advance what you intend to eat and try not to ever let yourself get too hungry.
- Don't deny yourself the pleasure of the foods you most enjoy—in small portions—even if they're not as nutritious. Avoiding certain foods altogether will eventually lead you to eat too much of them.

CHAPTER NINE
Creating a Culture That Pulses

If you're a leader or a manager, creating a new way of working begins with recognizing that renewal serves performance. You need to model renewal in your own behavior. At the same time, organizations must create policies, practices, and services that support and encourage people to eat right, work out regularly, renew intermittently, and get enough sleep.

- The big mind-set shift leaders need to make is from focusing too much on competency, the skills necessary for a given job, and too little on capacity, the fuel people need in their tanks to bring their skills fully to life.
- Commuting can take a huge toll on people's productivity, draining their energy during the early-morning hours, when they might otherwise be most effective. Organizations serve their employees and themselves by allowing employees to commute in off-hours or work from home.
- The collective energy of an organization follows a predictable path, and research suggests that there are optimal times of the week during which to take on the most challenging work and other times that makes sense for administrative tasks, for creative and strategic thinking, and for relationship building.

CHAPTER TEN
The War Between the States

How we feel profoundly influences how we perform. The problem is that much of the time we're not even aware of how we are feeling or what the impact those emotions are having on how we work and the people with whom we work. The more aware we are of what we're feeling, the more power we have to influence those feelings.

- There are four basic ways we can feel at any given time over the course of a day. They are depicted in what we call the Emotional Quadrants. The four states are: Performance Zone, Survival Zone, Recovery Zone, and Burnout Zone.
- The Performance Zone is the best place to be when you're working toward a clearly defined goal.
- Most of us spend a significant amount of time in the Survival Zone. This is where we default when we feel a sense of threat or danger. There are significant costs to our health, performance, and relationships from spending too much time in this zone.
- We think of leaders as "chief energy officers." The core challenge for leaders is to recruit, mobilize, inspire, focus, and regularly refuel the energy of those they lead.
- The antidote to falling reactively into the Survival Zone is to intentionally spend more time in the Renewal Zone.

CHAPTER ELEVEN
If You Ain't Got Pride, You Ain't Got Nothin'

A trigger is an event, behavior, or circumstance that consistently prompts negative emotions and propels us into fight or flight—the Survival Zone. We're biologically wired to sense danger, and we all experience triggers every day, to greater and lesser degrees.

- We readily notice what's wrong in our lives—and react to it automatically, often at a cost to more thoughtful deliberation and effectiveness.
- Gaining control of our triggers requires first becoming aware of the feelings that arise when we're triggered so that they don't take control of us before we can take control of them.
- The Golden Rule of Triggers is "Whatever you feel compelled to do, don't." That means resisting the urge to act when you're feeling triggered.
- Our core emotional need is to feel secure—to be valued and appreciated. The more we feel our value is at risk, the more energy we spend defending it and the less energy we have available to create value.
- The leader who is secure in his own value is freed to invest energy in empowering others and ultimately in fueling the organization's broader success.

CHAPTER TWELVE
The Facts and the Stories We Tell

A fact is something that can be objectively verified by any person. It is irrefutable. A story is something we create to make sense of the facts. We can't change the facts, but we do have a choice about what we make of them.

- We can develop the capacity to influence the stories we tell ourselves, so that they empower rather than undermine us.
- Awareness by itself can powerfully diminish our reactivity. By simply being curious about how we're responding, we move from being the subject of our feelings to making them the object of our observation.
- Realistic optimism balances a hopeful and positive perspective with a recognition that the desired outcome may or may not occur. This view can serve as a fuel for exerting the maximum effort to influence the best possible outcome.
- When we default reactively to telling negative stories, we almost invariably assign ourselves the role of victim. It feels better not to blame ourselves for disappointments, but the victim role undermines our power to influence our circumstances. The alternative is to intentionally look for where our responsibility lies in any given situation—and then take remedial action on any part of it that we're in a position to influence.
- Counterintuitively, we're strongest when we can freely acknowledge our shortcomings alongside our strengths. By accepting the whole of who we are, we no longer have to defend our value so vigilantly. Instead, we can use the best of the feedback we get to learn and grow.

CHAPTER THIRTEEN
A New Value Proposition

Every organization has a distinct emotional climate, and typically it's set from the top. A leader is effectively the "chief energy officer." The core responsibility of great leaders is to mobilize, focus, inspire, and regularly renew the energy of those they lead.

- The best leaders strike a balance between challenging their people to exceed themselves and regularly recognizing and rewarding their accomplishments.
- Leaders who default to negative emotions to motivate others may get the short-term performance they're seeking, but the costs over time are high.
- Because the impact of "bad" is stronger than "good," the first rule for an effective leader is the same as it is for doctors: above all else, do no harm. That means avoiding devaluing emotions such as anger, intimidation, disparagement, and shame.
- The most effective leaders are those who regularly recognize and show appreciation for the real accomplishments of their people.
- Leaders who avoid conflict often cause even more harm than those who are more direct. The key for leaders is to balance honesty and appreciation, always keeping in mind the value of the other person, even when being critical of a particular behavior.

CHAPTER FOURTEEN
A Poverty of Attention

Our attention is under siege. There is an inverse relationship between the increasing volume of information available to us and our ability to prioritize and make sense of it. We've lost control of our attention. When we default reactively or lazily to distraction, we diminish not just our cognitive capacity but also the depth of our experience and, ultimately, our effectiveness.

- Human beings are incapable of multitasking. Unlike computers, we're hard-wired to undertake tasks sequentially, and our brains are not able to focus on two separate cognitive tasks at the same time.
- We perform best when we're most singularly focused on a given task.
- Rather than setting our own agenda and sticking to it, we often react to the most immediate and visible demand on our attention. Prioritization is critical in the face of urgent demands.
- We retain information less effectively when we're presented with a great deal of it all at once. We do far better metabolizing information intermittently, in spaced cycles.

CHAPTER FIFTEEN
One Thing at a Time

The first step in taking more control of our attention is recognizing the costs of distraction. Focused attention is a capacity like any other. Much like a muscle, it gets stronger with practice and weaker when it is not exercised.

- Two kinds of distraction fracture our attention. One is external—what's going on around us. The other is internal—the endless chatter of our own minds. We must learn to address both.
- The most common and relentless source of interruption in most workplaces is e-mail. Our pull to it is so powerful that we must learn to turn it off entirely when we are doing the sort of challenging work that requires deeply absorbed attention.
- Our responsiveness to distractions is powerfully influenced by our desire for connection and our resistance to discomfort. Gaining more control of our attention is intimately linked to our capacity to delay gratification. The safer and more secure we feel, the more focused attention we can allocate to our long-term goals.
- Whenever possible, we ought to put our attention in the service of what's most important. At a practical level, this requires that we set aside regular time to reflect on and define our priorities and focus on the most challenging ones, preferably at the start of our days when our energy is typically highest.
- We must also contend with relentless internal chatter in our own minds. Meditation is an age-old form of attentional practice that helps us focus on one thing at a time.

CHAPTER SIXTEEN
Cultivating the Whole Brain

Logical, deductive, analytic attention is the province of the left hemisphere of the brain. There is a second kind of absorbed focus associated with the right hemisphere of the brain, which is typically undertrained and underdeveloped.

- The key capacities of the right hemisphere—creative and big-picture thinking, openness to learning, and empathy—are a largely untapped source of competitive advantage, both for individuals and for organizations.
- Creative thinking can be trained systematically. Doing so paradoxically requires that we let go of conscious control of our thinking process, something most of us initially find very difficult to do.
- In right-hemisphere mode, we can be deeply absorbed in a task, but we pay attention in a different way—seeing both the whole and the parts, noticing patterns, embracing paradox, ambiguity and complexity.
- To activate the right hemisphere, we must intentionally set aside time to quiet the mind—through meditation, drawing, daydreaming, or other activities that don't demand logical sequencing or a specific outcome.
- The highest levels of thinking require both hemispheres, each playing different roles at different stages of the process. The better we understand these stages, the more systematically we can train and enhance creativity in ourselves and others.

CHAPTER SEVENTEEN
Autonomy for Accountability

One of the best ways an organization can encourage both higher productivity and more innovation is to promote absorbed focus. Too often, employers collaborate with their employees to fracture their focus and distract their attention. Focus improves only when it becomes an explicit organizational priority. That requires creating policies and practices that support employees in focusing on one thing at a time.

- Key organizational practices that drive better focus include creating clarity around when people are expected to respond to e-mail; banning e-mail in meetings; encouraging firm start and stop times for meetings; and encouraging intermittent rest and renewal during the day.
- Open-plan offices may save companies money and break down hierarchy, but they also drive people to distraction and reduce productivity.
- The ideal workplace offers people the quiet and privacy of a separate office, along with more comfortable, informal environments for more collaborative work.
- Organizations that set aside separate spaces for creative thinking make a statement about the priority they've accorded innovation.
- Most people focus better when they're given more freedom to choose where and when they do their work and are held accountable only for the value they deliver.

CHAPTER EIGHTEEN
Who Are You, and What Do You Really Want?

Spiritual energy is the uniquely powerful source of energy we derive from deeply held values and a clear sense of purpose beyond our self-interest, which we embody in our everyday behaviors. Cultivating this source of energy requires effort and reflection, but it is also energizing and inspiring. Significance is not our birthright. We must find ways to invest our lives with meaning.

- Deeply held values define the person you aspire to be. They're what we're rooted in and what we stand for—an internal compass that helps us navigate the storms and the choices we all inevitably face.
- A clearly defined purpose ties our values to concrete actions that transform our aspirations into actions.
- We cultivate spiritual energy most effectively by moving between the inner work of defining and regularly reflecting on our values and the outer work of bringing our intentions to life in our everyday behaviors.
- Spiritual practice requires not just cultivating our best selves but also recognizing our basest instincts—and then having the courage to resist expedient choices in favor of ones that are consistent with our deepest values.
- False humility is manipulation aimed at winning praise. Genuine humility frees us of the need to protect an image or stand above others, allowing us instead to accept, embrace, and learn from our limitations.

CHAPTER NINETEEN
We're All in This Together

The most powerful and embracing source of purpose is one that serves something beyond our self-interest. Adding value to others, and to the commons, is a unique source of energy. It's also increasingly critical to our survival.

- We experience purpose most viscerally in the form of positive emotions. We all bring more energy to the activities we most enjoy, and enjoyment itself sustains our energy.
- Once you've defined what you most enjoy doing and do best, the spiritual challenge is to put those skills in the service of something beyond your immediate self-interest.
- Purpose provides a way to extend our sphere of influence not through the accumulation and exercise of power but by giving us a clear route to adding value to others.
- No job automatically provides a purpose, and no job precludes our finding a way to express our purpose through it. The role we fill isn't the route to purpose. Rather, it's the approach we take to whatever work we do.
- Taking care of others at the expense of taking care of ourselves undermines our ability to fully achieve the highest purpose. In the spiritual dimension, as in all the others, we must renew ourselves regularly.

CHAPTER TWENTY
Purpose for Passion

To fuel spiritual energy, an organization must define a set of shared values and a purpose beyond its continuing profitability. That begins with asking itself a variation on the questions that we pose to individuals: "Who are we?" (What do we stand for?) and "What do we really want?" (What is the purpose we're here to serve beyond our own survival and success?).

- There is a deep disconnect between what many companies say they stand for and what they actually do. This disconnect takes a toll on employee engagement, on productivity, and ultimately on organizational success.
- An organization is a living organism, a human community that can reach its highest purpose only when each individual feels fully valued and fully vested in a shared purpose.
- An organization that invests in its people across all dimensions of their lives—and rallies them around an inspiring purpose—is actually investing in itself. As individuals grow and increase their capacity, the organism as a whole becomes stronger.
- The most universally despised of all qualities among leaders is egocentricity—selfishness and self-absorption.
- The best evidence of an organization's values and purpose is to consider the behavior of its leaders. Transactional leaders focus narrowly on the "what"—how to get things done. Transformational and servant leaders are more focused on the purpose of their actions and on meeting the needs of their employees.
- Most employees are less inspired by a leader's personal charisma than by a compelling purpose to rally around every day. The most admired and effective leaders are those with the most inspiring vision and the greatest humility about themselves.
- A new way of working ultimately requires an evolutionary shift in the center of gravity in our lives—from "me" to "us."

Notes

CHAPTER ONE: MORE AND MORE, LESS AND LESS

6. *In 1993, Anders Ericsson:* K. Anders Ericsson, Ralf Th. Krampe, and Clemens Tesch-Romer, "The Role of Deliberate Practice in the Acquisition of Expert Performance," *Psychological Review,* 100, no. 3 (1993): 363–406. http://graphics8.nytimes.com/images/blogs/freakonomics/pdf/DeliberatePractice(PsychologicalReview).pdf.
6. *As Gladwell puts it:* Malcolm Gladwell, *Outliers* (New York: Little, Brown, 2008), 39.
7. *Ericsson himself concluded:* Ericsson, Krampe, and Tesch, "The Role of Deliberate Practice in the Acquisition of Expert Performance."
8. *"In field after field":* Geoffrey Colvin, *Talent Is Overrated* (New York: Portfolio, 2008), 3, 4.
8. *Our Four Primary Needs:* Abraham H. Maslow, "A Theory of Human Motivation," *Psychological Review* 50 (1943): 370–96. I owe a considerable debt to Abraham Maslow in framing the core energy needs. Maslow first framed what he called the "hierarchy of needs" in his 1943 paper "A Theory of Human Motivation," published in the *Psychological Review.* He cited five needs, from more basic to higher level ones and suggested that as one level of needs was reasonable well met, the next level tended to emerge. Physiological needs were at the bottom of his pyramid, followed by safety, love and belonging, esteem, and finally, self-actualization. I have redefined our core needs as survival, sustainability, security, self-expression, and significance. The highest one is spiritual, which was not part of Maslow's original model, but his core insights remain as relevant and brilliant today as they were when he first had them.
11. *When we published:* Tony Schwartz and Catherine McCarthy, "Manage Your Energy, Not Your Time," *Harvard Business Review,* October 2007.
14. *The Emotional Quadrants:* A slightly different version of this quadrant was designed by Jim Loehr, my coauthor for *The Power of Full Engagement,* and appears in that book as "The Dynamics of Energy." This book contains eight different quadrants that address each of the four dimensions of energy—physical, emotional, mental, and spiritual—at both the individual and organizational levels.
20. *Take Zappos.com, which sells:* www.zappos.com.
20. *The vast majority:* Author interview with Tony Hsieh, February 2009; http://about.zappos.com/meet-our-monkeys/tony-hsieh-ceo.

CHAPTER TWO: WE CAN'T CHANGE WHAT WE DON'T NOTICE

23. *"We are already the most":* Robert Kegan, *Immunity to Change* (Boston: Harvard Business Press, 2009), 6.
23. *"True development":* ibid., 26.

23. *"If something couldn't be"*: Ken Wilber, *A Brief History of Everything* (Boston: Shambhala, 1996), 190.
24. *As Daniel Goleman:* R. D. Laing, *The Politics of the Family and Other Essays* (London: Tavistock, 1971).
25. *We'll call him Carl:* Carl is a pseudonym, as are all names of people identified solely by a first name and without a named company affiliation.
27. *"Our efforts at self-justification"*: Carol Tavris and Elliot Aronson, *Mistakes Were Made (But Not by Me)* (Orlando, FL: Harcourt, 2008), 19.
28. *"To err is human"*: ibid., 10.
28. *Or as the psychologist:* ibid., 257.
28. *"Each violation of"*: Roy F. Baumeister, Todd F. Heatherton, and Dianne M. Tice, *Losing Control* (San Diego: Academic Press, 1994), 29.
28. *"The greatest of faults"*: Thomas Carlyle, http://en.wikiquote.org/wiki/Thomas_Carlyle.
29. *"I don't do nuance"*: Jacob Weisberg, *The Bush Tragedy* (New York: Random House, 2008), 104.
30. *In direct reaction:* Marcus Buckingham and Donald O. Clifton, *Now, Discover Your Strengths* (New York: Free Press, 2001).
30. *"There is always"*: Daniel Goleman, *Vital Lies, Simple Truths: The Psychology of Self-Deception* (New York: Simon & Schuster, 1985), 245.
30. *The Stoic philosophers:* Michael Murphy, *The Future of the Body* (Los Angeles: J. P. Tarcher, 1992), 558.
30. *"In Chinese philosophy"*: http://en.wikipedia.org/wiki/Yin_and_yang.
31. *Seng-ts'an, a Chinese:* Jonathan Haidt, *The Happiness Hypothesis* (New York: Basic Books, 2006), 78.
31. *"Loving oneself"*: James Hillman, *The Soul's Code,* (quoted in Jim Loehr and Tony Schwartz, *The Power of Full Engagement* (New York: Free Press, 2003), 162.

CHAPTER THREE: WE'RE CREATURES OF HABIT

33. *Ninety-five percent:* T. F. Heatherton et al., "A 10-Year Longitudinal Study of Body Weight, Dieting, and Eating Disorder Symptoms," *Journal of Abnormal Psychology* 106 (1997): 118.
33. *Twenty-five percent:* J. C. Norcross et al., "Ringing in the New Year: The Change Processes and Reported Outcomes of Resolutions," *Addictive Behaviors* 14 (1989): 205–12.
33. *Seventy percent:* John Kotter, "Leading Change: Why Transformation Efforts Fail," *Harvard Business Review,* January 1, 2007.
33. *In 1998, Baumeister:* M. Muraven, D. M. Tice, and R. F. Baumeister, "Self-Control as a Limited Resource: Regulatory Depletion Patterns," *Journal of Personality and Social Psychology* 74 (1998): 774–89.
34. *"Acts of choice"*: Roy F. Baumeister, *The Self in Social Psychology* (Philadelphia: Psychology Press, 1999), 325.
34. *In another series of experiments:* Mark Muraven and Roy F. Baumeister, "Self-regulation and Depletion of Limited Resources: Does Self-control Resemble a Muscle?" *Psychological Bulletin* 126, no. 2 (2000): 247–59.
34. *A series of studies:* ibid.
35. *Self-control:* ibid., 247; Roy F. Baumeister, *Losing Control* (San Diego: Academic Press, 1994), 19.

35. *That's precisely what happened:* K. Anders Ericsson et al., "The Role of Deliberate Practice in the Acquisition of Expert Performance," *Psychological Review* 100, no. 3 (1993): 363–406.
35. *Fully 95 percent:* John A. Bargh and Tanya Chartrand, "The Unbearable Automaticity of Being," *American Psychologist* 54, no. 7 (1999): 464.
35. *"Human beings":* John Gray, *Al Qaeda and What It Means to be Modern* (New York: The New Press, 2003), 108.
36. *"It is a profoundly erroneous truism":* Alfred North Whitehead, *An Introduction to Mathematics* (New York: H. Holt, 1911), 41.
37. *"To pay attention."* Baumeister, *Losing Control,* 52.
37. *"Even when engaged in":* Irving Kirsch and Steven Jay Lynn, "Automaticity in Clinical Psychology," *American Psychologist* 54, no. 7 (1999): 508.
37. *"Consciousness deserts all processes":* William James, *The Principles of Psychology,* Vol. 2 (New York: Henry Holt and Company, 1890); 496.
37. *"Most of moment-to-moment":* John A. Bargh and Tanya L. Chartrand, "The Unbearable Automaticity of Being," *American Psychologist* 54, no. 7 (1999): 464.
37. *one of the values:* Ericsson, "The Role of Deliberate Practice in the Acquisition of Expert Performance."
38. *In one study:* Peter M. Gollwitzer and V. Brandstatter, "Implementation Intentions and Effective Goal Pursuit," *Journal of Personality and Social Psychology* 73 (1997): 186–99.
39. *In another study:* Peter M. Gollwitzer, "Implementation Intentions: Strong Effects of Simple Plans," *American Psychologist* 54, no. 7 (1999): 496.
41. *"It is probably easier":* Baumeister, *Losing Control,* 26.
41. *"It matters whether":* ibid., 494.
41. *"When you go into a day":* David Besio, quoted in David Kessler, *The End of Overeating* (Emmaus, PA: Rodale, 2009), 298.
41. *"'When situation X arises'":* Gollwitzer, "Implementation Intentions," 494.
42. *"When someone comes to me":* Robert Kegan and Lisa Laskow Lahey, *Immunity to Change* (Boston: Harvard Business Press, 2009), 35.
42. *"What is the commitment":* ibid.
44. *Powerful as the evidence:* See chapter 6.
44. *"The leader must be more":* Kegan and Lahey, *Immunity to Change,* 81.

CHAPTER FOUR: FEELING THE PULSE

53. *"If I get any less":* Author interview with John Weiser.

CHAPTER FIVE: SLEEP OR DIE

57. *In a famous:* A. Rechtschaffen and B. M. Bergmann, "Sleep Deprivation in the Rat: An Update of the 1989 Paper," *Sleep* 25 (2002): 18–24.
57. *William Dement:* William C. Dement and Christopher Vaughan, *The Promise of Sleep* (New York: Dell, 2000).
58. *rocking chair marathon:* "40 Facts about Sleep You Probably Didn't Know . . . (or Were Too Tired to Think About)," The National Sleep Research Project (Australian Broadcasting Corporation, 2000), www.abc.net/science/sleep/facts.htm (accessed March 31, 2009).
58. *Amnesty International:* Michael M. Rosen, "Is Sleep Deprivation Torture?"

Techcentralstation.com, March 28, 2005, www.geocities.com/three_strikes _legal/torture_sleep_deprivation.html (accessed March 13, 2009).

58. *In his memoir:* Menachem Begin, *White Nights* (San Francisco: Harper & Row, 1979).
58. *"We all think":* Matthew Walker, quoted in interview with Lesley Stahl, "The Science of Sleep," *60 Minutes,* CBS, March 13, 2008, transcript, www.cbsnews .com/stories/2008/03/14/60minutes/main3939721.shtml, accessed March 17, 2009.
58. *The National Sleep Foundation:* For the National Sleep Foundation's recommendations, visit www.sleepfoundation.org/how-much-sleep-do-we-really-need.
58. *"The percentage of":* Mary Sykes Wylie, "Sleepless in America: Making It through the Night in a Wired World," *Psychotherapy Networker,* March–April 2008, 27.
58. *Diane Lauderdale:* Diane S. Lauderdale et al., "Objectively Measured Sleep Characteristics among Early-Middle-Aged Adults," *American Journal of Epidemiology* 164, no. 1 (2006): 8.
59. *"It's convenient to say":* David Dinges, quoted in "The Science of Sleep," *60 Minutes,* CBS, March 13, 2008.
59. *"Like a drunk":* Charles A. Czeisler and Bronwyn Fryer, "Sleep Deficit: The Performance Killer," *Harvard Business Review,* October 2006, 56.
59. *"Perhaps," he says:* Thomas Wehr, quoted in: Susan Brink, "Sleepless Society," *U.S. News & World Report,* October 2000, www.usnews.com, 1.
59. *That's true of:* K. Anders Ericsson, Ralf Th. Krampe, and Clemens Tesch-Romer, "The Role of Deliberate Practice in the Acquisition of Expert Performance," *Psychological Review* 100, no. 3 (1993): 376.
59. *"Practice does not":* Walker, quoted in, "The Science of Sleep," aired on *60 Minutes,* 3/13/03.
59. *Two recent studies:* Cheri Mah, "Extended Sleep and the Effects on Mood and Athletic Performance in Collegiate Swimmers," Annual Meeting of the Associated Professional Sleep Societies, Baltimore, June 9, 2008; Cheri Mah, "Extra Sleep Improves Athletes' Performance," Annual Meeting of the Associated Professional Sleep Societies, Minneapolis, June 14, 2007.
59. *"While this study":* Cheri Mah, quoted in "Extra Sleep Helps Give Stanford Athletes Peak Performance, Improved Alertness and Mood," June 9, 2008, www.medicalnewstoday.com/printerfriendlynews.php?newsid=110191 (accessed May 4, 2009).
60. *In* Dream On*:* Charles Leadbeater, *Dream On: Sleep in the 24/7 Society* (London: Demas, 2004), 21.
60. *Eve Van Cauter:* Eve Van Cauter et al., "Metabolic Consequences of Sleep and Sleep Loss," *Sleep Medicine* 9, suppl. 1 (September 2008): S23–S28.
60. *The Harvard Nurses' Health Study:* Sanjay R. Patel et al., "Association between Reduced Sleep and Weight Gain in Women," *American Journal of Epidemiology* 164, no. 10 (2006): 947–54.
61. *Nurses in the same study:* E. S. Schernhammer et al., "Rotating Night Shifts and Risk of Breast Cancer in Women Participating in the Nurses' Health Study," *Journal of the National Cancer Institute* 93, no. 20 (2001): 1563–68.
61. *Numerous other studies:* Johnni Hansen, "Light at Night, Shiftwork, and Breast Cancer," *Journal of the National Cancer Institute* 93, no. 20 (2001): 1513–15.
61. *David Dinges found:* H. P. Van Dongen et al., "The Cumulative Cost of Addi-

tional Wakefulness: Dose-Response Effects on Neurobehavioral Functions and Sleep Physiology from Chronic Sleep Restriction and Total Sleep Deprivation," *Sleep* 26, no. 2 (2003): 117.

61. *More striking still:* Frank Curran, "Sleep Deficit: The Performance Killer," *Harvard Business Review,* October 2006: 54.
61. *In one clever and fascinating:* U. Wagner et al., "Sleep Inspires Insight," *Nature* 427, no. 6972 (2004): 353–55.
62. *"basic rest activity cycle" (BRAC):* Nathaniel Kleitman, *Sleep and Wakefulness* (Chicago University of Chicago Press, 1987): 113.
62. *Many of the most devastating:* Jennifer Ackerman, *Sex Sleep Eat Drink Dream* (Boston: Houghton Mifflin: 2007), 167; S. Folkard and S. D. Rosen, "Circadian Performance Rhythms: Some Practical and Theoretical Implications," *Philosophical Transactions of the Royal Society, B,* 327, no. 1241 (1990): 543–53.
62. *A 2004 Work Hours:* C. P. Landrigan et al., "The Effect of Reducing Interns' Work Hours on Serious Medical Errors in Intensive Care Units," *The New England Journal of Medicine* 351, no. 18 (2004): 1838.
63. *"Ours is the only species":* Ackerman, *Sex Sleep Eat Drink Dream,* 179.

CHAPTER SIX: MAKING WAVES

67. *A decade after:* Nathaniel Kleitman, *Sleep and Wakefulness* (Chicago: University of Chicago Press, 1987).
67. *"ultradian" cycles:* Ernest Rossi, with David Nimmons, *The 20-Minute Break* (Los Angeles: J. P. Tarcher, 1991), viii.
67. *The Israeli sleep researcher:* Lavie Peretz, *The Enchanted World of Sleep* (New Haven, CT: Yale University Press, 1996), 51.
68. *That helps explain:* K. Anders Ericsson, Ralf Th. Krampe, and Clemens Tesch-Romer, "The Role of Deliberate Practice in the Acquisition of Expert Performance," *Psychological Review* 100, no. 3 (1993): 374.
70. *Professional tennis players:* Tony Schwartz and Jim Loehr, *The Power of Full Engagement* (New York: Free Press, 2003), 32–33.
70. *In one study:* Jon Kabat-Zinn et al., "Effectiveness of a Meditation-Based Stress Reduction Program in the Treatment of Anxiety Disorders," *American Journal of Psychiatry* 149, no. 7 (1992); pp. 936.
72. *"Our circadian clocks":* Sara C. Mednick, *Take a Nap! Change Your Life* (New York: Workman, 2006), 53.
72. *As far back:* ibid., 5.
72. *Winston Churchill:* ibid., 8.
72. *Evidence for the circadian influence:* ibid., 5.
73. *he found that:* ibid., xiii.
73. *Mednick's simple:* Sara Mednick et al., "Sleep-Dependent Learning: A Nap Is as Good as a Night," *Nature Neuroscience* 6 (2003): 678.
73. *In another experiment:* Sara Mednick et al., "The Restorative Effect of Naps on Perceptual Deterioration," *Nature Neuroscience* 5 (2002): 677–81.
73. *Perhaps the most striking:* M. R. Rosekind et al., "Alertness Management: Strategic Naps in Operational Settings," *Journal of Sleep Research* 4, suppl. 2 (1995): 64–65.
74. *Mednick has taken this research:* Mednick, *Take a Nap!,* 51.
74. *"sleep inertia":* ibid., 46.

74. *The best option:* ibid., 47.
75. *On average, Americans:* Steve Rushin, "One Nation in Need of Vacation," *Car and Travel,* September 2008, 36.
75. *"The idea of":* Mike Pina, quoted in Timothy Egan, "The Rise of Shrinking-Vacation Syndrome," *The New York Times,* August 20, 2006, www.nytimes.com/2006/08/20/us/20vacation.html?pagewanted=print.
75. *A congressional bill:* Steven Greenhouse, "Bill Would Guarantee up to 7 Paid Sick Days," *The New York Times,* May 15, 2009, www.nytimes.com/2009/05/16/health/policy/16sick.html.
75. *The European Union:* David Moberg, "What Vacation Days?," June 18, 2007, www.inthesetimes.com/article/3233/what_vacation_days (accessed May 17, 2009).
75. *As part of the Framingham Heart Study:* Elaine D. Eaker et al. "Myocardial Infarction and Coronary Death Among Women: Psychosocial Predictors from a 20-Year Follow-up of Women in the Framingham Study," *American Journal of Epidemiology* 135, no. 8 (1992), 854–64.
76. *A comparable study:* B. B. Gump and K. A. Matthews, "Are Vacations Good for Your Health? The Nine Year Mortality Experience After the Multiple Risk Factor Intervention Trial," *Psychosomatic Medicine* 62, no. 5 (2000); 608–12.
76. *A 2005 study of 1,500 women:* Vatsal Chikani et al., "Vacations Improve Mental Health among Rural Women: The Wisconsin Rural Women's Health Study," *Wisconsin Medical Journal* 104, no. 6 (2005): 21.
76. *at Ernst & Young:* Ben Rosen, "Career Value Study: The Grass Isn't Always Greener" (Ernst & Young, 2006).
77. *A recent study of 11,000 children:* Romina M. Barros et al., "School Recess and Group Classroom Behavior," *Pediatrics* 123, no. 2 (2009), 431.
77. *"We should understand:* Romina Barros, quoted in Tara Parker-Pope, "The 3 R's? A Fourth Is Crucial Too: Recess," *The New York Times,* February 23, 2009, www.nytimes.com/2009/02/24/health/24well.html.
77. *Thirty percent:* Barros et al., "School Recess and Group Classroom Behavior."
77. *Achievement First charter schools:* www.achievementfirst.org/af.

CHAPTER SEVEN: USE IT OR LOSE IT

79. *"How much you move":* Eric Heiden, Masimo Testa, and DeAnne Musolf, *Faster, Better, Stronger* (New York: Collins Living, 2008), 27.
79. *Steve Wanner:* Author interview with Steve Wanner.
80. *Simon Ashby:* Author interview with Simon Ashby.
80. *In a study of 15,000:* Heiden, *Faster, Better, Stronger,* 14.
80. *In another study:* K. Sundquist et al., "The Long-Term Effect of Physical Activity on Incidence of Coronary Heart Disease: A 12-Year Follow-up Study," *American Journal of Preventive Medicine* 41, 1 (2005): 219–25.
81. *In a third study:* "Exercising to Prevent Exercise Heart Attacks," *The New York Times,* November 9, 2000, Section A, p. 20.
81. *"Regular exercise":* Sampath Parthasarathy in *The Journal of the American Medical Association,* quoted in Heiden, *Faster, Bigger, Stronger,* 11.
81. *In a meta-analysis:* "Meta Study of Studies," *Journal of Psychiatric and Mental Health Nursing* 11 (2004): 476–83.
81. *aptly named SMILE:* James Blumenthal et al., "Exercise and Pharmacotherapy

in the Treatment of Major Depressive Disorder," *Psychosomatic Medicine* 69, no. 7 (2007): 592–93.

81. *Agencies ranging from:* For the most up-to-date fitness recommendations, visit the American College of Sports Medicine (www.acsm.org), the American Heart Association (www.americanheart.org), and the President's Council on Physical Fitness (www.fitness.gov).
82. *In the two most recent:* U.S. Department of Health and Human Services, *Physical Activity and Health: A Report of the Surgeon General* (Atlanta: U.S. Department of Health and Human Services, Centers for Disease Control and Prevention, National Center for Chronic Disease Prevention and Health Promotion, 1996).
82. *Overall, the World Health Organization:* Heiden, *Faster, Better, Stronger,* 27; for up-to-date information from the World Health Organization, visit https://apps.who.int/infobase/report.aspx.
82. *A study published in:* X. Jouven et al., "Heart Rate Profile during Exercise as a Predictor of Sudden Death," *The New England Journal of Medicine* 352, no. 19 (2005): 1951.
84. *periodization:* Heiden, *Faster, Better, Stronger,* 105; Steven J. Fleck, "Periodized Strength Training: A Critical Review," *Journal of Strength and Conditioning Research* 13, no. 1 (1999): 82.
84. *Interval training is:* Jason R. Karp et al., "Interval Training for the Fitness Professional," *Strength and Conditioning Journal* 22, no. 4 (2000): 65.
85. *"supercompensation":* Heiden, *Faster, Better, Stronger,* 54.
86. *In one study:* Peter Jaret, "A Healthy Mix of Rest and Motion," *The New York Times,* May 3, 2007.
86. *Dallas Bed Rest and Training Study:* D. K. McGuire et al., "A Thirty Year Follow-Up of the Dallas Bed Rest and Training Study," *Circulation* 104 (2001): 1350–57.
87. *Just as we lose approximately:* Heiden, *Faster, Better, Stronger,* 21; also see www.fitdynamics.com/gpage.html.
87. *Between 18 and 33 percent:* Virtual Health Care Team, "Falls and Hip Fractures: Incidence of Falls and Associated Morbidity & Mortality," www.vhct.org/case4007/index.htm (accessed May 23, 2009).
88. *In one of a series:* Maria A. Fiatarone et al., "Exercise Training and Nutritional Supplementation for Physical Frailty in Very Elderly People," *The New England Journal of Medicine* 330, no. 25 (1994): 1769–75.
88. *By contrast, there have been:* James F. Fixx, *The Complete Book of Running* (New York: Random House, 1977).
88. *Arthur Jones:* Ellington Darden, *The New High Intensity Training* (Emmaus, PA: Rodale, 2004).
89. *evidence suggests that a single set:* "Weight Training Guidelines: American College of Sports Medicine Recommendations and Position Stand," accessed May 24, 2009. www.exrx.net/WeightTraining/Guidelines.html; Elizabeth Quinn, "Basic Strength Training Principles," www.about.com, updated on October 3, 2007, http://sportsmedicine.about.com/od/strengthtraining/a/strength_strat.htm; www.mayoclinic.com/health/strength-training/AN00893.

CHAPTER EIGHT: LESS IS MORE

91. *Consider this:* K. M. Flegal and R. P. Troiano, "Changes in the Distribution of Body Mass Index of Adults and Children in the US Population," *International Journal of Obesity and Related Metabolic Disorders* 24, no. 7 (2000): 808.
91. *In response to similar increases:* For the most up-to-date estimates on global obesity statistics, visit www.who.int/nutrition/topics/obesity/en/index.html; http://apps.who.int/bmi/index.jsp; www.worldheart.org/press/facts-figures/obesity.
92. *In the United States:* "Chartbook on Trends in the Health of Americans," *Health* (United States, 2007); "Prevalence of Overweight and Obesity among Adults: United States, 2003–2004," cdc.gov/mmwr/preview/mmwrhtml/mm5345aa.htm (accessed December 3, 2008).
92. *In France:* Elaine Sciolino, "France Battles a Problem That Grows and Grows: Fat," *The New York Times,* January 25, 2006; Elizabeth Rosenthal, "Even the French Are Fighting Obesity," *The New York Times,* May 4, 2005; both articles at www.nytimes.com.
92. *In a National Cancer Institute:* K. F. Adams et al., "Overweight, Obesity, and Mortality in a Large Prospective Cohort of Persons 50–71 Years Old," *The New England Journal of Medicine* 355, no. 8 (2006): 763–78.
92. *For every pound:* Ali Mokdad, Frank Vinicor, et al., "Diabetes Trends in the U.S.: 1990–1998," *Diabetes Care* 23, no. 9 (2000): 1278–83; Denise Grady, "Diabetes Rises: Doctors Foresee a Harsh Impact," *The New York Times,* August 24, 2000.
92. *The incidence of type 2:* www.doctorslounge.com/endocrinology/diseases/diabetes.htm; for the most up-to-date estimates of the prevalence of type 2 diabetes worldwide, visit www.who.int/mediacentre/factsheets/fs312/en.
92. *A National Institutes of Health study:* Diabetes Prevention Program Research Group, "Reduction in the Incidence of Type 2 Diabetes with Lifestyle Intervention or Metformin," *The New England Journal of Medicine* 346, no. 6 (2002): 393–403.
94. *In a study titled:* Eva Weisz, "Energizing the Classroom," *College Teaching* 38, no. 2 (1990): 74–76.
94. *In a second study:* ibid.
95. *A series of researchers:* Jorge Cruise, *The 3-Hour Diet: How Low Carb Makes You Fat and Timing Will Slim You* (New York: HarperResource, 2005), 5; "Eat More Often to Combat Overeating," *Environmental Nutrition* 23, no. 4 (2000): 8; A. J. Fogteloo et al., "Impact of Meal Timing and Frequency on the Twenty-four Hour Leptin Rhythm," *Hormone Research* 62, no. 2 (2004): 71–78; D. J. Jenkins et al., "Metabolic Advantages of Spreading the Nutrient Load: Effects of Increased Meal Frequency in Non-Insulin-Dependent Diabetes," *The New England Journal of Medicine* 55, no. 2 (1992): 461–67; D. P. Speechly and R. Buffenstein, "Acute Appetite Reduction Associated with an Increased Frequency of Eating in Obese Males," *International Journal of Obesity-Related Metabolic Disorders* 23, no. 11 (1999): 1151–59.
95. *Mark Fields:* Author interview with Mark Fields.
96. *"People eat in units":* Lisa Young, *The Portion Teller* (New York: Morgan Road Books 2005), 12.

97. *Consider the beloved bagel:* ibid., 2.
97. *Part of the problem:* ibid., 46.
97. *A second issue:* Brian Wansink, *Mindless Eating* (New York: Bantam Books, 2006), 48.
97. *"Everyone—every single one":* ibid., 1.
98. *In one study:* ibid., 16–18.
98. *In another study:* ibid., 36.
98. *Even the size of the plates:* ibid., 67.
99. *In an even more elaborate:* ibid., 52.
99. *In his extraordinary book:* David Kessler, *The End of Overeating* (Emmaus, PA: Rodale, 2009) 14.
100. *"Fat," Drewnowski explains:* Adam Drewnowski, quoted in Kessler, *The End of Overeating,* 13; A. Drewnowski, "Energy Intake and Sensory Properties of Food," *American Journal of Clinical Nutrition* 62, no. 5 (1995): 1081S–85S; A. Drewnowski and M. R. Greenwood, "Cream and Sugar: Human Preferences for High-Fat Foods," *Physiology and Behavior* 30, no. 4 (1983): 629–33.
100. *Another researcher:* A. Scalafini and D. Springer, "Dietary Obesity in Adult Rats: Similarities to Hypothalamic and Human Obesity Syndromes," *Physiology and Behavior* 17, no. 3 (1976): 461–71.
100. *In another study:* D. E. Larson et al., "Spontaneous Overfeeding with a 'Cafeteria Diet' in Men: Effects on 24-Hour Energy Expenditure and Substrate Oxidation," *International Journal of Obesity and Related Metabolic Disorders* 19, no. 5 (1995): 331–37.
100. *"Hyperpalatable foods":* Kessler, *The End of Overeating,* 141.
101. *"Eat":* Michael Pollan, *In Defense of Food* (New York: Penguin Press, 2008), 1.
101. *The glycemic Index:* To learn more about the glycemic index, visit www.glycemicindex.com.
101. *"When layer upon layer":* Kessler, *The End of Overeating,* 49.
101. *The psychologist Walter Mischel:* J. Metcalfe and W. Mischel, "A Hot/Cool-System Analysis of Delay Gratification: Dynamics of Willpower," *Psychological Review* 106, no. 1 (1999): 12.
102. *A Cinnabon, to take:* Kessler, *The End of Overeating,* 74–77.
102. *The speed with which we lose:* Wansink, *Mindless Eating,* 238.
102. *"Focusing single-mindedly":* Kessler, *The End of Overeating,* 156.
102. *"The emotional drivers":* ibid., 147–48.
103. *Wansink and his colleague:* Wansink, *Mindless Eating,* 78.
103. *"If we see that temptress":* ibid., 79.
103. *"Many times our resources":* Russell Fazio, quoted in Kessler, *The End of Overeating,* 199.
103. *"When you use all":* Kessler, *The End of Overeating,* 232.
103. *"We can't sustain":* ibid., 207.
103. *Gary Farro:* Author interview with Gary Farro.
105. *"When you go into a day:* David Besio, quoted in Kessler, *The End of Overeating,* 298.

CHAPTER NINE: CREATING A CULTURE THAT PULSES

110. *Among all of:* Sony Consumer Electronics, http://presscentre.sony.eu.
111. *"The results":* Andy Benson, Sony UK's commercial director, www.independent electricalretailer.co.uk/news/fullstory.php/aid/719/Andy_Benson_Commercial _Director,_Sony_UK.html.
114. *Derek Mann:* Author interview with Derek Mann.

CHAPTER TEN: THE WAR BETWEEN THE STATES

125. *It's triggered by the:* Joseph LeDoux, *The Emotional Brain* (New York: Simon & Schuster, 1996), 256.
126. *the amygdala prompts:* Jonathan Haidt, *The Happiness Hypothesis* (New York: Basic Books, 2006), 30.
128. *The same is true:* http://en.wikipedia.org/wiki/W._Edwards_Deming.
128. *"The more intense":* Daniel Goleman, *Emotional Intelligence* (New York: Bantam Books, 1995), 268.
129. *In another study:* R. F. Baumeister and M. R. Leary, "The Need to Belong: Desire for Interpersonal Attachments as a Fundamental Human Motivation," *Psychological Bulletin* (1995): 508.
129. *In a metareview:* Bruce J. Avolio and Fred Luthans, *The High Impact Leader* (New York: McGraw-Hill, 2006), 51.
130. *"My shtick, of course":* John McEnroe, *You Cannot Be Serious* (New York: Putnam, 2002), 194.
131. *We feel better:* S. Talbott, "Cortisol Control: What Salmon Can Teach You about Proper Training and Recovery," *American Fitness* 21, no. 6 (2003): 29–31.

CHAPTER ELEVEN: IF YOU AIN'T GOT PRIDE, YOU AIN'T GOT NOTHIN'

133. *"Bad Is Stronger than Good":* Roy Baumeister, Ellen Bratslavsky, and Catrin Finkenauer, "Bad Is Stronger than Good," *Review of General Psychology* 5, no. 4 (2001): 323.
133. *"Over and over":* Jonathan Haidt, *The Happiness Hypothesis* (New York: Basic Books, 2006), 29.
134. *"It is evolutionarily":* Baumeister, Bratslavsky, and Finkenauer, "Bad Is Stronger than Good." 325.
137. *"In the course of that work":* James Gilligan, *Violence: Reflections on a National Epidemic* (New York: Vintage, 1996), 105–106.
137. *Elijah Anderson, a sociologist:* Elijah Anderson, *Code of the Street* (New York: W. W. Norton & Company, 1999), 33, 34, 70, 75, 76.
138. *"We want them to acknowledge":* William B. Irvine, *On Desire* (New York: Oxford University Press, 2006), 35.
138. *Or, as Daniel Goleman:* Daniel Goleman, *Social Intelligence* (New York: Bantam Books, 2006), 229.
139. *"Belongingness can be almost":* R. F. Baumeister and M. R. Leary, "The Need to Belong: Desire for Interpersonal Attachments as a Fundamental Human Motivation," *Psychological Bulletin* 117, (1995): 498.
140. *The key to healthy:* John Bowlby, *A Secure Base* (London: Routledge, 1988), 11.
141. *"A great deal of":* Baumeister and Leary, "The Need to Belong," 521.
141. *"To remain within":* Bowlby, *A Secure Base,* 27.

142. *"A common defense"*: Terrence Real, *I Don't Want to Talk about It* (New York: Fireside, 1997), 55.
142. *In one study:* Jean M. Twenge and W. Keith Campbell, *The Narcissism Epidemic* (New York: Free Press, 2009), 30, 2, 34, 43–45.

CHAPTER TWELVE: THE FACTS AND THE STORIES WE TELL

150. *Optimism can indeed:* Roy Baumeister, Ellen Bratslavsky, and Catrin Finkenauer, "Bad Is Stronger than Good," *Review of General Psychology* 5, no. 4 (2001): 355.
150. *Or, as the psychologist:* Christopher Peterson, *A Primer in Positive Psychology* (New York: Oxford University Press, 2006), 127.
150. *"A healthy psychological"*: Daniel Gilbert, *Stumbling on Happiness* (New York: Knopf, 2006) 178.
150. *"realistic optimism"*: Sandra L. Schneider, "In Search of Realistic Optimism: Meaning, Knowledge, and Warm Fuzziness," *American Psychologist* 53, no. 3 (2001): 256–63.
151. *"I never lost"*: Jim Collins, *Good to Great* (New York: HarperBusiness, 2001), 85–86.
151. *"Over and over"*: Jonathan Haidt, *The Happiness Hypothesis* (New York: Basic Books, 2006), 64.
154. *"Everyone carries a shadow"*: John Welch, *Spiritual Pilgrims* (New York: Paulist Press, 1982), 119.
154. *Here's how I put it:* Tony Schwartz and Jim Loehr, *The Power of Full Engagement* (New York: Free Press, 2003), 152.
154. *"Healthy self-esteem"*: Terrence Real, *I Don't Want to Talk About It* (New York: Fireside, 1997), 44.
157. *"Most of us:* Gilbert, *Stumbling on Happiness,* 127.
158. *"The fact is"*: ibid., 165.
158. *After Lance Armstrong lay:* Lance Armstrong and Sally Jenkins, *It's Not about the Bike* (New York: Berkley, 2001), 259.
158. *As Alan Mulally:* Author interview with Alan Mulally.

CHAPTER THIRTEEN: ORGANIZATIONAL ENERGY

163. *Jeff Blake:* Author interview with Jeff Blake.
163. *Matthew Lang:* Author interview with Matthew Lang.
164. *Roy White:* Author interview with Roy White.
165. *Sarah Henbrey:* Author interview with Sarah Henbrey.
166. *In the past we:* Author interview with Roy White.
166. *David Patton:* Author interview with David Patton.
166. *How people feel:* Author interview with Alan Mulally.
167. *"People seem to need"*: R. F. Baumeister and M. R. Leary, "The Need to Belong: Desire for Interpersonal Attachments as a Fundamental Human Motivation," *Psychological Bulletin* (1995): 520.
167. *The neuroanatomist:* Jill Bolte Taylor, *My Stroke of Insight* (New York: Viking, 2006), 113, 114, 118.
168. *Doug Conant:* "Lighting a Fire under Campbell," *BusinessWeek*, December 4, 2006, www.businessweek.com/magazine/content/06_49/b4012086.htm.
169. *"If I realize"*: Author interview with Amy Pascal,
170. *"Guys, this company"*: Author interview with Alan Mulally.

CHAPTER FOURTEEN: A POVERTY OF ATTENTION

178. *"Every one knows what":* William James, *The Principles of Psychology* (New York: Holt, 1890), 403–404, www.archive.org/details/theprinciplesofp01jameuoft.
179. *"What information consumes":* Herbert A. Simon, "Designing Organizations for an Information-Rich World," September 1, 1969 http://zeus.zeit.de/2007/39/simon.pdf.
180. *The psychologist Mihaly:* Mihaly Csikszentmihalyi, *Flow* (New York: Harper & Row, 1991), 84–85.
180. *"The skillful management:* Winifred Gallagher, *Rapt* (New York: Penguin Press, 2009), 2.
180. *"The way we live":* Maggie Jackson, *Distracted* (New York: Prometheus Books, 2008), 13.
181. *"Learning occurs best":* John J. Medina, *Brain Rules* (Seattle: Pear Press, 2008), 132, 133.
182. *"It's not that":* David Strayer, quoted in "In Study, Texting Lifts Crash Risk by Large Margin," *The New York Times,* July 27, 2009, www.nytimes.com/2009/07/28/technology/28texting.html?pagewanted=1&_r=1.
183. *"Texting is in":* Rich Hanowski, quoted in "In Study, Texting Lifts Crash Risk by Large Margin," *The New York Times,* July 27, 2009, www.nytimes.com/2009/07/28/technology/28texting.html?pagewanted=1&_r=1.
183. *finding by the Nielsen Company:* Nielsen Company, 2008, http://en-us.nielsen.com/main/insights/consumer_insight/August2009/breaking_teen_myths.
183. *Linda Stone, a former:* www.lindastone.net.
185. *Jackson also notes:* Jackson, *Distracted,* 91.
185. *"Training can help":* ibid., 79–80.
187. *Edward Hallowell, a psychiatrist:* Edward Hallowell, *CrazyBusy* (New York: Ballantine Books, 2007), 6.
187. *"We are allowing:* Jackson, *Distracted,* 235.
187. *"To value a spit-focus life":* ibid., 92.
187. *"In the name of efficiency":* ibid., 81.
187. *"Paying rapt attention":* Gallagher, *Rapt,* 10.

CHAPTER FIFTEEN: ONE THING AT A TIME

189. *"the ability to persist":* David Lykken, "Mental Energy," *Intelligence* 33, no. 4 (2005): 331–35.
189. *"The goal of":* K. Anders Ericsson, Ralf Th. Krampe, and Clemens Tesch-Romer, "The Role of Deliberate Practice in the Acquisition of Expert Performance," *Psychological Review* 100, no. 3 (1993): 363–406.
192. *Mischel came to call:* Walter Mischel, quoted in Jonah Lehrer, "Don't!: The Secret of Self-Control," *The New Yorker,* May 18, 2009.
193. *"Young kids":* ibid.
194. *Mihaly Csikszentmihalyi captures:* Mihalyi Csikszentmihalyi, *Flow* (New York: Harper & Row, 1991), 63, 211.
198. *"the human mind:* William James, *The Principles of Psychology* (New York: Holt, 1890), www.archive.org/details/theprinciplesofp01jameuoft.

CHAPTER SIXTEEN: CULTIVATING THE WHOLE BRAIN

206. *"Prior to this"*: Jill Bolte Taylor, *My Stroke of Insight* (New York: Viking, 2006), 133.
207. *"[T]here appear to be two"*: Roger W. Sperry, "Lateral Specialization of Cerebral Function in the Surgically Separated Hemispheres," quoted in Betty Edwards, *Drawing on the Right Side of the Brain* (Los Angeles: J. P. Tarcher, 1989), 32.
210. *"You already know"*: ibid., 7.
210. *"Drawing is the time-bound"*: Betty Edwards, *Drawing on the Artist Within* (New York: Simon & Schuster, 1986), xiii.
211. *"If ever there was"*: Jerome Bruner, *Contemporary Approaches to Creative Thinking: A Symposium Held at the University of Colorado* (Palo Alto, CA: Atherton Press, 1962).
212. *"the power or faculty"*: *Merriam-Webster's Collegiate Dictionary,* 11th ed. (Springfield, MA: Merriam-Webster, 2003), 658.
213. *"Solving a problem"*: Author interview with John Kounios.
213. *"You want to"*: ibid.
213. *Hannah Minghella:* Author interview with Hannah Minghella.
214. *"Preconceptions"*: Edwards, *Drawing on the Artist Within,* 26.
214. *"Our left mind's language center"*: ibid., 20; Taylor, *My Stroke of Insight,* 143–44.
215. *"Our right brain"*: ibid., 143.
215. *"not capable of experiencing"*: ibid., 70.
215. *"In the absence"*: ibid., 49.
215. *"Freed from all perception"*: ibid., 141.
216. *"being in the light"*: Author interview with Amy Pascal.
216. *"The female brain"*: Simon Baron-Cohen, *The Essential Difference* (New York: Basic Books, 2003), 1, 5.
217. *"The formulation of"*: Albert Einstein, quoted in Edwards, *Drawing on the Artist Within,* 3.
218. Saturation, *the gathering:* George Kneller, quoted in ibid., 185.
218. *"One of the paradoxes"*: George F. Kneller, *The Art and Science of Creativity* (New York: Holt, Rinchart and Winston, 1965), 126.
219. *Urged by his patron:* Michael Gelb, *How to Think like Leonardo da Vinci* (New York: Dell, 1998), 159.
219. *"Using the two"*: Edwards, *Drawing on the Artist Within,* 8.

CHAPTER SEVENTEEN: AUTONOMY FOR ACCOUNTABILITY

222. *"The expectations have really changed"*: Author interview with David Hendler.
222. *"When we banned e-mail"*: Author interview with Juan Carlos Dalto.
223. *"Two principal types"*: Author interview with Roy White.
225. *Andreas Ditter:* Author interview with Andreas Ditter.
225. *Sarah Henbrey:* Author interview with Sarah Henbrey.
226. *Derry Newman:* Author interview with Derry Newman.
227. *"The ability to learn"*: Arie de Geus, *The Living Company* (Boston: Harvard Business School Press, 1997), 157.
229. *Hew Evans:* Author interview with Hew Evans.
231. *"The employer's job"*: Cali Ressler and Jody Thompson, *Why Work Sucks and How to Fix It* (New York: Portfolio, 2008), 71, 43, 57.

CHAPTER EIGHTEEN: WHO ARE YOU, AND WHAT DO YOU REALLY WANT?

238. *"He who has"*: Friedrich Nietzsche, http://en.wikiquote.org/wiki/Friedrich_Nietzsche.
239. *"It did not:* Viktor Frankl, *Man's Search for Meaning* (Boston: Beacon Press, 1962), 77.
240. *"There's plenty to criticize"*: Michael Lewis, "In Defense of the Boom," *The New York Times,* October 27, 2002, www.nytimes.com/2002/10/27/magazine/27Defense.html?pagewanted-10.
243. *"To know ourselves"*: Ian McCallum, *Ecological Intelligence* (Cape Town: Africa Geographic, 2005), 175.
243. *It is important:* ibid., 45, 14, 79.
243. *"There is no sun"*: Albert Camus, *The Myth of Sisyphus,* 1942, http://history.hanover.edu/courses/excerpts/111camus.html.
243. *"I must have"*: Carl Jung, *Modern Man in Search of a Soul* (Orlando, FL: Harcourt, 1955), 35.
244. *"Every time we"*: Lyall Watson quoted in McCallum, *Ecological Intelligence,* 82.
245. *"It does not matter"*: ibid., 99.
246. *"Only those who will risk"*: T. S. Eliot, http://en.wikiquote.org/wiki/T._S._Eliot.

CHAPTER NINETEEN: WE'RE ALL IN THIS TOGETHER

249. *"Don't be trapped"*: Steven Jobs, 2005, http://news.stanford.edu/news/2005/june15/jobs-061505.html.
251. *"Is it necessary"*: Drew Gilpin Faust, Baccalaureate Address to the Class of 2008, Harvard University, 2008, www.president.harvard.edu/speeches/faust/080603_bacc.php.
254. *Adam Williams:* Author interview with Adam Williams.
255. *Pedro Jesus:* Author interview with Pedro Jesus.
256. *"We are obliged"*: Ian McCallum, *Ecological Intelligence* (Cape Town: Africa Geographic, 2005), 221.
256. *"A person with* ubuntu*"*: Archbishop Desmond Tutu, *No Future Without Forgiveness* (New York: Doubleday, 1999), 31.
259. *"Picture a pasture:* Garret Hardin, "The Tragedy of the Commons," *Science* 162, no. 3859 (1968): 1243–48.

CHAPTER TWENTY: PURPOSE FOR PASSION

262. *"These leaders"*: Laura Reeve, "Spiritual Values and Practices Related to Leadership Effectiveness," *The Leadership Quarterly* 16 (October 2005): 625–53.
264. *In two-thirds:* Jim Collins, *Good to Great* (New York: HarperBusiness, 2001), 36, 39.
264. *Servant leadership starts:* Robert Greenleaf, "The Servant as Leader," 1970, pp. 63–84, http://www.alfsv.org/downloads/Greenleaf_servant_as_leader.pdf.
264. *Alan Mulally:* Author interview with Alan Mulally.
266. *David Bishop:* Author interview with David Bishop.
266. *Keith LeGoy:* Author interview with Keith LeGoy.
267. *"We've done well"*: Transcript of speech, 2009.

267. *"There are lots":* Transcript of speech, 2009.
269. *"For two years":* Author interview with Roy White.
270. *"The work we did":* Author interview with Fujio Nishida.
270. *Steve Dowdle:* Author interview with Steve Dowdle.
270. *Roy Dickens:* Author interview with Roy Dickens.
271. *"I've seen the value":* Author interview with Mathew Lang.
271. *In Roy White's view:* Author interview with Roy White.
271. *"What is the future":* Author interview with Fujio Nishida.
272. *I was never:* Eugene O'Kelly with Andrew Postman, *Chasing Daylight* (New York: McGraw-Hill, 2006), 132.
273. *"We have to wake up:* Ian McCallum, *Ecological Intelligence* (Cape Town: Africa Geographic, 2005), 3, 1.

Bibliography

Ackerman, Jennifer. *Sex Sleep Eat Drink Dream: A Day in the Life of Your Body.* Boston: Houghton Mifflin Company, 2007.

Anderson, Elijah. *Code of the Street: Decency, Violence and the Moral Life of the Inner City.* New York: W. W. Norton & Company, 1999.

Armstrong, Lance, and Sally Jenkins. *It's Not about the Bike: My Journey Back to Life.* New York: Berkley, 2001.

Avolio, Bruce J., and Fred Luthans. *The High Impact Leader: Moments Matter in Accelerating Authentic Leadership Development.* New York: McGraw-Hill, 2006.

Baron-Cohen, Simon. *The Essential Difference: Male and Female Brains and the Truth About Autism.* New York: Basic Books, 2003.

Baumeister, Roy F., ed. *The Self in Social Psychology.* Philadelphia: Psychology Press, 1999.

Baumeister, Roy F., Todd F. Heatherton, and Dianne M. Tice. *Losing Control: How and Why People Fail at Self-Regulation.* San Diego: Academic Press, 1994.

Begin, Menachem. *White Nights: The Story of a Prisoner in Russia.* Translated by Katie Kaplan. San Francisco: Harper & Row, 1979.

Bowlby, John. *A Secure Base: Parent-Child Attachment and Healthy Human Development.* London: Routledge, 1988.

Buckingham, Marcus, and Donald O. Clifton. *Now, Discover Your Strengths.* New York: Free Press, 2001.

Collins, Jim. *Good to Great: Why Some Companies Make the Leap—and Others Don't.* New York: HarperBusiness, 2001.

Colvin, Geoffrey. *Talent Is Overrated.* New York: Portfolio, 2008.

Covey, Stephen. *The 7 Habits of Highly Effective People.* New York: Free Press, 1989.

Csikszentmihalyi, Mihaly. *Flow: The Psychology of Optimal Experience.* New York: Harper & Row, 1990.

de Geus, Arie. *The Living Company.* Boston: Harvard Business School Press, 1997.

Dement, William C., and Christopher Vaughan. *The Promise of Sleep: A Pioneer in Sleep Medicine Explores the Vital Connection Between Health, Happiness, and a Good Night's Sleep.* New York: Dell, 2000.

Edwards, Betty. *Drawing on the Artist Within: A Guide to Innovation, Invention, Imagination, and Creativity.* New York: Simon & Schuster, 1986.

——. *Drawing on the Right Side of the Brain: A Course in Enhancing Creativity and Artistic Confidence.* Los Angeles: J. P. Tarcher, 1989.

Eliot, Lise. *Pink Brain, Blue Brain: How Small Differences Grow into Troublesome Gaps—and What We Can Do About It.* Boston: Houghton Mifflin Harcourt, 2009.

Fixx, James F. *The Complete Book of Running.* New York: Random House, 1977.

Frankl, Viktor. *Man's Search for Meaning: An Introduction to Logotherapy.* Boston: Beacon Press, 1962.

Gallagher, Winifred. *Rapt: Attention and the Focused Life.* New York: Penguin Press, 2009.

Gelb, Michael. *How to Think like Leonardo da Vinci.* New York: Dell, 1998.

Gilbert, Daniel. *Stumbling on Happiness.* New York: Knopf, 2006.

Gilligan, James. *Violence: Reflections on a National Epidemic.* New York: Vintage, 1996.

Gladwell, Malcolm. *Outliers: The Story of Success.* New York: Little, Brown, 2008.

Goleman, Daniel. *Emotional Intelligence.* New York: Bantam Books, 1995.

——. *Social Intelligence: The New Science of Human Relationships.* New York: Bantam Books, 2006.

Gray, John. *Al Qaeda and What It Means to Be Modern.* New York: New Press, 2003.

Haidt, Jonathan. *The Happiness Hypothesis: Finding Modern Truth in Ancient Wisdom.* New York: Basic Books, 2006.

Hallowell, Edward. *CrazyBusy: Overstretched, Overbooked, and About to Snap! Strategies for Handling Your Fast-Paced Life.* New York: Ballantine Books, 2007.

Heiden, Eric, Massimo Testa, and DeAnne Musolf. *Faster, Better, Stronger: 10 Proven Secrets to a Healthier Body in 12 Weeks.* New York: Collins Living, 2008.

Hillman, James. *The Soul's Code: In Search of Character and Calling.* New York: Warner Books, 1997.

Irvine, William B. *On Desire: Why We Want What We Want.* New York: Oxford University Press, 2006.

Jackson, Maggie. *Distracted: The Erosion of Attention and the Coming Dark Age.* New York: Prometheus Books, 2008.

Jung, Carl. *Modern Man in Search of a Soul.* Orlando, FL, 1955. First published 1933.

Kegan, Robert, and Lisa Laskow Lahey. *Immunity to Change: How to Overcome It and Unlock the Potential in Yourself and Your Organization.* Boston: Harvard Business Press, 2009.

——. *How the Way We Talk Can Change the Way We Work: Seven Languages for Transformation.* San Francisco: Jossey-Bass, 2001.

Kessler, David. *The End of Overeating: Taking Control of the Insatiable American Appetite.* Emmaus, PA: Rodale, 2009.

Kleitman, Nathaniel. *Sleep and Wakefulness.* Chicago: University of Chicago Press, 1987. First published 1939.

Kneller, George F. *The Art and Science of Creativity.* New York: Holt, Rinehart and Winston, 1965.

Laing, R. D. *The Politics of the Family and Other Essays.* London: Tavistock, 1971.

Lavie, Peretz. *The Enchanted World of Sleep.* Translated by Anthony Berris. New Haven, Conn.: Yale University Press, 1996.

LeDoux, Joseph. *The Emotional Brain: The Mysterious Underpinnings of Emotional Life.* New York: Simon & Schuster, 1996.

Lewis, Michael, ed. *Panic: The Story of Modern Financial Insanity.* New York: W. W. Norton & Company, 2008.

McCallum, Ian. *Ecological Intelligence: Rediscovering Ourselves in Nature.* Cape Town: Africa Geographic, 2005.

McEnroe, John. *You Cannot Be Serious.* New York: Putnam, 2002.

Medina, John. *Brain Rules: 12 Principles for Surviving and Thriving at Work, Home, and School.* Seattle: Pear Press, 2008.

Mednick, Sara C., with Mark Ehrman. *Take a Nap! Change Your Life.* New York: Workman, 2006.

Murphy, Michael. *The Future of the Body: Explorations into Further Evolution of Human Nature.* Los Angeles: J. P. Tarcher, 1992.

O'Kelly, Eugene, with Andrew Postman. *Chasing Daylight: How My Forthcoming Death Transformed My Life: A Final Account.* New York: McGraw-Hill, 2006.

Pollan, Michael. *In Defense of Food: An Eater's Manifesto.* New York: Penguin Press, 2008.

Real, Terrence. *I Don't Want to Talk about It: Overcoming the Secret Legacy of Male Depression.* New York: Fireside, 1997.

Ressler, Cali, and Jody Thompson. *Why Work Sucks and How to Fix It.* New York: Portfolio, 2008.

Rossi, Ernest, with David Nimmons. *The 20-Minute Break: Reduce Stress, Maximize Performance, and Improve Health and Emotional Well-being Using the New Science of Utradian Rhythms.* Los Angeles: J. P. Tarcher, 1991.

Schwartz, Tony. *What Really Matters: Searching for Wisdom in America.* New York: Bantam, 1995.

Schwartz, Tony, and Jim Loehr. *The Power of Full Engagement: Managing Energy, Not Time, Is the Key to High Performance and Personal Renewal.* New York: Free Press, 2003.

Tavris, Carol, and Elliot Aronson. *Mistakes Were Made (But Not by Me): Why We Justify Foolish Beliefs, Bad Decisions, and Hurtful Acts.* Orlando, Fla.: Harcourt, 2008.

Taylor, Jill Bolte. *My Stroke of Insight: A Brain Scientist's Personal Journey.* New York: Viking, 2006.

Twenge, Jean M., and W. Keith Campbell. *The Narcissism Epidemic: Living in the Age of Entitlement.* New York: Free Press, 2009.

Wansink, Brian. *Mindless Eating: Why We Eat More Than We Think.* New York: Bantam Books, 2006.

Weisberg, Jacob. *The Bush Tragedy.* New York: Random House, 2008.

Welch, John. *Spiritual Pilgrims: Carl Jung and Teresa of Avila.* New York: Paulist Press, 1982.

Whitehead, Alfred North. *An Introduction to Mathematics.* New York: H. Holt, 1911.

Wilber, Ken. *A Brief History of Everything.* Boston: Shambhala, 1996.

Young, Lisa. *The Portion Teller: Smartsize Your Way to Permanent Weight Loss.* New York: Morgan Road Books, 2005.

Acknowledgments

TONY SCHWARTZ

I have spent most of my adult life thinking about the ideas contained in this book. Along the way I've been influenced, inspired and enriched by some extraordinary thinkers whose work I've read and studied. There are many more of them than I can mention here, but the most significant include Ian McCallum, Roy Baumeister, Jim Collins, Anders Ericsson, Jonathan Haidt, Daniel Gilbert, Daniel Goleman, Betty Edwards, Terrence Real, and David Kessler. I've also been deeply influenced by some of the great seminal psychological thinkers, including Carl Jung, Abraham Maslow, and John Bowlby.

I've had the incredible good fortune to meet, and in some cases work with, a number of the thinkers who've influenced me the most. Often they've been outside the mainstream. Ken Wilber remains a powerful influence on my thinking about the nature of integrated adult development, across multiple lines. Irv Dardik introduced me to the profound idea that human beings operate at their best when they move between rhythmic energy expenditure and energy renewal. The irrepressible Michael Murphy brought together an amazing range of Eastern and Western thinkers and practitioners at the Esalen Institute, which he cofounded in 1962. It was through Murphy that I met many of the people whose work I wrote about in an earlier book, *What Really Matters: Searching for Wisdom in America.*

Robert Kegan, a professor and scholar at Harvard, is perhaps the leading academic thinker about adult human development. I've been especially affected by his work with his longtime collaborator Lisa Lahey, focused on how people change for the better (and what stands in their way). Jim Loehr is a sports psychologist whose work I also wrote about in *What Really Matters.* Out of his experiences with athletes, Jim had several brilliant insights about the importance of renewal, and the role of rituals in making change that lasts. Starting in 1999, Jim and I worked together to extend those ideas and apply them in the corporate world. We described our work in *The Power of Full Engagement,* the book we coauthored in 2003. My goal in this book has been to widen, deepen, and extend that earlier work. The opportunity to collaborate with Jim, after twenty-five years as a journalist, changed the trajectory of my life in every imaginable way, all of them for the better.

When I parted ways with Jim in 2003 to found the Energy Project, the one person I took with me was Catherine McCarthy, one of my two collaborators on this book. Catherine is also our COO and runs the Energy Project day to day. She's a person of many talents, infinite energy, and amazing passion. We have been true partners every step of the way and I'd be lost without her. Wherever I fall short, Catherine excels. Jean Gomes, my other collaborator on this book, runs the Energy Project in Europe. Jean is a restlessly creative thinker with a wide-ranging mind. It was in our work together, informed by his long consulting experience with large companies, that we moved the Energy Project from working solely with individuals to addressing organizations and their leaders as well. The richness of the work that Jean's Energy Project team has done throughout Europe is evident throughout this book.

I have deep respect—and beyond that, real love—for every member of our Energy Project team. Annie Perrin is a superb facilitator and coach, incredibly insightful and attuned. We rely on her for her insights into both our clients and ourselves. Corry Devin runs our marketing, and she is a quiet force of nature. Sheryl King manages our client relationships and is excellent at everything she does. Sheryl also fact-checked, gathered footnotes, and helped drive this book to the finish line. Jane Sparrow is Jean Gomes's Catherine, among many other things, and Michelle Pfeifer has been my amazing assistant from the beginning; in addition to keeping our company's finances straight, she keeps me moving forward against all odds. Erin Kunkel did a little of everything in her year with us, including a great deal of research for this book. Kevin Small, our independent marketing maven, helped us navigate a world we barely understood.

Our designers, Christopher Simmons and Tim Belonax, created the distinctive look that characterizes everything from our workbooks and PowerPoint slides to our marketing materials. We also richly value our relationships with all of those who've facilitated our work, most especially Andrew Deutscher and Laurie Coe.

Many of the ideas and strategies I've described in this book grew out of work we did with key clients. Ben Jenkins, the retired president of Wachovia Bank, was a wonderfully enthusiastic early supporter and an exemplar of the practices we teach. So was David Furman, his head of HR. The same is true of Arkadi Kuhlman, the CEO of ING Direct, and Jim Kelly, the COO, who brought us into their company in its infancy, and ours. At Ernst & Young, Cathy Salvatore has been a continuing supporter, and so has Mike Hamilton. Art Tulley is an E&Y partner who, like Ben Jenkins, has not only championed our work but also seeks to model it in his own leadership.

The incredibly energetic Evan Wittenberg and Catherine Brown brought us into Google, and we're thrilled that they have also become facilitators of the work inside Google, along with more than a dozen of their colleagues. At Ford, our sponsor from the start was Lena Allison. We also deeply appreciate and admire CEO Alan Mulally and Mark Fields, the president of the Americas. Bill Bratton, the former police chief at the LAPD, brought us into his department, and we were supported there by two unique cops and exceptional human beings, Sandy Jo MacArthur and Mark Perez.

Bridget Duffy was a fierce advocate for our work at the Cleveland Clinic, as was Marc Gillinov, a world-renowned surgeon but also a true seeker. What a wonderful synchronicity that Dominic Randolph, the head of the Riverdale Country School, where I attended high school, reached out to see if we'd be interested in working with his students and faculty, unaware that I was one of his alumni. The collaboration has been exhilarating, and Dominic has become a valued friend. Debbie Bolger has done a brilliant job overseeing the program we call "The One Big Thing" at Riverdale. At the resort Miraval, our partners Philippe Bourgignon and Michael Tompkins have helped us create a program for executives that blends the best of our work with the best of Miraval's programs.

Sony Europe's head of HR, Roy White, was a passionate and visionary advocate for our work at a time when the company was struggling deeply. Fujio Nishida, the president of Sony Europe, also became a supporter and a role model. Our most comprehensive work has been with Sony Pictures, where CEO Amy Pascal had a vision for the company she wanted to create and invested in us to help her realize that dream. Nearly every employee of Sony Pictures ultimately went through some form of our curriculum. We're enormously grateful to Amy and chairman Michael Lynton, and to Kesa Tsuda and Todd Pitts, the original HR executives who never wavered as our champions. We're also thankful to George Rose, successor as head of HR, for continuing to support the work, and especially to Sonya Narang and Annalee Siller, who oversaw the rollout.

My agent, Alice Martel, is a bundle of enthusiasm, support, and fierce advocacy. At the Free Press, where this is my second book, I've enjoyed a great partnership with Martha Levin, Suzanne Donahue, Dominic Anfuso, Carisa Hays, and Christine Donnelly. Emily Loose is one of the few editors who really edits. She has made this book immeasurably stronger. And thanks, too, to Maura O'Brien, for keeping the ship afloat.

I have benefited, both personally and professionally, from many friends, all of whom I've talked with about these ideas, in some cases for years. Thanks to Michael Fiori and Jane Eisen, Mitch Lee, Rachel Newton Bellow, John Weiser, Ian Michner, Michael Weinstein, and Victor Garcia. Brian Buffini has been not just an endlessly generous friend but also a valued mentor.

I feel very grateful to my brother, Jim, and my sister, Cassie, two people who have grown as much as anyone I know and with whom my relationship is closer and richer as a result. Nathan Salant Schwartz has been many things to me over the past two decades—a source of amazing insights, a constant support in difficult times, and someone who gently but firmly holds me accountable whenever I try to kid myself. I love and admire him.

My two daughters, Kate and Emily, are now in their twenties, and they've been subjected to these ideas and practices all their lives. Both of them have cheered me on, worked with me at times, read this manuscript, and shared their penetrating insights. It's a joy that Emily has come to work with us. I also deeply value my soon-to-be son-in-law, Omri Roden, who has been part of our family for nearly a decade. Despite my many shortcomings as a father, my daughters have both turned into extraordinary young women, and my love and admiration for them is endless.

Finally, there is, Deborah, my wife of thirty-one years. The writing of this book coincided with a very difficult period during which Deborah was recovering from a stroke that occurred at a time when she could not have seemed healthier, happier, or more productive. It's hard to find wisdom in such a random, devastating event. The closest I can come is that the more challenging life becomes, the more important it is to apply the principles I've written about in this book. Difficult as it is to face pain, it's always ultimately the better choice. We've been tested—Deborah and I and our children—and we've survived, individually and as a family. Almost losing Deborah has reminded me over and over how essential love is in my life—and in all lives.

JEAN GOMES

Five years ago, urged by my wife, Sally-Ann, I picked up the phone to talk to Tony Schwartz about the possibility of taking his work to one of our long-standing clients, Sony Electronics in Europe. In the months that followed, we rapidly established common ground and a way of sparking off each other creatively that was both exceptionally productive and deeply enjoyable. The pilot at Sony was a huge success and sowed the seeds of a deep friendship, the formation of the Energy Project Europe, and some of the most rewarding experiences of my career. I'm privileged to contribute to this work.

I'm also deeply appreciative to have worked with some great leaders including Fujio Nishida, President of Sony Electronics Europe, Steve Dowdle, M.D. at Sony UK, Andreas Ditter in Sony Pictures in Germany, Matthew Lang at Sony South Africa, Simon Ashby in the UK, Steve Dalton, who runs Sony's factory in Wales, and Roy White and Sarah Henbrey, who led the cultural adoption of our work by thousands of people at Sony Europe. Derry Newman, who heads up solarcentury, has adopted our work in a similarly profound way in his pioneering company. I'm also indebted to David Paynter, who for many years was my boss, then mentor, and now occasional inspirational coach.

Jane Sparrow, our managing director, embodies our work in her life, bringing passion and focus to every dimension of what we do. Similarly, our team, including Kevin Witham and Steve Clark, have inspired hundreds to make profound changes in their lives.

When it comes to counting my blessings, my wife, Sally-Ann, is the center of my life. In setting up the Energy Project with me, she combined infinite enthusiasm, meticulous attention to detail, and a ceaselessly positive attitude. Together, we have grown with our understanding of what the Energy Project teaches and found greater satisfaction and meaning in our lives. That brings me to our wonderful children, Lauren and Saffron. My deepest hope is that when they look back in twenty or thirty years they can see that the way the world works has been positively influenced by these ideas.

CATHERINE MCCARTHY

Early in 2000, I began to ask people around me whether or not they loved their jobs. At the time, I was working as a consultant in a small firm in Chicago with wonderful colleagues and interesting clients, but there was a large part of me that did not feel fulfilled. I began a quest to find a job that felt more like a calling. Soon after, I was introduced to Tony Schwartz and Jim Loehr, who were collaborating on how to bring the ideas of renewal and rituals into the corporate world. My connection to the work was immediate. I knew my calling was to use the science of high performance to help people improve their lives on and off the job.

When Tony asked me to join him in building the Energy Project, I jumped at the chance. The last six and a half years have been immensely rewarding. I am eternally grateful to Tony for seeing potential in me, giving me the room to grow, and allowing me to accompany him on this amazing journey building our company. I'm honored to have been a part of this book, and Tony's generosity, personally and professionally, has changed my life forever. I'm also deeply appreciative of the team we have at the Energy Project and at the Energy Project Europe. Their dedication to our shared mission inspires me on a daily basis.

This book would not exist without our clients—the leaders and individual contributors who have been willing to explore a new way of working. Their courage to challenge their own habits and assumptions and the status quo in their organizations is a constant source of positive energy for me.

Last, I must acknowledge my husband, Paul. He has been an unending source of support, love, advice, reassurance, humor, optimism, and clarity throughout the seventeen years that we've known each other. His presence in my life has made me a better person through and through.

Index

Page numbers in *italics* refer to illustrations.

The Energy Project

TOOLS FOR CHANGE

GO TO WWW.THEENERGYPROJECT.COM/RESOURCES

The Energy Audit™

How effectively are you managing your energy—physically, emotionally, mentally, and spiritually?

Take our twenty-question assessment and receive your results immediately by e-mail. Learn which behaviors you can address immediately to improve your performance, effectiveness, and engagement, on the job and off.

The Energy Audit for Leaders

How well are you energizing others, so they're capable of performing at their best?

This assessment will show you how well you're managing the energy of those you lead. Your results, sent immediately by e-mail, will suggest specific steps you can take to fuel higher engagement, productivity, and satisfaction.

Creating Rituals that Last

Change is hard. We must overcome ingrained habits, often unrecognized resistance, and a range of external forces that support the status quo. How can you adopt new behaviors to improve your productivity and satisfaction in the face of all these obstacles? In this podcast, Tony Schwartz offers a step-by-step guide to building rituals that last.

The Energy Project

TOOLS FOR CHANGE

GO TO WWW.THEENERGYPROJECT.COM/RESOURCES

Ten Rituals for Performing at Your Best

Would you like to know the most effective rituals to drive higher performance and satisfaction—and how precisely to build them? Take a look at the list we've compiled, developed out of our work with thousands of people like yourself.

Transforming the Way You Work Calendar

Transforming the Way You Work Calendar

Do you want to more easily incorporate into your daily life the rituals you've designed to improve your energy, engagement, and focus? Use this weekly calendar to track your key rituals, color coded to capture the four key dimensions of energy management.

Renewing on the Road

Traveling for work often interferes with the positive routine that are effective for us at home—especially around managing our physical energy. In this video podcast you'll get some key tips on how to eat, exercise, renew, and sleep when you're on the road.

About the Authors

Tony Schwartz is president and CEO of the Energy Project, which helps individuals and organizations perform at their best. Tony's previous book, *The Power of Full Engagement: Managing Energy, Not Time,* coauthored with Jim Loehr, was a number one *Wall Street Journal* bestseller, spent four months on the *New York Times* bestseller list, and has been translated into twenty-eight languages. Tony also coauthored the number one worldwide bestseller *The Art of the Deal* with Donald Trump and wrote *What Really Matters: Searching for Wisdom in America.*

Jean Gomes is chairman of the Energy Project Europe. He has spent the past twenty-five years consulting with some of the world's leading organizations on strategy, leadership development, and organizational and culture change. He has also coached more than fifty CEOs and senior leaders around the world.

Catherine McCarthy is chief operating officer of the Energy Project. She is the coauthor of *Leading at the Edge,* a book based on Ernest Shackleton's Antarctic expedition, which outlines ten key strategies for helping leaders and teams optimize performance in the face of adversity.

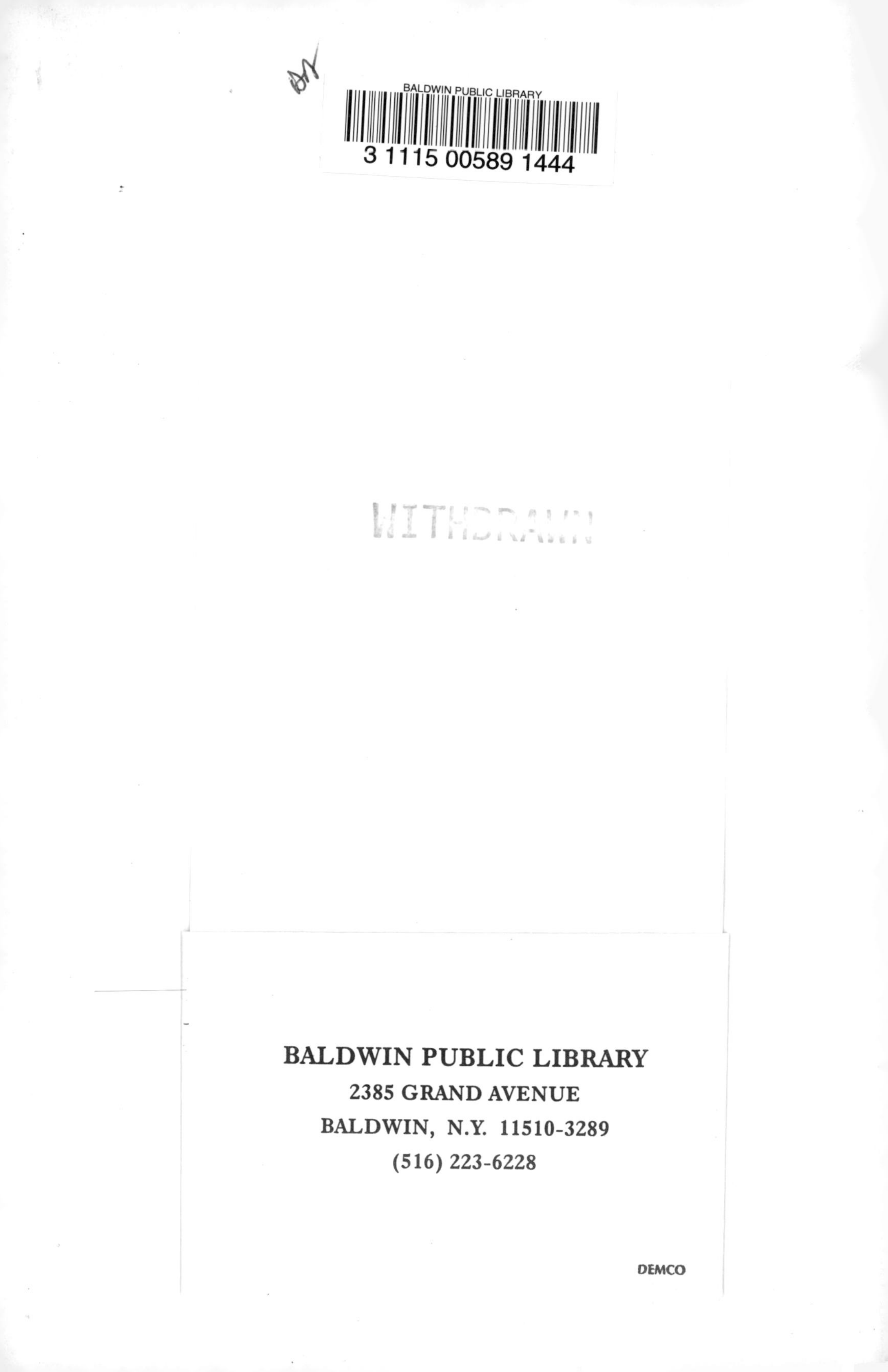